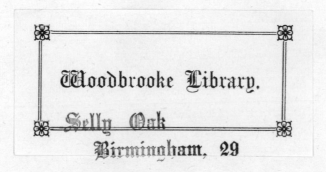

THE CHRISTIAN HOPE

THE
CHRISTIAN
HOPE

The Presence
and the Parousia

by

J. E. FISON, M.A., B.D.

Sub-Dean and Canon Residentiary of Truro
Cathedral

LONGMANS, GREEN AND CO
LONDON • NEW YORK • TORONTO

LONGMANS, GREEN AND CO LTD
6 AND 7 CLIFFORD STREET LONDON W 1
ALSO AT MELBOURNE AND CAPE TOWN
LONGMANS, GREEN AND CO INC
55 FIFTH AVENUE NEW YORK 3
LONGMANS, GREEN AND CO
215 VICTORIA STREET TORONTO 1
ORIENT LONGMANS LTD
BOMBAY CALCUTTA MADRAS

First published 1954

Printed in Great Britain by Neill & Co. Ltd., Edinburgh

CONTENTS

v

NOTE

I OWE to Rochester the opportunity of writing this book and to Truro the chance to get it ready for printing. The upheaval of the move from Rochester to Truro has meant many more encroachments upon the time, temper and goodwill of the publishers and printers than I could have wished. For their patience, courtesy and skill I am truly grateful.

J. E. F.

INTRODUCTION

THIS book is written in the conviction that there is nothing distinctively Christian about an outlook on the future, whether of the individual soul or of the world as a whole, which is not centred in Jesus Christ. This is not to deny the importance of immortality, resurrection and the last judgment, but it is to assert emphatically that not one of these doctrines is distinctively Christian at all, however profoundly the Christian gospel may have modified or enhanced their significance.

The only distinctively Christian doctrine about the future, which finds expression in the ancient creeds or hymns of the church, is the terse Latin *Inde venturus*. It is the coming again of Jesus Christ which is at the centre of the Christian hope from the earliest times, and it is at its centre not as the terminus of a movement either of the whole world or of the individual soul towards God, but as the spearhead of God's own loving movement and advance towards the whole world and every single individual soul within it.

Is this doctrine of the 'second coming' just a relic of a naïvely primitive Christian outlook, needing to be scrapped to-day in favour of a more comprehensive and intelligible dogma, at least of the coming of the kingdom of God or of the consummation of all things in Christ, if not of universal progress towards perfection? Can such doctrines so supersede the ancient dogma as to express fully without it the original great expectation of the Christian church? Is the retention of *Inde venturus* as an article of the creed unnecessary and irrelevant, or is it still so much the heart of the Christian gospel about the future that without it any attempt to express the Christian hope loses all its original vital significance?

The appearance of Dr. C. H. Dodd's great work on *The Interpretation of the Fourth Gospel* [1] inevitably raises acutely the question as to whether it is possible to discard the whole primitive futurist expectation of the parousia or coming again of Jesus Christ and rest content with the realized presence through the Paraclete. Despite the repetition of the credal formula in church, this is what in fact large sections of contemporary Christendom have tacitly done.

But before we acquiesce in such an apostasy (for that is what by

C.U.P., 1953, published only after production of this book had begun.

ix

the strict verbal standards of the creed it is) we should pause and ask whether any such intention was really in the mind of the writer of the Fourth Gospel. He is even more silent about the birth of Jesus Christ at Bethlehem and about the institution of the eucharist at the Last Supper than he is about the parousia or coming again of our Lord.

It is therefore a very arbitrary criticism, which is prepared at all costs to retain the Bethlehem nativity, as well as the pre-existent Logos, and the dominical institution of the eucharist, as well as the discourse at the feeding of the five thousand and the feet-washing at the Last Supper, and is at the same time only too glad to avail itself of the Johannine silence to scrap the parousia altogether in favour of the presence and the Paraclete.

Surely the purpose of the Fourth Gospel is at least as much to educate Christians as to evangelize pagans,[1] and it is the outlook even more of the church than of the world at the end of the first century A.D. which determines its particular emphasis and point of view. Its stress on the Logos of God no more invalidates the Christ of Bethlehem than its emphasis on the presence and the risen life renders superfluous the doctrines of the parousia and the future resurrection.

It was accepted as a gospel because it spoke to the condition of the church for which it was written, and it did this because it corrected tendencies towards either an arrested development or a lopsidedness in doctrine which, if unchecked, might easily have stunted or warped the whole Christian outlook. Its corrective needs, however, to be used to-day with discrimination, for, though all Christians need it at some point, they do not all need it equally at every point.

Some should heed the Prologue, which is the Christmas gospel at the eucharist, as the antidote to sentimentalism: others should notice the feet-washing and the great commandment in the context of the Last Supper, and realize the danger of unethical sacramentalism: still others should pay attention to its message of eternal life here and now and curb their apocalyptic day-dreaming and wishful thinking about the future.

It is this latter eschatological corrective which is needed as badly by the sects in the middle of the twentieth as by the great church at the end of the first century A.D. But what the sects need to-day is not what the great church needs: if they need to see the future through the eyes of St John, she needs once again to have her eyes opened to the secret of the Synoptists.

[1] Despite C. H. Dodd, *The Interpretation of the Fourth Gospel* (C.U.P., 1953), p. 9.

The Fourth Gospel is deadly as a substitute for the Synoptic gospels, but it is invaluable as their complement and corrective. For this is the wonder of Holy Scripture: if we allow its different parts to speak to us in isolation, the one from the other, then we find ourselves bewildered and overwhelmed by the multitude of problems which confront us; but if we allow the whole to speak to our condition as a unity, then those problems are simplified and at any given moment of history a single issue is seen to embrace them all.

To-day this issue is nothing less than the redemption of charity, which has become debased in its meaning, to its true significance and glory. St Paul would teach us that the touchstone of ethics is the middle wall of partition: St John would show us that the touchstone of worship is the presence through the Paraclete: the Synoptists would make clear that the touchstone of eschatology is the parousia: and the whole Old Testament would drive us back to the touchstone of theology itself, the very meaning of the holy name of YHVH.

These are not different problems to be tackled separately: they are all aspects of the one issue which must be faced as a whole, even if the cost of facing it and realizing its significance is the cross itself. Only so can the glorious gospel of the charity of God be redeemed from its debased to its true significance, and seen as the way of salvation both for the whole world and for every individual soul within it.

As far as the Christian hope is concerned, this means that the great church must rediscover the secret of the parousia; for only so can she redeem the eschatological charity of God to its true significance in the very end and so minister to the contemporary world at its point of deepest need. As an incentive and aid to such a ministry this book may help if it is understood not as an all-out offensive along the whole eschatological front, but as a probing reconnaissance in enough force to reveal by its survey some of the glaring weaknesses and some of the glorious opportunities of the Christian church to-day. May others expose its errors and defects, and if it has succeeded in opening up any new territory, may the break-through be exploited to the full!

CHAPTER I

THE NEED OF THE WORLD

THIS book is being written in the year of grace 1952, in the year of our Lord 1952, in the year of our Saviour and of our salvation 1952. Is this comparatively recent [1] method of reckoning time sensible or stupid? Is it true or is it complete nonsense? Is it up-to-date gospel or out-of-date irrelevance? No one can avoid thinking about such questions if he wants to understand the Christian outlook on the world to-day.

Ought the whole idea of relating our lives to a particular historical event and of evaluating them with reference to that event to be abandoned? Is history, in fact, irrelevant to our creed? Ought all references to events, past, present or future, to be cut out of it and replaced either by a series of philosophical propositions about the values of truth, beauty and goodness, or by a series of scientific propositions about the origin, nature and destiny of the world in which we live?

Once such questions are asked they raise the whole problem of revelation. If there is such a thing as revelation, what sort of a thing is it? No one can answer this question without going deeper still into the problem it raises. For the nature of revelation depends on the nature of God. It is the kind of God we believe in which determines the kind of revelation we are prepared to accept. It is the Christian conviction that the least inadequate way of speaking about God is to use the language of personal love, and once that position is accepted and that language used, the problem of revelation is clarified.

For the revelation of love, though it may be expressed in verbal form in a love letter or in ritual form in a kiss or in visual form in a look, is not to be identified with any or all of these. They are indeed the normal and necessary modes of its expression. But that which is expressed lies behind them, though it is conveyed through them. It is not something which is exhausted by them, but it is something which can only be expressed through them. The media of the expression of love are events even more than words, or, rather, they are events interpreted by words.

[1] O. Cullman, *Christ and Time* (S.C.M., 1951), pp. 17 f.

Revelation is like that. It is not propositional, but personal.[1] It needs propositions in order to express its meaning. But its meaning is not caught, in the sense of being fully comprehended, in any proposition. For the proposition, when it is genuinely apostolic and not merely apologetic, is a pointer towards and not a proof of the personal love, which it interprets and expresses. It is in historical events and their interpretation that we see into the heart of the biblical revelation of personal love, which culminated in the incarnation and atonement of our Lord Jesus Christ.

To cut out the historical element from the Christian creed is to cut out the core of the Christian revelation and the heart of the Christian good news. But the historical event referred to as happening 'under Pontius Pilate' and interpreted in the Christian creed is no isolated event. Other historical events led up to it in the history of the old Israel and other historical events have followed after it in the history of the new Israel. They have significance for our understanding of it and it has significance for our interpretation of them.

It happened 'once for all',[2] but what happened once for all in time under Pontius Pilate gives the Christian his clue as to what is happening all the time. It is not from the abstract values of a timeless eternity that he deduces the significance of the concrete events of historical time. It is from a concrete event in historical time that he divines the significance of both the values in which he believes and also of the world in which he lives.

So it is with love. It is its self-disclosure in a single event which if rightly sensed and interpreted reveals and 'gives away' the significance of its whole attitude. It is not the significance of its whole general attitude which reveals the significance of its single particular action. It is exactly the other way round. To replace the person by the proposition, the historical event by the timeless value, the particular moment by the general principle, is to establish perhaps a satisfactory *modus vivendi* in a logical world of our own choosing, but at the cost of missing all opportunity of entering the lovely world of God's choice.

So it is throughout the Bible, and so it was from the beginning and so it will be at the end. It is impossible to hold one view about God's revelation in A.D. 30, and another about his revelation in 4004 B.C. and another about his revelation in A.D. 2002. He is the same, and if the clue given in A.D. 30 is right, he is personal love, revealing himself personally to those who are willing to receive his

---

[1] The ultimate justification for such a statement is the Johannine claim of Jesus himself: 'I am . . . the truth' (John 14, 6).
[2] Jude 3.

revelation. This is therefore what he was at the beginning and what he will be at the end.

Distortions of his revelation due to human misunderstandings of him may be ignorant or malicious.[1] But propositional error should not blind us to personal truth. The propositions will be inevitably limited by human language as well as by human sin. Love never imposes its revelation on anyone, and so there is always a proportion between a revelation received and the spiritual and mental and social and cultural state of the receiver. Therefore the proposition must not be disregarded because it is inadequate, whether in Genesis about the beginning or in Revelation about the end. On the other hand it must not be so relied on as to be identified with the revelation itself.

Revelation and interpretation are indissolubly connected in the event of revelation and at the moment of revelation. Later on and in retrospect they can be sifted, though never by any infallible criterion. There is thus a place and an essential place for interpretation, but if the revelation is of love, then the interpretation, whether in Bible or in creed or in intuitional experience, can never be the revelation. To identify the interpretation with the revelation is idolatry: to separate the revelation from the interpretation is apostasy. Loyalty to the core of revelation is compatible with and indeed demands the continual revision of the circumferential interpretation of it. This is the essential character of progressive revelation in the Bible, and this is why the climax of biblical revelation is not found in a word or a deed but in a person, who through word and deed revealed God as completely as such a revelation of love was possible in terms of our human understanding of life.

Jesus Christ is God's self-disclosure.[2] In him God in more senses than one 'gave himself away'. But the self-disclosure of love is never ostentatiously fool-proof: it is always self-effacingly reticent. Its self-disclosures will pass unnoticed except for those who have eyes to see them and ears to hear them. That is why 'all revelation is of a Now and for a Now. It is not in itself information about the past or the future'.[3] Revelation about the past could never be by

---

[1] Cf. D. L. Sayers, *The Mind of the Maker* (Methuen, 1941), pp. 83 f.: 'Unfortunately his creation is only safe from the interference of other wills so long as it remains in his head . . . misquotation arises from carelessness or bad memory; misinterpretation from lack of understanding; deliberate distortion from a perverted intention; we may call them mechanical (or material) defect, intellectual error, and moral wickedness.'

[2] John 1, 18.

[3] Cf. J. A. T. Robinson, *In the End, God* (James Clarke, 1950), p. 30 and footnote: 'This doctrine of revelation, here summarily stated without argument, may well turn out to be one of the "assured results" of modern scientific theology. It is that accepted, for instance, by such authorities as W. Temple, E. Brunner, J. Baillie and A. Richardson.'

propositions giving a verbatim report to any present person or generation of what happened 'in the beginning'.

Right interpretation of love's present self-disclosure is the only clue any individual or any group in any generation ever has about love's past self-disclosure. A right interpretation of creation therefore involves a thinking out, whether by discursive reasoning or by intuitional insight, of the implications of love's self-disclosures in history in their bearing upon the nature of love's self-disclosure at the beginning of history. That is why the Bible begins with two different accounts of creation,[1] each interpreting love's action 'in the beginning' in the light of its interpretation of love's activity in the present.

Similarly when it comes to a description of the end, there can be no pre-view either in propositional terms or even in archetypal images of what will happen then. There can only be a divine self-disclosure in the present, which will have a bearing upon the future, the implications of which will be differently drawn, for example, in the Revelation of St John the Divine and in the Gospel according to St John.

To look rightly at the future we need, therefore, to look rightly at the present. But right thinking about the present will not depend so much upon the things which go to make up the present as upon the presence of him who discloses himself to those who have eyes to see him, and ears to hear him, in and through the things of the present. All talk about a revelation of love is meaningless apart from this. But if this be granted, then right thinking about the future will not depend so much upon the correctness of the logical deductions drawn from the propositions which interpret the presence as upon a true understanding of the implications of the present self-disclosure of love for all future self-disclosures of love right up to the very end.

The limits of all expressions of truth in propositional form must be faced, for whereas in logic presence and absence are contradictory, in love they are complementary. So far from the absence of love being the necessary precondition of its coming, the actual facts are exactly the reverse. It is the presence of love which carries with it the corollary of its coming. Love cannot be present without also being absent. Love's presence now in the present implies therefore love's coming then in the future. Without faith in the real presence, belief in the real *parousia* (παρουσία)[2] is phantasy: without faith in the real *parousia*, belief in the real presence is idolatry. This

---

[1] Gen. 1, 1–2, 4a and Gen. 2, 4b ff.

[2] The Greek word *parousia* (παρουσία) can mean either presence or coming.

must be so, if the real presence is the presence of love: it cannot be so, if it is anything else.

Revelation therefore depends on God, and if God is personal love, then revelation is in event rather than in word, though the event must be interpreted by the word. The event is only revelatory to those who catch a glimpse of its meaning, though the revelation is in the event quite apart from whether anyone catches a glimpse of it or not. Those who catch a glimpse of its meaning thereby necessarily interpret the revelation to themselves, and to that extent interpretation is bound up with revelation even in the actual moment of love's self-disclosure, quite apart from the place which interpretation plays in handing on the meaning of that self-disclosure to others.

Judged by human standards, love often seems to be the weakest of all things.[1] That is precisely why it is the strongest. It never tries to get its own way [2] and therefore in the end it always does. Something like that is the truth of the Christian gospel, preached by Jesus on the mount of the Beatitudes and practised by him on the mount of Golgotha. Either that gospel is true or it is false; either it is up-to-date or it is out-of-date; either it is relevant to the world's needs or it is totally irrelevant. We are back again where we started. The clue to everything was given, so Christians believe, in the self-disclosure of the love of God in Jesus Christ nearly two thousand years ago. That clue is not a general idea about love but a particular demonstration of love. It is something which occurred at a particular moment of time and at a particular place in space.

In Anno Domini 1952 we cannot avoid facing the inescapable facts with which such a method of dating confronts us, both in its past reference to what happened 'once for all' under Pontius Pilate and in its contemporary relevance to what is happening all the time here and now in the world to-day. To put the issue in a sentence: what have the events which occurred in Palestine over nineteen hundred years ago to do with the events which are occurring in the world to-day?

The main outline of the events in Palestine nineteen hundred years ago is not in dispute, nor is the main outline of world events to-day. There is throughout the world a head-on collision between the aggressive forces of world communism and those who oppose them. The astonishing and alarming thing is that in country after country, in trade union after trade union, the communist advance continues. It is easy to write this off as due either to the diabolic ingenuity of its machinations or to the desperate poverty of its

[1] 1 Cor. 1, 26 ff.   [2] 1 Cor. 13 5

dupes. But this is not to explain but to explain away the way in which a minority movement, and often a very small minority movement at that, goes on and on securing such spectacular successes. A far deeper and more significant explanation is gradually beginning to force itself upon our dulled conscience and blurred vision. The success of the communist drive is due to the totalitarian faith that grips its devoted *corps d'élite*, the communist party. The dialectical materialism of Karl Marx has gripped his followers with a force and a compulsion which are quite incomprehensible to the average tolerant democrat of the western world, who imagines he has left far behind and has in fact quite outgrown the wars of religion, which marked the bigoted and unenlightened fanaticism of his ancestors.

Yet it must be obvious, even to such a democrat, that neither dollars nor guns nor extra butter are proving by themselves adequate to stop this menace, which from the standpoint of western civilization seems like a flood to threaten to engulf the whole world. The agelong tradition of China has gone [1] down before it; the ramparts of Islam are tottering, as even the most superficial observer of Near and Middle Eastern affairs must realize: the one Asiatic country which offers hope of a rival rallying point is India. And in India it is touch-and-go whether a non-communist Congress will succeed in its aims. If it does, it will only be by the skin of its teeth and thanks both to the spiritual testimony of Mahatma Gandhi and to the political decision of Mr. Attlee to quit India by a fixed and definite date.

In Africa (and South America too) the situation is still 'fluid', but the traditional camouflage of the war communiqué language is only too apt a description of the situation in the 'dark continent'. Africans look for a faith upon which to build up their future, and where do they find it? Missionaries from Europe have done much for them, as they usually recognize. But if they visit Europe itself, many of them are greatly disillusioned. Christianity seems 'played out' and already in its western [2] homelands a thing of the past. And in their own country it is so-called Christians from Europe or America who perpetrate in deed in most places, even if in word only in a few, that fatal policy of racial segregation and exclusiveness, which is the hall-mark of a civilization which has lost its nerve and is inwardly on the decline and outwardly on the defensive.

Racial discrimination (no matter how understandable) as an instrument either of conscious policy or of unconscious influence

---

[1] I wrote 'is going' in the first draft of this chapter in 1949.

[2] It cannot be too often repeated (*a*) that Christianity is an eastern religion, (*b*) that Jesus was a Jew, (*c*) that the only indigenously western religion is Marxist communism.

hands over Africa free, *gratis* and for nothing to the communist agitator. It is not the slightest use Christians proclaiming oneness in Christ and in his church in the apostolic language,[1] if they are not prepared for the apostolic implications [2] of their conduct to be drawn out in their own home. This issue of 'the middle wall of partition',[3] whether it is of race or colour or class, is at least as old as the Acts of the Apostles, and really honest *apartheid*, disgraceful though it is for a Christian people, has at least the sanction of post-exilic Judaism [4] and is an improvement in honesty on those hypocritical assurances of spiritual unity which their utterers have no intention of putting into practice in terms of physical and embodied realities.

For Europe and for all those parts of the world which have been predominantly colonized from Europe the real issue to-day is not that between communism and democracy but something much more radical, the deep world-wide cleavage between the white peoples and all others. White hegemony was a world possibility as long as white leadership provided something which not only materially but also morally and spiritually seemed worth copying.[5] But two world wars have shattered the claims of such leadership to deserve world support or imitation. It is therefore quite certain that the nemesis of world communism, with all the attraction that it seems to offer to the underprivileged everywhere, awaits the *hybris* of western materialism unless the latter can offer a positive alternative not only to the communist economic theories and practice but also to the communist ideological doctrines and faith.

Only those possessed by a living faith can venture towards the creation of one world of free and equal peoples with sufficient speed to outstrip their communist rivals. Mere political or economic alternatives to communism are by themselves bankrupt in face of the depth of the emergency confronting the world, unless they are built upon a real and vital religious faith. There is no escaping the stark and unavoidable issue; the only alternative to the world-wide communist *internationale* is the world-wide Christian church.

---

[1] Col. 3, 11.   [2] Gal. 2, 11 ff.   [3] Eph. 2, 14.

[4] Ezra 9, 1–10, 44; Neh. 13, 1 ff. It is noteworthy (*a*) that this racial exclusiveness is emphasized when the Jewish culture and religion is on the defensive, (*b*) that the places where the colour bar is most prominent to-day, viz. South Africa or the Southern States of the U.S.A., are precisely those places in which the Christians are predominantly 'fundamentalist' in their biblical outlook. Thus by putting the Old Testament on a level of practical equality with the New and by levelling the differences within the Old Testament itself, biblical sanction can be found to justify behaviour which runs clean contrary to apostolic practice.

[5] Cf. A. J. Toynbee, *A Study of History* (O.U.P., vols. i–iii, 2nd ed. 1935, vols. iv–vi, 1st ed. 1939), vol. i, pp. 191 f., vol. iii, pp. 244 ff., and 'where there is no creation, there is also no mimesis' (vol. iv, p. 5).

This is not to deny the importance of other religions. If God is one, he is one and the same in all places and at all times. He may be interpreted very differently, but the fundamental difference is not between rival interpretations of him, whether on the one hand these are primitive and animistic or developed and monotheistic, or whether on the other hand they are crude like Jael's [1] or lovely like St John's. Such differences are real differences of interpretation, but they do not necessarily involve any contradiction of revelation. The fundamental cleavage is between those who are interpreting a revelation, however crudely or beautifully, and those who are strangers to all such revelation; it is between those whose knowledge about God, however primitive, is based upon true knowledge of him, and those whose knowledge about him, however developed, has no such foundation. The difference in the Old Testament between Yahweh and Baal is not that Yahweh is moral and Baal is not. It is that Yahweh is alive and Baal is not. It is only the living God who can reveal himself at all, and it is certainly only the living God who can become the loving God.

But when all this has been said (and it needs saying very badly indeed in days when the interpretation of the faith is so often mistaken for its dynamic), it still remains true that it is only in Christianity of all the religions in the world that God has been unequivocally interpreted as love. Even in Christianity itself there has always been the constant temptation for the church to revert to something lower than the revelation given in our Lord Jesus Christ, or to find in another than him the secret of who God is and of what he is like. He either ceases to be fully personal, as is certainly the case with the religions of India, or he ceases to be fully ethical, as in the arrested development of Judaism and in the perverted development of Islam.

The fact that Christians do not live up to their faith and that others do in fact live better lives than Christians do (whether it is true or not—and it might be claimed that on the whole it is the exception that proves the rule) is no disproof of the claim that in both faith and practice Christianity is the one live alternative to communism to-day. Christians should be grateful for the spiritual values of the Indian sub-continent which have so far resisted the materialistic dogmas of the Marxists; but Hindus should not be blind to the fact that it is precisely the strongholds of orthodox Hinduism which are the great obstacle to the development of that secular India in which alone Mr. Nehru sees any alternative to communism. Christians in the west cannot help wondering whether,

[1] Judg. 5, 24 ff.

if India is secularized and so loses her ancestral faiths, she will not be in the end an easier prey to communism than if she were resolutely committed to the rigidities of orthodox Hinduism.

As far as Islam is concerned, Christians should recognize with gratitude and at the same time with shame (as they look at their own past and present record) that on the crucial contemporary issue of the breaking down of those racial barriers, which so divide our modern world and so envenom all human relationships within it, Islam may well have a big contribution to make.[1] On the other hand, Moslems should face up both to the intellectual sterility of Islam in face of the vast movements of modern thought and the vast advances of modern techniques, and also to its inability so far to provide any positive spiritual antidote to western secularism, despite the use of religious ideas to cloak nationalist ambitions.[2]

It is at first sight strange that a religion, which has no caste system comparable to the caste system of India and which imposes no segregation (except between the sexes) comparable to that imposed by so much protestant Christianity[3] between different races and colours where these live together, should now be used as a lever to exaggerate rather than to lessen the differences between nations. But the reason is not far to seek, for these very differences are fundamentally in theory at least not national, but religious. It is against the nations which are not of 'the house of Islam' that the Moslem erects his barriers. And on his own premises he is justified, for they belong to 'the house of war', and a *jihad* is no further from the minds of some Moslems than is an Inquisition from the minds of some Christians.

Neither the religions of India nor those of the Arab world[4] can seriously dispute the claim of Christianity to be the only possible existing rallying ground for those who are looking not for an eclectic system but for a dynamic faith, with which to oppose communism not with a rival ideology of hate but with the real gospel of love. But, although this is so, it is no good pretending that the divided and quite literally hopeless condition of many parts of the Christian

---

[1] Cf. A. J. Toynbee, *Civilization on Trial* (O.U.P., 1948), pp. 184–212.

[2] Despite (a) the mysticism of the Sufis and (b) the missionary enthusiasm of the Ahmadiyah sect.

[3] Cf. A. J. Toynbee, *A Study of History*, vol. i, pp. 211 ff., and especially 'the race feeling engendered by the English Protestant version of our Western culture became the determining factor in the development of race-feeling in our Western Society as a whole' (p. 211). In the light of this, Wilberforce's great achievement of the emancipation of all slaves within the British Empire takes on the appearance not so much of a triumph of disinterested altruism as of an act of tardy and long overdue penance.

[4] Including Zoroastrianism with its non-Arabic Persian origin and its later Parsee development in India.

church gives sober ground for confidence in any success other than that guaranteed through death by the resurrection from the dead. And indeed the Christian faith is never apostolically based on any other foundation than that, however valuable apologetically may be the evidences of the progress of its culture and civilization or the statistics of its conversions and baptisms.

If we reject the Christian church as the one live option to the communist *internationale*, where else can we look? An eclectic faith, formed by a synthesis of the best of all religions, and perhaps of all idealist philosophies as well, neither shows any sign of generating the dynamic needed nor could it possibly be made to fit into any interpretation of Christianity which gave full value to the unique once-for-all character of the revelation of God in our Lord Jesus Christ. Furthermore, such an eclectic faith, though it might hold the conscious allegiance of the understanding of its adherents, could never grip by its rational and ethical and idealistic truths those depths of the unconscious, which need the symbols and images of historic religion if they are to come to expression and through such turbines generate the power needed for world regeneration.

As for the rival alternative religions to Christianity, it is no part of the creed of anyone who believes in the salvation offered to mankind in the unique disclosure of the love of God in our Lord Jesus Christ to deny the revelations of that selfsame love which have been given partially not only to the Jews but also to those who share the primitive natural religious outlook of mankind, however differently interpreted, and to those who are still living worshippers within some other non-Christian historic religion. But to admit all this gladly, as we should, rather than grudgingly, as we so often do, by no means implies that the challenge of communism for the soul of the world can be met as adequately by them as by Christianity. On the contrary, if it is a personal faith we need, then Christianity is better than the religions of India; if it is an ethical faith, then Christianity is an improvement upon either the arrested development of Judaism (which if it had been true to itself would not have crucified Jesus Christ) or the perverted development of Islam (which, however understandable in its origins, is nevertheless a deviation from the authentic Judæo-Christian stock from which it stems).

There is in fact no live option to communism to-day except the Christian church. And to express it in terms of such rivalry between Christianity and communism by no means implies that Christians are committed necessarily to the belief that the communists are either the sole or even the chief devils of the piece. In the light of the parable of our Lord about the mote and the beam [1] it is not for us to judge. What we can with certainty say is that the advance of communism to-day, like the advance of Attila the Hun in the fifth century A.D., and like the advance of Sennacherib the Assyrian in the eighth century B.C., is indeed 'the scourge' of God or 'the rod' of his anger upon us.[2] The scourge, if only we will understand its meaning, can be for our chastening and salvation.[3] But if we are blind to its significance and refuse to face its challenge to build one world upon better and surer foundations than it can offer, then it can only be for our destruction. And in that case our civilization will be no exception to Professor Toynbee's general rule: its destruction will be due far more to our own wilful and suicidal unwillingness to face facts and to carry out the clear implications of our own faith than to any diabolical ingenuity of our Machiavellian rivals.

If anything like this is a true picture of the actual situation with which we are confronted in A.D. 1952, then we need at once to come to grips with the issues involved. They are primarily ideological, not economic. They are primarily matters of faith, not matters of conduct; though in this struggle a faith that does not work, e.g. in terms of real brotherhood and genuine human friendship, is condemned to an utterly futile sterility and cannot long survive. It will be worth while, therefore, to look for a possible touchstone of conduct before we find a touchstone of faith. Each may give us a clue as to that *punctum stantis aut cadentis ecclesiæ* in our new Elizabethan age which may stand comparison with the doctrine of justification by faith in the reign of Queen Elizabeth I.

As far as conduct is concerned, it is salutary to keep the parable of the mote and the beam before our minds and, if we do, then the converging testimony of hostile communist propaganda on the one hand and friendly impartial investigation on the other suggests that we are likely to find at least one of the main practical causes of the predicament of the non-communist world in the behaviour of the white peoples who dominate that world in power towards the coloured peoples who dominate it in population. Professor Gunnar Myrdal's exhaustive study of the Negro question [4] in the United States of America is as much evidence of this as is the attitude of most if not all the non-European members of the United Nations towards South Africa.

It is at the point of the colour-bar right within our so-called democratic world rather than at the point of the iron curtain at its

[1] Matt. 7, 1 ff.   [2] Isa. 10, 5.   [3] Heb. 12, 5 ff.
[4] Cf. Gunnar Myrdal, *An American Dilemma* (1944), condensed authoritatively in A. Rose, *The Negro in America* (Secker and Warburg, 1948).

frontier that we face the issue of 'the middle wall of partition',[1] with which the early church was confronted. It had to face the issue as between Jew and Gentile (not between Gentile and barbarian). We have to face the issue as between white and black (not between one side of the iron curtain and the other). If we were to face up to what we can do something about, we might find there was something we could do about the thing about which at present we feel unable to do anything. It is so much easier to talk about the big issues of which we are powerless spectators than to do something about the smaller issues in which we could be effective actors.

The upshot of Professor Myrdal's study is that, so far as the relations between black and white in the United States of America are concerned, it is true that the root of the whole problem is not economic or material, but psychological and spiritual. Behind all the other difficulties lies the basic fear of the whites lest there should be any sexual intercourse between the races which might lead to racial miscegenation.[2] The abhorrence professed by the whites for such sexual relationship has both its tragic and its ironical aspects. On the one hand there are the millions of mulattoes,[3] and on the other hand there is the psychologically compensatory cult of the natural or artificial tan of the bodies of white people, which seems to have grown up *pari passu* with the hardening of the lines of colour prejudice.

[1] Eph. 2, 14.

[2] A. Rose, *op. cit.*, *passim* and especially pp. 22 ff., 194–197: 'Sex and race fears are, however, even to-day the main defense for segregation and the whole caste order' (p. 197), and also his conclusion: 'Our handling of the Negro problem has much more effect on Asia and on Africa than it has on Europe, however. Most of the inhabitants of these continents are colored (in appearance, if not in race). Hatred of "white" people is intense in Asia and Africa, not only because the whites have set themselves up as racially superior but also because the whites are seen as conquerors and as tyrants. Hatred against whites is identified with the struggle for national freedom. The colored peoples of the world have always had divided feelings about America: they have admired our treatment of the Philippine Islands, our attitude after the Boxer Rebellion in China, our lack of imperialist aims, and our democratic government at home. At the same time they have resented deeply our treatment of the Negroes and our theories of the racial inferiority of darker peoples.

'Until recently what the colored peoples thought of us did not make much difference. Now it has become of crucial importance to us. Whatever Russia's faults she has no color prejudice. Again and again she has demonstrated that she does not regard colored people as inferior, that she respects their culture. Laws against discrimination or the manifestation of prejudice are strictly enforced. To the colored people of the world suffering under the double yoke of prejudice and colonial exploitation from white people, this attitude of Russia's has a strong appeal. It is doubtful, however, if it is as appealing as the promise of real democracy America can hold out—provided we can hold out also the promise of equality to the individual regardless of color' (p. 320).

[3] Cf. W. E. B. du Bois, *The Souls of Black Folk* (A. C. McClurg, Chicago, 1924), p. 106: 'The rape which your gentlemen have done against helpless black women in defiance of your own laws is written on the foreheads of two millions of mulattoes, and written in ineffaceable blood' (quoted by A. Rose, *op. cit.*, p. 25).

If this problem of the relations between the white peoples of the world and all others is in one way or another at the root of so many other troubles to-day, it most certainly undermines the claim of the non-communist world to be genuinely democratic, and it bears a striking resemblance to the basic practical problem of conduct which in one way or another undermined all over the Mediterranean world the claim of the Jews to be the champions of the one true and universal faith in the time of Jesus Christ.   The attempt to 'compass sea and land to make one proselyte'[1] was as futile for Pharisees then as it is for missionaries to-day, unless coupled with a willingness to face and overthrow by mutual and reciprocal and embodied love the 'middle wall of partition'[2] which divides blacks and whites to-day as surely as it divided Jews and Gentiles two thousand years ago.   The attempt by segregated white and black churches in the United States of America to evangelize the people of Africa, when they are unwilling to worship or eat together in America, would be laughable if it were not so tragic.   And any missionary society frowning upon, even if not explicitly forbidding, any form of mixed marriage 'in Christ' has obviously in principle excluded itself from all chance of speaking to the condition of the peoples of many countries at their point of greatest need.[3]

It was precisely because Christianity knew how to deal with this basic problem in the form in which it confronted the early church, and because the apostles had the courage to carry out the implications of their Lord's practice and teaching, that it was the Christian religion which took the place of the Jewish religion and in the end succeeded where Judaism had failed, and persuaded the world that it had the secret of which it was most in need.   Here was the one faith that in a time of disintegration, division and collapse had the secret of constructive unity.

The issue had to be faced not only in the church but also in the home.   St Paul's stand-up fight with St Peter at Antioch[4] suggests that a celibate missionary without a home found the solution rather easier than a married man with a home.   But it was then, as it still is now, the man with a family who can finally establish and root the church in any community.

First-century Christianity had the secret of uniting 'in Christ'

---

[1] Matt. 23, 15.   [2] Eph. 2, 14.
[3] The point is not whether a particular mixed marriage is good or bad, wise or unwise.   It is whether in principle all mixed marriages are frowned upon.   How do the missionary societies of all the Protestant churches stand up to this test?   And how would those Catholic and Anglican societies, which have a better record, fare if their missionaries were not so often vowed to celibacy?
[4] Gal. 2, 11 ff.

both Jews and Gentiles, both barbarians and Scythians, both slaves and freemen, and even both men and women.[1] There was as much temptation then as there is to-day to be content with a church on one side only of the great dividing issues of humanity, of one race or of one sex or of one class; but this easier way was resolutely rejected, and almost the whole of the story of the early church recorded in the New Testament is concerned with that rejection. Instead of being a church of one race or even of one empire, the Christian church in the end won the title of 'the third race', not because of its racial exclusiveness, but because its membership cut across all racial divisions whether of the civilized world within the Roman empire or the barbarians without.

It was the creation of this one universal society across the frontiers which divided mankind which was the supreme practical achievement of the first Christians. If the practical issue which they so triumphantly succeeded in solving is still as much the touchstone of conduct to-day as it was two thousand years ago, then it is not impossible that the doctrinal issue which they solved may be the touchstone of faith to-day, especially if the basic problems of humanity remain as constant as they appear to do, and if the era in which Christianity arose is at least comparable with our own in being an era of the decline of a dominant civilization.[2]

If we look at the doctrinal scene presented by the declining Græco-Roman civilization, we may perhaps be led to investigate the re-discovery of hope as being at the very heart of the good news which Christianity brought to the Levant and so to the whole Mediterranean world two thousand years ago. Faith then was in tolerably good supply. The Jews had successfully resisted all attempts to stamp out their peculiar religion, and had so completely turned the tables on the Hellenizers that all over the Mediterranean world they were an active and aggressively distinctive element in the body politic in the time of Jesus Christ. At the same time the Roman empire was being flooded by mystery cults, whether of Greek or oriental or synthetic origin, and even the fabricated cult of the emperor was providing some substitute for the old Lares and Penates of Rome which had fallen into as much disrepute as the old Olympian gods of Greece, who had gone down like ninepins before the biting

---

[1] Gal. 3, 28.
[2] This, I think, is the sure conclusion to be drawn from Professor Toynbee's *A Study of History*, based upon the theory of the philosophical comparability of civilizations and of their relative historical contemporaneity as a species of organized society. It does not carry with it Oswald Spengler's determinism, nor does it necessarily imply acceptance *in toto* of Professor Toynbee's complete pattern of the rise and fall of civilizations.

sarcasm of the Greek comedians and the splendid reconstructions of the Greek philosophers. In fact the motive behind the recall to religion issued in the name of the imperial cult was not the fear that there would soon be no religion in the Empire, but the fear that there would soon be too many religions within the Empire and that these would threaten its unity rather than cement it. Religious faith was not at all in decline in the world in which Jesus Christ was born.

As for love, the genuine article is always in such short supply that facile attempts to prove that it was a powerful factor in the life of the Roman empire in the first century A.D. are bound to fail. Nevertheless equally facile attempts to write that century off the record of history as a forlorn and loveless era are equally wide of the mark. For it is undoubtedly true that the world was not often so near the Platonic ideal of the rule of a philosopher-king as when the Roman empire enjoyed the famous *quinquennium Neronis* [1] and when the Stoic philosopher, Seneca, was the emperor's tutor. Here was a philosophy which combined high ideals with practical politics, and as such brought the brotherhood of man within the range of possibility in a way not often seen in history.[2]

At the very point of the ancient world's greatest need, across the barriers of nation or class, the Stoic faith gained ground. It was a grand ideal, but it lacked the depth of dynamic faith to appeal to the masses. But in view of what it did to extend the boundaries not only of thought but also of practical sympathy and love across the narrow frontiers of nations, it would be unjust to speak of love as the virtue in shortest supply in the Roman empire in the first century A.D., even though Christianity brought such an entirely new conception of its meaning into the ancient world as to necessitate the coining of an completely new vocabulary with which to express it.[3]

No; of the three theological virtues it was not faith and it was not love, but it was hope which was in shortest supply in the ancient world to which Christ came, and it is precisely in the same position to-day. It was the lack of a positive and adequate future hope in this world which led to 'the failure of nerve' of the Græco-Roman civilization and to that preoccupation with its defence which used

---

[1] Cf. H. Furneaux, *The Annals of Tacitus* (O.U.P., 1907), vol. ii, pp. 55 ff.

[2] Cf. Sir A. Grant, *The Ethics of Aristotle* (Longmans, 1885), vol. i, pp. 304 ff., especially 'We have seen how it' (*sc.* Stoicism) 'held up the delights of an inner life as preferable to all tangible and palpable enjoyments, however innocent they might be; we have seen how it drew the mind away from external realities into an abstract ideal; how it delighted in the conception of moral progress and the triumph of will; how it developed the thought of duty and the responsibility of the individual; how deserting the restrictions of national politics it raised itself to conceive of all mankind in one brotherhood, each member standing in direct relation to God . . .' (pp. 370 f.).

[3] Cf. A. Nygren, *Agape and Eros* (S.P.C.K., 1931), part I, p. 43.

up the energies of the best emperors during the first three centuries of the Christian era. The Empire became a vast static bureaucratic system, looking for nothing better than the maintenance of the *status quo*. Even the great Augustan peace was at least in Italy itself the peace of exhaustion after the hundred years of civil strife which began with the murder of Tiberius Gracchus in 130 B.C. and only ended with Augustus' victory at Actium in 30 B.C. And as far as the vision of the *pax Romana* was concerned, there was nothing beyond the frontiers of the Empire. All hope stopped short there. What had Rome to offer the barbarians in this life except subjection to the sword? And what had the genius of the emperor to offer anyone after this life?

Indeed quite apart from the cyclical view of time,[1] which ruled out any confident hope in an historical future in this life, there was no hope of life beyond the grave except among the Jews and the initiates of some of the mystery cults. These latter had no hope to offer in this life, but from the first their popularity partly depended upon the assurance they gave of life beyond the grave.[2] And as for the Jews, the official conservative Sadducees were now the exception to prove the general rule of a hope in a life after death, though it was a hope jealously and exclusively guarded by most of the Jews for themselves alone. In this life the only hope they saw was to be achieved by a fury of either proselytizing or nationalist zeal. The missionary and the nationalist zealots were fiery and fanatical, but the gospel of hope which they commended was a gospel to be received if not at the point of the pike, at least at the dictation of the *torah*. If Saul [3] the Pharisee was the pattern of the one, Simon the Zealot (if we knew more about him) or Judas Iscariot (if Miss Dorothy Sayers [4] is not right about him) might well be the pattern of the other.

It was hope that the declining Græco-Roman civilization needed most of all the virtues. It was hope that in this world it could never find as long as the cyclical view of time prevailed. If there was a golden age it lay in the dim and distant past, and the most that could be hoped for was its recurrence at the end of perhaps 36,000 years.[5] Only among the Jews was there any real sense of history moving forward with a purpose. But there was little in the nature of that purpose to offer much attraction to any self-respecting Gentile. It

---

[1] Cf. J. Baillie, *The Belief in Progress* (O.U.P., 1950), pp. 422 ff., and the quotation from Aristotle, *Physics*, Bk. IV, 14, 223b, Καὶ γὰρ ὁ χρόνος αὐτὸς εἶναι δοκεῖ κύκλος τις.
[2] Cf. J. Baillie, *And the Life Everlasting* (O.U.P., 1934), pp. 107 ff.
[3] Phil. 3, 5 ff.
[4] Cf. D. L. Sayers, *The Man Born to be King* (Gollancz, 1943), pp. 30 ff.
[5] Cf. J. Baillie, *The Belief in Progress*, p. 47.

is the absence of hope from all the ancient pagan cultures which
is the most remarkable thing about them from the standpoint of
anyone brought up in the Judæo-Christian tradition.

'Remember', wrote St Paul to the Christians at Ephesus, 'that
when you were pagans . . . you had no hope' (ἐλπίδα μὴ ἔχοντες).[1]
He was writing to Greeks, but the words would have been equally
appropriate if addressed to Indians or Chinese, Babylonians or
Egyptians. For none of these peoples did future time hold any
promise of better things, but at best the prospect of wearisome
sameness and at worst the threat of doom.[2] It was to such a people
'without God' (and that meant particularly 'without hope')[3] that
the Christian gospel came, and the point of its relevance to the needs
of the world was its offer of a ringing and confident, but never
forced or fevered, hope.

It offered hope in a fulfilment of God's purpose on earth, in which
there was no most-favoured-nation treaty clause restricting God's
favours to his favourites. It offered hope in a fulfilment of God's
purpose beyond this earth in 'a new heaven and a new earth',[4]
in a life after death, far more wonderful than anything of which the
pagan world had ever dared to dream and far more sensible than
anything the Jewish world had imagined. If it was 'the middle
wall of partition'[5] which was the touchstone of the conduct of the
early church, it was eschatology which was the touchstone of its
doctrine. Its hope was clear, definite and universal. It knew what
it hoped for, and it knew it not by any magical pre-view of the shape
of things to come, but by a clear and distinct idea of the meaning
of things as they are. The early Christians were content to leave
on one side the wilder apocalyptic speculations about the details
of the future with which hawkers always seek to satisfy man's
curiosity about the unknown, for they were confident that these
were not what mattered. For them nothing mattered in the world
in comparison with the revelation of God's love in the person of
Jesus Christ himself.

It goes without saying that if the view of revelation, already
outlined as the self-disclosure of love, is right, then it is wrong to
look for an answer to the question as to what they hoped for in
terms of any advance or inside information about the shape of things
to come, even when the pre-view can claim biblical or ecclesiastical
sanction. We shall look for the answer in terms not of any future
propositional speculation of logic, but in terms of a present personal

---

[1] Eph. 2, 11 f.
[2] J. Baillie, *The Belief in Progress*, p. 50 f.
[3] Eph. 2, 12.   [4] Rev. 21, 1.   [5] Eph. 2, 14.

2

relationship of love. If the latter is unreal, then the former can only be speculative, but if the latter is real, then its reality carries with it the reality of the former also.

The fact that of the three theological virtues it is hope which is in shortest supply will not deceive us into imagining that a future hope which is unrelated to present faith can carry any conviction whatever, except to a fanatical bigot or a fantastic dreamer. And even where faith and hope are interrelated, we shall not imagine for one minute that their logical interdependence is necessarily any guarantee of their validity, unless they are both the interpretative response to the revelation of love, which can never be glimpsed except by those who are 'in love' themselves.

Keeping 'faith, hope, love, these three' [1] thus indissolubly connected, we shall face the fact that the relevance of the Christian gospel to the world's need to-day is doctrinally at the point of hope, even if ethically it is (as we have seen) at the point of love. But we shall not expect to be able to present the Christian hope as a living alternative either to the hopelessness of our modern pagan non-communist democracy or to the false hope of modern Marxist communism, unless that Christian hope is itself the corollary of present faith, and unless both faith and hope are the implications for the present and the future of the revelation of love itself.

It is a living eschatology, and that means a loving eschatology, which the Christian church needs more than anything else to-day. And its interpretation of the future will only be living if it is the fruit of such an understanding of the present as realizes that the revelation disclosed in it is essentially loving. Only the present presence will give the future parousia the generating power of a creative idea: on any other basis it will lose its vitality and be either at best an optional extra to round off a neat theological system contriving to make the best of the *status quo*, or at worst the most completely paralysing inhibitor of any present creativity whatever. Unless, in other words, the Christian eschatological parousia is matched by the Christian mystical presence, it will be powerless to provide the hope that is needed both by the church and by the world at the level at which it is needed.

It is one thing to meet evil with evil, to use the weapons of carnal [2] warfare to win a carnal victory, to introduce one rival fanatical hope to defeat another fanatical hope: it is quite another thing to meet evil and overcome it with good, to use the weapons that are not carnal to win a spiritual victory, to offer the weakness of the hope of love to defeat the strength of the hope of hate (whether that hatred

[1] 1 Cor. 13, 13.   [2] 2 Cor. 10, 4.

is expressed militarily or intellectually). The first way is not the way of Christ, though it may often be the way of the world and even of the worldly church. The second is still the way of Christ, and unless the Christian theologian bends his energies to serve Christ's way rather than to impose his own or any other, he has nothing to offer as a constructive contribution towards a solution of our present problems.

It was at the conclusion of a most impressive broadcast on 'Why Marxism attracted the Russians' that Mr. Christopher Hollis said: 'It will be a waste of time overthrowing Bolshevism unless it is overthrown by a trained theologian.' [1] The whole of the rest of his argument focused the trained theologian's task upon the crying need of providing the world with a sane and invigorating hope based upon a clear and coherent eschatology. Mr. Hollis emphasized the notorious, but none the less strange, fact that of all people in the world it was the Russians who were the first nation to embrace the teaching of Karl Marx and make it the dogmatic basis of their national policy. This was to run flat in the face of Marx's thesis that the necessary precondition of a successful communist revolution was a stage of capitalism, through which Russia as a matter of fact had never passed. In the face of this strange fact that Russia, which adopted Marx's doctrines, herself contradicted them in doing so, it is most important to ask the fundamental question as to why it was that the Russians embraced communism in the way they did.

There must have been many contributory factors which were responsible for this; but at least one of them, and probably one that was more important than most others, was that the Russians were, as Mr. Hollis put it, a profoundly messianic people: 'they are incomparably more millennium-minded than are we of the west.' This is what linked them in sympathy not with the logical, but with the illogical element in the communist hope for the future expressed in the Marxist doctrine of the last things.

To understand this, it is important to remember Karl Marx's own personal history. His family was Jewish, but his parents became Christians, and his own best piece of school-work is reported to have been an essay on the passage in St John's Gospel which ends with the words of Christ to his disciples, 'Ye are my friends, if ye do the things which I command you'.[2] Two factors must have greatly influenced the future prophet of communism: the behaviour of Gentile Christians towards his newly converted Jewish family, and the tradition of agelong Judaism, from which it sprang.

---

[1] *The Listener* (January 22, 1948), p. 131.
[2] John 15, 14; cf. E. H. Carr, *Karl Marx* (Dent, 1934), p. 5.

Anyone who has had opportunities to study to-day at first hand the interrelations of Christians and Jews, and especially the behaviour of Christians to Jewish converts to Christianity, can hardly doubt that here in Marx's case was a powerful influence towards the hard and biting ruthlessness of his final challenge to contemporary capitalism.   So often the Jewish convert to Christianity remains an outcaste from both communities.   Ostracized by his own fellow-Jews for the great apostasy, he is alternately fawned upon as an exhibit or despised as an inferior by the community which claims the name of Jesus Christ but so easily forgets that Jesus was himself a Jew.

There is no need to go all the way with the anti-Semites, who perform the crowning indignity, in Léon Bloy's graphic phrase, of slapping our Lord 'on the face of his mother'.[1]   There is abundant evidence to-day, as there has been all down the history of the Christian church, of the continual reappearance of that 'middle wall of partition'[2] between Jew and Gentile, to the smashing of which the main energies of the two greatest of the apostles, St Peter and St Paul, were primarily devoted.   We have forgotten time and time again that love is no one-way-traffic dole of giving, but a two-way-traffic street of mutual give and take, and that to 'love our neighbour' in this way in theory is quite valueless unless we are prepared to love him in practice as well.   If we are, we are quite likely to be not the givers of favours to others, but the recipients of favours from them, as the parable of the half-caste non-conformist whom we call the Good Samaritan makes abundantly plain.[3]

Had the Christian church welcomed Marx and his family on terms of mutual respect and love, and had he had actual experience in boyhood of the unity of Christian fellowship and communion in a voluntary and free association of friends, such as the subject of his boyhood essay depicts, then history might have run very differently.   For who knows whether the 'iron curtain' of to-day may not owe its origin to the 'middle wall of partition'[4] still existing in the Christian church of the Rhineland just over one hundred years ago?

Certainly here is one factor which goes far to explain Marx's manner, if not his matter.   But there is another, and this goes far deeper and certainly does something to explain his matter as well as

---

[1] Cf. A. Béguin, *Léon Bloy: A Study of Impatience* (Sheed and Ward, 1947): 'Anti-Semitism, a quite modern development, and the most horrible buffet that our Lord has received in his Passion, which is still going on: it is the most outrageous and the most unpardonable because he receives it ON THE FACE OF HIS MOTHER and from Christian hands . . .' (p. 136).

[2] Eph. 2, 14.   [3] Luke 10, 25 ff.   [4] Eph. 2, 14.

his manner. Russian Christian messianism and Russian communist messianism are both connected with Jewish messianism, and in the second case Karl Marx himself is the connecting link. His hopes for the future are not reasoned conclusions which can be supported in logical argument. They are dogmatic assertions quite illogically connected with the Marxist analysis of the contemporary scene. There is no logical reason why capitalism should give place to a classless society. On the contrary, everything in history and logic suggests that the removal of one class will pave the way for the supremacy of another, and that the behaviour of the latter will end by differing little from the behaviour of the former.

Why did Marx say 'No' to this? Why did he dogmatically affirm the contrary? For the answer to these questions we must turn from his relations with Christians in the Germany of his youth to his Jewish background and heredity. In many ways, as has so often been pointed out, Marx is the last of the great Hebrew prophets, and in so far as he stands in that great succession, his hopes for the future are based not upon the logic of reason, but upon the intuition of faith, with which all down history and in the teeth of every apparently insuperable objection, both material and logical, the Jews have clung tenaciously to the conviction that a glorious future awaited the chosen people in what might be described as the messianic age.

Whether this vision was the real climax of a religion of hope or the compensatory refuge of a religion of despair, it was certainly the hope that gripped Marx. He transferred it from a racial to a social proletariat, and no doubt the nominal Christianity of his early days provided the stepping-stone that eased the transition. It is his dogma of the last things that has gripped the minds and fired the imagination of his Russian followers. And the fact that the Marxist eschatology is of this world and not of the next, for the community rather than for the individual, only serves to strengthen its link with the Old Testament. For it is one of the most remarkable things about the Old Testament that the Jews refused the temptation to indulge in speculation about life after death, though such speculation abounded in other parts of the Near East all around them. Right up till the very end the outlook of the Old Testament is for this world and for the nation rather than for the next world and the individual. Even if in the very end the individual does come into his own and even if then a future opens up beyond the grave, that fact only serves to throw into higher relief the confidence held by the Jews for nearly a millennium in a future confined to this life. Such a hope flies in the face of every conceivable objection, whether in history or in logic.

It is just this illogical dogmatic conviction about the end that links the Jewish and the Russian outlooks. And it is here that the 'trained theologian', whom Mr. Hollis desires,[1] must get to grips with Marxism if Bolshevism is to be overthrown to any useful purpose. Unless some better alternative to the Marxist dogma of the last things can be put forward, the best that the opponents of communism can do is to drive out one devil with the certainty, guaranteed by Jesus himself, and endorsed on every page of contemporary history, that the 'swept and garnished'[2] house thus left empty will be occupied by at least half a dozen other devils far worse than the first.

And here we come up against the real difficulty. The western church unlike the eastern orthodox church, to which Russian communism owes so much of unacknowledged debt,[3] has always been so preoccupied with Christ's first coming that it has for all practical purposes neglected his second coming altogether. And when, as always happens in times of doubt and loss of faith, his first coming is regarded merely as an historical event in past time and not as a contemporary fact of eternity revealed in past time, then of course there is every reason for the Russian protest against the obstacle to all progress that such historical archaism inevitably produces. In this sense, in the phrase of Oswald Spengler, which Mr. Hollis quotes, Russian communism is 'an apocalyptic revolt against antiquity'.[4]

If we are to counter this apocalyptic revolution of futurism against archaism, we can only do so if we have a more adequate and a more securely grounded and at the same time an equally triumphant confidence in the future. And we do not have to go to Russia and the Marxists to see the need for such a true eschatology. We need it to counter the false pride of a present deified institution if we are to be preserved from the fatal consequences of political or ecclesiastical *hybris*,[5] and at the same time to retain our faith in the divine society and in God's present activity both in the church and in the world.

We need it, too, to direct the non-communist surge of new hope in the lands only recently aware of their possibilities and only now becoming self-conscious of their nationhood. The spirit of the

---

[1] *The Listener* (January 22, 1948), p. 131.
[2] Matt. 12, 44.
[3] Cf. A. J. Toynbee, *Civilization on Trial* (O.U.P., 1948): 'Under the Hammer and Sickle, as under the Cross, Russia is still "Holy Russia" and Moscow still "The Third Rome". *Tamen usque recurret*' (p. 183).
[4] *The Listener, loc. cit.*
[5] Cf. A. J. Toynbee, *A Study of History*, vol. iv, pp. 512 ff.

students and scholars who sought the new learning of Europe and who were prepared to wander [1] the length and breadth of the continent to find it at the time of the Renaissance is now the spirit of the students and scholars who come from 'darkest Africa' to our shores with a desperate and wistful earnestness to discover the treasures of our learning to-day. They are full of hope for their continent. How can their enthusiasm be directed aright except by those who share their hope and are able to base it upon surer foundations?

As far as the western world itself is concerned, the optimistic evolutionary liberalism of a past European era may still linger in the isolationism of the Middle West of the United States of America, though contemporary evidence suggests to an outsider that it is giving way either to a timid and defeatist pessimism or to mass hysteria in many political quarters which have no present awareness of the historical religious roots of American political optimism. Where there is such awareness, there is a tendency for religion to retreat from the whole range of contemporary life, and from the manifold complexities and responsibilities involved in living in it, in order to cultivate a narrow area within which a forcing-house enthusiasm can be artificially worked up and sustained. We need not be surprised that the pathetic hunger of the masses should turn to all the sects in legitimate search for the food, of which they have for so long been starved by the church. It might well be that the 'displaced persons' who through suffering can contribute to our day the spiritual revival which alone can save our civilization would be rightly looked for in the most abundantly prolific of all the areas of the world in producing sects which are filled with what are to us fantastic visions of the future. The Negroes in the United States of America might stand comparison in this respect with both the Jewish exiles in Babylonia and the early Christians in the Roman empire far better than most other communities in the world.[2]

Clearly it is a surer and a saner hope for the future which is in every case the need of our times, if we are to match the hour not only with the cause but with the men. There is a moving passage in Martin Buber's profoundly searching critique of Christian missions to Jews,[3] which bears on the same point. 'For us', he says, writing as a Jew, 'at no definite point in history has a saviour appeared, so that a new redeemed history began with him. Because we have

[1] Cf. H. Waddell, The Wandering Scholars (6th ed. 1932) (Constable).
[2] Cf. A. J. Toynbee, Civilization on Trial, p. 15, and A Study of History, vol. v, pp. 192 ff.; W. L. Sperry, Religion in America (C.U.P., 1945), pp. 181 ff., 287 ff.
[3] M. Buber, Mamre (Melbourne University Press and O.U.P., 1946), pp. 18 ff.

not been stilled by anything which has happened, we are wholly orientated towards the coming of that which shall come.'[1]

Of course this whole future orientation may take the form of a futurism, which is ultimately as disastrous as the most reactionary archaism.[2] All fanatical forcing of the future must remain foreign to the spirit of the true followers of Jesus of Nazareth. But this is no excuse whatever for falling back upon the past and relying on it in such a way as to ignore the future orientation of life which is as characteristic of the New Testament as of the Old, and far more richly developed in the New Testament than in the Old.

To this extent at least Buber's criticism is well founded and he needs taking seriously to heart as he goes on to claim that 'thus divided from you' (i.e. Christians) 'we have been assigned to you for your help'. He ends by quoting Franz Rosenzweig's direct challenge to the Christian church: 'You who live in an *ecclesia triumphans* need a silent servant who reminds you every time you believe you have partaken of God in bread and wine, "Sir, remember the last things".'[3] Such criticism is fair both negatively because of the historic attitude of the Christian church to the Jews, and also positively because it is true to the element of surprise which is central to the whole eschatological outlook of the New Testament. Karl Barth is in this respect true to St Paul, and indeed to the whole of the New Testament, when he emphasizes 'the great preliminariness'[4] with which the performance of the eucharistic action is everywhere coloured. It is a striking tribute to the scriptural character of the Book of Common Prayer that in 'The Order of the Administration of the Lord's Supper or Holy Communion' it emphasizes the eschatological significance of the sacrament with the explicit reference to its *interim* character, 'until his coming again'.

Buber's emphasis is one-sided, but equally certainly it is an emphasis badly needed to correct the western church, which has been all too easily 'stilled'[5] by the past historical event of the historic coming of Jesus Christ into a total failure to enter into the intense future expectation of the early church. To the modern western Christian, whether he be catholic or protestant, Karl Barth is well entitled to put his challenging application of the Pauline

---

[1] M. Buber, *op. cit.*, p. 30.

[2] The state of Israel provides something like a laboratory experiment of these tensions at work in their most extreme form. Here ultra-modern communist experimentation is seen side by side with ultra-reactionary religious conservatism, and each is driven into the archaism of the forced revival of the ancient Hebrew language.

[3] M. Buber, *op. cit.*

[4] K. Barth, *The Resurrection of the Dead* (Hodder and Stoughton, 1933), p. 71.

[5] M. Buber, *loc. cit.*

time limit, 'till he come'.[1] 'Can this action', he asks of the celebra-
tion of the Lord's Supper, 'be performed in the church without
shuddering at the great preliminariness with which this, our world,
"in the night when the Lord Jesus was betrayed", was characterized
for ever?'[2]

It is not good enough just to dismiss Barth's challenge or to ignore
Rosenzweig's reminder. Theoretically no doubt we can rebut his
suggestion of arrogance and complacency in an *ecclesia triumphans*
by referring him to the theological textbooks to prove that the
church he refers to is now not yet triumphant and not yet even
expectant, but simply 'militant here in earth'. But to this the reply
from the Jewish standpoint is obvious that all down the centuries
since the time of Jesus Christ it has again and again and again been
only too true that the Jews have had to deal with precisely the
arrogance of an *ecclesia triumphans*, forgetful in practice, if not in
theory, of the nature of its triumph and of the need for 'fear and
trembling before the narrow door which leads to life'.[3] It has been
'militant here in earth' in all too true and literal a sense from the
Jewish point of view, but the weapons of its warfare have been
precisely those characterized by the apostle as 'carnal'[4] and utterly
rejected by him.

And there is the added rejoinder that Rosenzweig and Buber are
well justified in making against the Christian church, that no church
which lacks the note of vivid expectation is true to the gospel. The
relegation of such hope either to the dim and distant future as an
ideology or to the dim and distant past as a mythology is a betrayal
of the New Testament outlook. It is inconceivable that any fair
criticism of the Gospels can expunge from the outlook of the first
Christians and of our Lord himself that note of tingling and of
trembling hope, which finds graphic, if colloquial, application in
Oswald Chambers' famous phrase: 'In my study am I a wool-
gatherer or like a man looking for his Lord?'[5]

No: the western church must face seriously the challenge brought
to it not only by Marxist communism but also by Jewish messianic
mysticism, that it has lost a vital insight into reality and one which
was profoundly dynamic in the first creative centuries of Christianity.
The eloquent plea of Father Lev Gillett[6] for a genuine dialogue
with Judaism is the sort of response that is needed from Christians
to the Jewish approach of Professor Martin Buber[7] towards that

---

[1] 1 Cor. 11, 26. [2] K. Barth, *loc. cit.* [3] *Ibid.* [4] 2 Cor. 10, 4.
[5] O. Chambers, *So Send I You* (Simpkin, Marshall, 1930), pp. 5, 37.
[6] Cf. L. Gillett, *Communion in the Messiah* (Lutterworth Press, 1942), pp. 1 ff.
[7] M. Buber, *I and Thou* (T. and T. Clark, 1937), e.g. pp. 109 ff.

meeting in a relationship of mutual and reciprocal love, which is the secret of life itself. There may well be more of the messianic spirit and outlook among some Jews who do not know the Messiah than there is among many Christians who do. If Justin Martyr could enter into a dialogue with Trypho in A.D. 150, how much greater is the need to-day to abandon the one-way traffic street of our evangelistic or apologetic monologue and to endeavour to enter that two-way traffic street of truly reciprocal dialogue with modern mystical Judaism! It is not a *Tractatus adversus Judæos* which is needed, or even a *Demonstratio contra Judæos*, but a *Dialogos pros Tryphona*. The cause of Christ himself is better served by 'irenic conversations'[1] than by embattled polemics at most times of church history and not least to-day.

The need for such conversations forces itself on anyone with experience of Palestine in recent years. There is no question that the tumultuous destructive forces of a fanatical and terrorist futurism can only be met constructively by an equally forward-looking creative Christianity. The volcanic fires of a material messianism burn in the hearts of those who inherit the double energy of both a Jewish and a Marxist faith and are bent on the inauguration of an immediate earthly millennium, no matter what the means employed or what the loss of life involved. One side of this messianic explosion is material and terrorist, but there is another, to be found in many Jewish agricultural colonies, which may be material but is not terrorist at all, and has sometimes a mystical understanding of Judaism which is a vital spiritual force to-day.

Arthur Koestler[2] has not overdrawn his picture of the way in which these two elements in modern Judaism seem so inextricably intertwined. The idea of some old rabbis inquiring of a terrorist leader whether it would be possible to seize the Temple Area in Jerusalem and hold it for the six hours or so necessary to perform the sacrifice which would ensure the coming of the Messiah is not the far-fetched nonsense that it seems to most western democrats. It is not fantastic at all to those who have first-hand acquaintance with either Jewish apocalyptic expectations or Christian sectarian and millenarian fanaticism. It is just such an outlook with an emphasis on eschatology in general and upon the second coming in particular which characterizes so many of the protestant sects.

It is idle for theologians to dismiss this and similar attitudes, whether in Christianity or Judaism, as the product of a wayward and fantastic exegesis of the letter of the obscurer parts of Holy

[1] L. Gillett, *op. cit.*, p. 1.
[2] A. Koestler, *Thieves in the Night: Chronicle of an Experiment* (Macmillan, 1946).

Scripture and so to avoid the obligation to take up its challenge with all the seriousness it deserves. The fact is that, however mistakenly, the sects are ministering to the hunger of the soul of western man for some assurance of the future. And a hungry man will turn to food, however unpalatable and indigestible, rather than remain in semi-starvation before an impressive list of vitamins, however correct the diet it outlines may be. Only a living future hope can supply his need. Abstract theological speculations, which have no root in his contemporary awareness, cannot possibly satisfy him. If evidence for these contentions is needed it is not far to seek. For the popularity of the Negro Spiritual is conclusive proof that, even if some Negroes have outgrown its hope and turned in desperation to another, modern western man is pathetically and desperately hungry for it.

Thus we see something of the eschatological issue to-day, and are prepared for the emphasis laid by Mr Hollis [1] on the importance in the nineteenth century of the apocalyptic sects in influencing the mental attitude of the Russian people. Their futurism combined with eastern orthodox mysticism to produce the climate of opinion in which, as Mr. Hollis says, 'it would not have been in the least surprising if Christ really had appeared'. Anyone with any first-hand acquaintance of those who share the same belief in the western world, whether among Adventists or among those of a more orthodox evangelicalism, knows how real and how naively childish (or child-like) and how utterly illogical (despite its scriptural proof-texts) such an attitude is. Yet it is not a new phenomenon, nor may it be written off merely as a recrudescence of a chiliastic heresy of the second century or a Fifth Monarchy movement of the seventeenth.

The fact is that the perpetual hunger of the soul for food has not been satisfied by the western church in its average teaching about the last things. Either the future has been ignored, as it so often is to-day, or it has been preached as the cast-iron corollary of logic, based on orthodox intellectual propositions about the past and the present. Precisely because of its hard logic it has been felt by many sensitive and Christian souls to miss the one thing needful, the mystical love which is vital to any true understanding both of the presence and of the parousia.

It is here that the apparent illogicality of love comes in and links the illogicality of communist eschatology with the illogicality of the eschatology of sectarian Christianity. 'To the western mind', as Mr. Hollis so admirably sums it up, 'the most childish part of communism is its belief that a political and economic revolution

[1] *The Listener* (January 22, 1948), pp. 131 ff.

can effect a radical transformation of human nature. It is only if we read the history of nineteenth-century Russia and Russian literature that we understand that the Russians were expecting such a transformation anyway, long before they had even heard of Lenin or of Karl Marx.' [1]

What Mr. Hollis describes as the eschatological outlook of simple Russian believers in the nineteenth century is still true to-day of the outlook of the largely sectarian inter-denominational evangelical Christianity of the western world. Thirty years ago it seemed to many that except among biblical or perhaps among sacramental fundamentalists there was no living doctrine of the last things to be found in the Christian church.[2] To-day the position is greatly changed, and the climate of our theology has become almost too logically or too respectably eschatological.

There is thus still hope that the 'trained theologian' will show us a 'more excellent way' than the trained dialectical materialist, so that 'the overthrow of Bolshevism' will not be 'the waste of time' that Mr. Hollis so rightly says it otherwise inevitably must be.[3] But if the theologian is to do so, it must be by facing and not by dodging the eschatology of the Bible as a whole and of the New Testament in particular. That means facing it at the level of mystical love of which it speaks and out of which it was born and inside which alone it is intelligible. The time is short, as for the true eschatology of lovers' time it always must be. The rival eschatology of Karl Marx is in the field. It is high time that the Christian church awoke to the situation and either honestly abandoned hope or else proclaimed the gospel of the Advent hope.

[1] The Listener (January 22, 1948), pp. 131 ff.
[2] Cf. J. E. Fison, The Blessing of the Holy Spirit (Longmans, 1950), pp. 1–9.
[3] The Listener, loc. cit.

CHAPTER II

THE PERSPECTIVE OF THE BIBLE

IF the church is thus to proclaim the Advent hope, that hope must be correctly placed in its true setting among the last things. Biblical eschatology only develops under a sense of the agonizing and acute tension caused by the contradiction between what is and what ought to be.[1] And this acute tension is only a matter of life and death for those who both recognize that the contradiction is radical and also still believe that it can be and will be overcome.

This goes for Marxism as well as for theism, and it is therefore important to set out in perspective the eschatological doctrine which is the final product of biblical theism. Such a doctrine will not be the logical compensation in the future for what is lacking in the present.' It will be the apparently illogical fulfilment of what is present. It will be the love which is known to be lacking by its presence (not by its absence) which will be the basis of a true future hope rather than the love which is absent now, for whose present absence its future presence will provide adequate compensation.

The biblical outlook is never dualistic, and the contradiction between what is and what ought to be is thus never metaphysical, but always moral. But the moral distinction is radical. And on this point Ecclesiastes is the solitary exception, which conclusively proves the rule that there is no deterministic materialism in the biblical outlook. Bertrand Russell's famous statement that 'only on the firm foundation of unyielding despair can the soul's habitation be safely built'[2] can claim no warrant in holy scripture except in Ecclesiastes and only in Ecclesiastes, when its positive assertions[3] of faith are excised from the original text.

The iron predestination of some theological systems, which have forgotten that the Bible interprets election as a romance,[4] is untrue to the living reality of biblical faith and fundamentally untrue to the whole Old Testament revelation of the living God. The idea that what is determines what shall be and that therefore what ought to be is merely wishful thinking, a dream incapable of fulfilment, is

---

[1] Cf. T. W. Manson, *The Teaching of Jesus* (C.U.P., 1931), pp. 244 ff.
[2] B. Russell, *Mysticism and Logic*, pp. 47 f. (quoted by T. W. Manson, *loc. cit.*).
[3] E.g. Eccles. 12, 1, 13 f.   [4] Hos. 11, 1 f.

contradicted by every item on the great calendar of faith, recorded in Hebrews 11. The biblical idea is the exact opposite of this, and it has seldom found finer expression than in D. S. Cairns' powerful advocacy of its constructive and revolutionary character.[1]

There is nothing in the Bible of the resignation of the Moslem *kismet*. Biblical faith indeed accepts what is, but only as the precondition of giving God a chance of transforming it into what it ought to be and can be. Perhaps it was in reaction against a one-sided misunderstanding of the Bible that Spinoza, a Jew, denied the distinction between what is and what ought to be in the interests of what might be described as a higher pantheism. Where God's laws of nature tend to be obscured by emphasis upon man's sin, there may be need of such a protest on behalf of the Creator and the natural order. But Spinoza's ultimate reduction of the contradiction between what is and what ought to be to an illusory distinction, based solely upon our imperfect knowledge, cannot possibly be made to square with the biblical outlook. This is governed throughout by the nature of God and of his revelation and of his relationship with his creation. As his nature is progressively revealed as love and is always understood as personal, it is more and more realized that it is not a predestined fate but a purposeful Father who is working out his plans in past, present and future.

The Old Testament only hints at the fullness of the New Testament doctrine of the last things. But at the outset it is important to get clear some of the salient features of the final eschatological picture and to try to see them in perspective. Otherwise we are likely to miss the wood for the trees and to allow the bewildering difference in detail to blur the fundamental unity of the outline as a whole. There are three central motifs in the New Testament picture of the end: the parousia (or the second coming of Christ), the resurrection, and the judgment.[2] The fundamental conception lying behind all three is that the end of history will be both its fulfilment or *telos* and also its *finis* or full stop. In other words, it will reveal the true meaning of history, which at any given moment in history is only capable of ambiguous or partial revelation, and it will at the same time by so doing upset all our ideas of the meaning of history.

Both these truths, as we shall see, find expression in the Christian conviction that Jesus is the Christ. For this implies, first, that the eternal has been revealed in time, and secondly, that as a matter of historical fact, this revelation came as a surprise even to those who

---

[1] D. S. Cairns, *The Faith that Rebels* (S.C.M., 1928).
[2] Cf. R. Niebuhr, *The Nature and Destiny of Man* (Nisbet, 1943), vol. ii, ch. X, pp. 297 ff.

were expecting it. Niebuhr [1] impressively handles the Pauline confession: 'we preach Christ crucified, unto Jews a stumblingblock and unto Greeks foolishness; but unto them that are called, both Jews and Greeks, Christ the power of God, and the wisdom of God.' [2] In this passage St Paul contrasts the Jews who see a meaning in history with the Greeks who see no meaning in it,[3] and over against both sets Jesus as the clue to its meaning. Jesus Christ is the vindication of the Jewish conviction that history has a meaning, but 'Christ crucified' is the refutation of all Jewish attempts to understand and interpret that meaning.

For the Jews it was the cross which was the 'stumblingblock'. At their best they realized that revelation was not in sets of propositional forms, whether expressed in scientific or in theological terms, but in events, interpreted by those sensitive enough to perceive the meaning of the self-disclosure of God in each particular event. But though the best Jews knew this, the development of post-exilic Judaism with its more and more rigid ritual form and propositional expression tended to obscure it. And it was always fatally easy either to misinterpret the revelatory events or deliberately to reject their true meaning even when that was understood.

As for the Greeks, 'Christ crucified' was to them an irrelevant and nonsensical expression, for they saw no meaning in history at all. Therefore to them Jesus Christ was 'foolishness' for two reasons: on the one hand there was 'the scandal' of the nature of the meaning of history disclosed on Calvary (this was a scandal to both Jews and Greeks), and on the other hand there was 'the scandal of particularity', in Gerhard Kittel's great phrase.[4] To the Greeks the whole conception of a revelation of the eternal at a particular point of historical time was incredible; if they thought of revelation philosophically at all, they thought of it in terms not of historical events, but either of abstract ideas or of mystical states. But there is no possibility of coming to terms with the eschatological perspective of the Bible if we jump headlong into the prologue of St John without being previously baptized, and baptized by total immersion, into the whole Hebraic background of thought, which the Fourth Gospel presupposes.

It is this Hebraic background of thought which should make us pause before laughingly and patronizingly dismissing the cruder materialistic apocalyptic and millenarian views of the

[1] *Op. cit.*, vol. ii, chs. I, II, pp. 1 ff.
[2] 1 Cor. 1, 23 f.
[3] Cf. H. A. L. Fisher, *A History of Europe* (Arnold, 1936) p. v.
[4] G. K. A. Bell and A. Deissmann, *Mysterium Christi* (Longmans, 1930), pp. 31 ff.

sects in favour of the supposedly higher spirituality of the philosophers. All too easily this contemptuous superiority towards the fantastic dreams of the future passes into a contemptuous superiority towards the historic facts of the past and leads to a denial of the crass materialism of the incarnation. Before we know it we have thrown overboard the whole secret of the Hebrew faith in the *shekinah* of God, which is finally disclosed in the incarnation.[1] We have lost the biblical faith in the living God and substituted for it an idea of God taking the form either of a projection upon the universe of our conclusions about the universe, or of a deification of some induced mystical experience.

We have thought to meet God at the rendezvous of our choosing and in doing so have, either intentionally or not, dodged the rendezvous of his appointment. We have volunteered for the cross of our own choice in order to avoid the cross of his design. We have even preferred heroic crucifixion on our own rather than face humdrum crucifixion 'with Christ'.[2]

This is to lose all chance of ever meeting with the living God, however keen our intellectual grasp, however holy our mystical contemplation, and however intense our ascetic devotion to the dead god. For we have substituted for the living relationship of love a dead objectivity of logic, perfectly safe but absolutely impotent; the creation of our own minds, an object among objects, whether a proposition or an experience. We have lost the world of the personal, and compared with the loss of that, the gain of acquiring an intellectually respectable ethical monotheism as opposed to an outgrown animistic or polytheistic outlook is as nothing.

Not for one moment may we imagine in our spiritual arrogance that we can live without the world of objects (whether those objects be 'hes' or 'shes' or 'its'), but not for one moment may we idolatrously and blasphemously imagine that that world of objects is any adequate substitute for the world of persons, in which any object may at any moment step up to us and meet us in the living and reciprocal personal relationship of 'I and Thou'.[3] The religion of escape and logic is but a hairbreadth removed from the religion of reality and love, and it is so easy either to miss the narrow way of the latter or to despise the stepping-stones of the former.

If we recognize with the Bible that the medium of the divine

---

[1] John 1, 14; cf. E. Hoskyns and F. N. Davey, *The Fourth Gospel* (Faber and Faber, 2nd ed. 1947), pp. 147 ff.

[2] Gal. 2, 20.

[3] Cf. M. Buber, *I and Thou* (T. and T. Clark, 1937); 'In all the seriousness of truth, hear this: without IT man cannot live. But he who lives with IT alone is not a man' (p. 34).

revelation is the historical and the personal, then we shall the better appreciate the significance of the cruder apocalyptic and millenarian ideas which continually crop up throughout church history, and not least in our own day, with a quite pathetic wistfulness and a quite desperate eagerness.   The great element of truth in all millenarianism is its insistence upon the historical, the temporal and the earthly as the vehicle of the divine revelation and the scene (for any genuinely biblical faith) of the divine vindication.

Because so often such an outlook has been tarred with the brush of a 'pie in the sky when you die' compensation in heaven for a hell upon earth, there is no excuse for dismissing it from the biblical perspective, when it is expressed in such triumphant tones as in the final verse of the Advent hymn 'Thou art coming, O my Saviour'.[1] Beyond this there may well lie 'a new heaven and a new earth ',[2] but only on the yonder and not on the hither side of it. Here is a glimpse into the only faith that can meet the Marxist millennial dream on its own level—the earth—and offer more solid grounds for hope there before passing on to the infinite vistas of eternity beyond, of which the Marxist has no inkling.   It is quite useless to go on to these vistas, however, unless we have faced the Marxist on his own ground and at his own earthly level first.   And this is what Christianity, alone of all existing religions, can do.

It was not Karl Marx, but Charles Kingsley, a clergyman of the Church of England, who first (as far as I can discover) [3] used the phrase, 'Religion is the opium of the people'.   And this now popular communist slogan is only too true unless the Christian outlook on the future and the Christian doctrine of the end is an expression of a reality-facing and not of a reality-escaping religion. The perspective of the Bible as a whole bids us hope for a future which is the corollary of a present reality or of a real presence, and not a compensation for a present lack of reality or a real absence.

We may not abandon the materialism of the Christian faith in favour of an escape into a more spiritual, but utterly unreal, de-historicizing of the biblical revelation.   Any true doctrine of the end,

---

[1]
O the joy to see Thee reigning,
　　Thee, my own belovèd Lord!
Every tongue Thy name confessing,
Worship, honour, glory, blessing
　　Brought to Thee with one accord,—
Thee, my Master and my Friend,
　　Vindicated and enthroned,
Unto earth's remotest end
　　Glorified, adored, and owned.
　　　　F. R. Havergal (*Hymns Ancient and Modern*, 203).
[2] Rev. 21, 1.
[3] Cf. A. Miller, *The Christian Significance of Karl Marx* (S.C.M., 1946), p. 40.

3

conceived along biblical lines, is bound to assert that the final consummation is, as Professor T. W. Manson has well expressed it, 'not a compensation for the sufferings of the faithful in the present, but the result of them'.[1] In this respect the doctrine of the end merely throws into high relief the contrast, the knife-edged contrast, between the true and the false, which runs right down through the whole Christian outlook from beginning to end.

On the one hand there is the faith which either fervently and evangelistically or wistfully and pathetically asserts the reality of the friendship of Jesus because of the lack of all human friends. And on the other hand there is the faith which has found through the friendship of Jesus the gateway to such depth and width of human friendship as apart from him would have been inconceivable. The one way is a cul-de-sac and the other is a thoroughfare. And this particular metaphor is capable of indefinite extension of application. How often, for example, emphasis upon forgiveness through the blood of Christ gives no real release of conscience to the sinner, but merely provides a make-weight, balancing Christ's merits against man's sense of guilt, and so providing at best a tolerable *modus vivendi*, which is an utter travesty of the thrilling initiation into the balanced rapture[2] which it should signify!

The true biblical perspective on the last things is not so enamoured of grace, to use von Hügel's fine phrase, that it despises nature. It holds to that unity of the temporal and the eternal in the realm of God, which is expressed in the central Christian dogma of the incarnation. The final formulation of that dogma in the definition of Chalcedon as to the unity of Christ's one person and the distinctness of his two natures may be to-day merely a negatively valuable defence against heresy. But it does at least safeguard the essential biblical truth, which refuses either to confuse or to separate the natural and the supernatural worlds.

The peril of apostasy is plain. Either the supernatural, of which the eschatological is in many ways the touchstone, is lost in the natural and there results almost inevitably the elimination of anything that could really be called biblical eschatology at all. Or, alternatively, the supernatural and the natural split asunder until there is no real unity or connection between them. Eschatology in the latter case is safeguarded, but it is an isolated appendage to the rest of theology and not integrated into any outlook on the present at all. It is left in illogical contradiction to the rest of the secular and religious framework of ideas and beliefs, that go to form

[1] T. W. Manson, *The Teaching of Jesus*, p. 256, and cf. ch. XIII *passim*.
[2] Cf. K. E. Kirk, *The Vision of God* (Longmans, 1931).

the contemporary twentieth-century outlook of the western world. This is exactly what has happened in the sects of Christendom, whether inside or outside the orthodox theological pattern of belief.

Now it is precisely in the avoidance of both these errors that the biblical eschatological perspective at its best and truest speaks to our present condition. A watered-down supernaturalism results in the loss of all eschatological conviction and is in part responsible for the impotence of the Christian church to face up to the challenge of contemporary secular or religious messianic dreams. And on the other hand a heightened supernaturalism safeguards an adequate eschatology of the future at the price of a total abandonment of all real claim to any divine action in the present. In either case it is relationship with the living God and response to his revelation which has disappeared, either because he is lost in the abyss of sheer transcendence or because he becomes so immanent that he ceases to be personal. The dangerous personal world of loving relationship is abandoned in favour of the safe impersonal world either of the propositional formulæ of liberal protestantism and of scholastic catholicism, or else of the induced experience of evangelical pietism or catholic mysticism.

In the Bible the nature of the eschatological expectation is conditioned by the nature of the theological conviction. It is the kind of God, believed in in the present, which determines the kind of end, hoped for in the future. The way the Jews arrived at their eschatological outlook was quite definitely via their outlook on God and not vice versa. The growth of their belief in life after death was 'not from Immortality of no matter what kind to God, but from God to a special kind of Immortality'.[1] One of the most remarkable and almost uncanny features of the Old Testament is its reticence as to the future until it has secured a present faith in God, regardless of consequences and ulterior motives, whether of reward or punishment. It is not till the nation as well as the individual has learnt the terrible but triumphant secret of Job's cry, 'Though he slay me, yet will I trust in him',[2] that it can be entrusted with the wonderful prospect of a life beyond the grave. Only so will it keep its head among the fantastic apocalyptic details of the eschatological panorama.

It is essential to keep in mind this utter dependence of eschatological future hope upon theological present faith. For it is the kind of God believed in at any particular period of biblical history which is clearly reflected in the doctrine of the end, both as to its essential

[1] F. von Hügel, *Essays and Addresses on the Philosophy of Religion* (Dent, 1924), p. 197.
[2] Job 13, 15, A.V.

content and as to the form and manner of its realization. We are neither given sketch maps of the beginning in Genesis nor blue prints of the end in Revelation. We are given in both Genesis and Revelation insights into the beginning and the end drawn from present understanding of him who is himself both 'the Alpha and Omega' [1] and also 'the same yesterday, and to-day, and for ever'.[2]

The Christian faith is that at the crucial focus of revelation the secret of the end as well as of the beginning was manifested in Jesus Christ. Here is the secret of the true messianism, in which the eternal is manifested in time and all theology becomes eschatological and eschatology interprets and illumines every item of theological dogma rather than adds another item of its own as an appendage to all the rest.

It is the unity of present and future in the eternal life, manifested and offered in Jesus Christ, that is the secret of New Testament eschatology. In church history present and future split asunder, as inevitably they must unless they are maintained as a unity at that level of love, expressed in prayer and worship, at which alone we can now transcend the apparent contradictions of temporal logic and experience at least by anticipation and as a first instalment [3] the reality of the Holy Spirit and of that eternal life of which the fullness is hereafter. Eschatology loses all its dynamic and creative power when the insights of present faith in the realm of love are replaced by the reasons for future hope in the realm of logic.

It is to the great credit of modern biblical and liturgical scholarship and research that we are now rediscovering the unity of the whole New Testament outlook, as expressed in its ethic, its worship and its doctrine. And that unity is only intellectually comprehensible and experimentally verifiable on an eschatological understanding of the significance of the life and death and resurrection of Jesus Christ, into which the early church entered and of which the first Christians partook in their living and thinking and daily prayer and practice, and above all in their central eucharistic act of worship.

At every eucharist every Christian was there, at the centre of the great eschatological crisis of history, face to face with the living God. He was not confronted by the abstractions of a metaphysician's theories, but by the immediacy of eternal love in the historical actuality of the person and passion of our Lord Jesus Christ. There at the Lord's supper he was at 'the judgment seat of Christ' [4] and in the real presence of the Lord. And because he was there now, he would not face the unknown when he faced the judgment seat and

---

[1] Rev. 1, 8; 21, 6; 22, 13.   [2] Heb. 13, 8.
[3] Cf. 2 Cor. 1, 22; 5, 5; Eph. 1, 14.   [4] Rom. 14, 10.

the parousia hereafter. In this lay the comfort and the assurance of the New Testament gospel. Justification by faith is no Pauline perversion of the gospel:[1] it focuses its whole message in a blaze of eschatological light. But it is a perversion of the gospel, if it is taken out of its eschatological setting in the total context of the life of the early church. It was because the early Christians on every Lord's day believed that at the Lord's supper they ate either damnation [2] or salvation to themselves that the reality of the abiding consequences which would be revealed on the eschatological day of the Lord was so vivid to them. No one who lived in the presence needed to work himself up into a fever about the parousia.

Thus to the first Christians the final expression of the eschatological gospel is the Johannine doctrine of eternal life, which with the parousia, the judgment and the resurrection is so much a present fact in the Fourth Gospel that we are apt to set it in a context of Greek idealism rather than recognize it for what it is, the final term of an essentially Hebraic eschatology. The last things have arrived, as no Greek could possibly believe they could ever arrive. But they are the *last* things: Jesus is the Messiah, but the Messiah indicates the present realization of the future eschatological hopes of Israel. Apart from that eschatological reference it is only a title of honour and of office, devoid of any final significance whatever either for Israel or for mankind.

Right at the end of his ministry Jesus does 'give away' his messianic secret without any equivocation whatever.[3] To the high priest's question 'Art thou the Christ, the Son of the Blessed?' he replies 'I am: and ye shall see the Son of man sitting at the right hand of power and coming with the clouds of heaven'. This has been interpreted traditionally as a reference (and perhaps the only unequivocal reference on Jesus' own lips) to the second coming or parousia. But this twofold coming is entirely foreign to the proof text in Daniel from which the last part of the quotation comes.[4] In Daniel there is only one coming, and that coming is of 'one like unto a son of man' (whoever he may be) 'to the ancient of days'. Daniel describes one single movement from the earth to God in heaven, and modern scholars have sought to reinterpret Jesus' own confession in this sense.[5]

This is a bold attempt to recover the original eschatological unity

---

[1] Jesus himself expressed the whole truth in a sentence at the end of the parable of the Pharisee and the Publican far more clearly than St Paul ever succeeded in doing with all his rabbinical arguments; cf. Luke 18, 9–14.
[2] 1 Cor. 11, 29.   [3] Mark 14, 62.   [4] Dan. 7, 13 f.
[5] E.g. notably G. Dix, *The Shape of the Liturgy* (Dacre Press, 1945), p. 262, and quoting W. K. Lowther Clarke in *Theology*, vol. xxxi, pp. 61 ff., 125 ff.

of the New Testament, which has certainly in church history become split up in terms of a twofold coming, with no essential unity of conception governing the whole idea or integrating it into the rest of Christian doctrine. But much more probably the traditional view is right. Jesus is quite deliberately reinterpreting Daniel and re-orientating the direction of his prophecy so that it now refers to a coming from heaven to earth and not from earth to heaven.[1] But in his mind this coming is no distant future compensation, such as logic would require, for his imminent departure and absence. On the contrary, as the Matthæan and Lukan additions to the Markan narrative make perfectly plain,[2] it is the secret of all that is going to happen from that very moment of his trial right onwards till the end of time.

It is the presence of love, not its absence, that both necessitates and guarantees its parousia. Nothing else can do it, and because nothing else can and everything else tries to, the original eschato-logical unity of love in the whole biblical outlook has been broken up in the traditional interpretations of logic. In consequence, what was once the inspiration of a living hope and a dynamic faith has tended to become the dope of the bigoted dogmatics of either an over-excited and fevered futurism or of a complacent and sleepy archaism. Only if we can recover the biblical perspective in all its richly com-prehensive unity and present reality of love can we compete with the rival messianisms of the present day and meet the hunger of 'modern man' more truly 'in search of a soul', in Jung's graphic phrase,[3] in respect of his eschatological hope than in respect of anything else.

If we are to recover this perspective of the Bible, we do well to pay attention to von Hügel's [4] valuable emphasis upon the contrast between two divergent interpretations of the shape of things to come, each of which has found a place within the Christian eschatological scheme. Time may be thought of either as a stream which we cross each in our own individual lives, or as a stream down which we travel in our own individual lives. In the first case we cross the stream and the transit is individual. In the second we enter the stream and are carried down by it in a movement that is collective. Any doctrine of the end must attempt to combine these two apparently conflicting aspects of a reality which we cannot deny even if we cannot stand outside it and so see it as a whole and formulate a coherent theory of its working.

---

[1] The placing of the quotation from Daniel 7, 14 after, and not before, the quotation from Psalm 110, 1 strongly supports the traditional view.
[2] Matt. 26, 64; Luke 22, 69.
[3] C. G. Jung, *Modern Man in Search of a Soul* (Kegan Paul, 1933).
[4] F. von Hügel, *Essays and Addresses on the Philosophy of Religion*, pp. 137 ff.

It is because of this double aspect of time that Christian eschatology tends, as von Hügel says,[1] either to stress the individual transit of the individual soul and so to emphasize its final destination as being either heaven or hell after a greater or less emphasis on purgatory, or on the other hand to emphasize the movement of the collective whole and so to lay stress upon the renovated earth, the millennium and the resurrection of the body. The state of hell has the emphasis in the former outlook which the fact or the event of judgment has in the latter. And whereas for the latter the mystical element in religion and the doctrine of the immortality of the soul have always been hard to integrate into the effective eschatological perspective, for the former it has been the resurrection of the body, which has tended to slip into the background as an irrelevant and unnecessary encumbrance upon an otherwise genuinely spiritual outlook.

Behind these divergencies of emphasis there lies the fundamental difficulty, which has always beset the Christian church, of integrating the Hebraic Old Testament outlook developed by Jewish apocalyptic into a world of thought which until recently has been dominated in the western world by the influence of Greek philosophy. The Fourth Gospel is proof that the New Testament itself had to face this issue, and the first four œcumenical councils of the Christian church are all the time grappling with this one problem. It is obvious that a living religion must express itself in terms which can be understood by the world in which it lives and which it seeks to influence. If it fails to face this issue, it is bound to become intellectually sterile. But if it does face it, there is always the danger of being disloyal to the core of revelation in the attempt to make its circumferential meaning intelligible in its teaching and evangelism.

A simple either/or will not suffice to deal with the complexity of the problems involved. And it is just because the either/or solution is too narrow to cover the full range of ideas and facts involved that neither the church view of heaven, purgatory and hell nor the sect view of millennium and resurrection has ever been able to stamp out its rival. Indeed both views manage to pay a homage of lip-service to the whole range of eschatological ideas and try to accommodate them all, even if without any effective relevance to each other, within their comprehensive pattern of the future.

This makes over-sharp distinctions always untrue, and yet without undue exaggeration it may be said that on the whole the great church has proclaimed a future with a relevance confined almost entirely to the fate and destiny of the individual soul. This very un-Hebraic

[1] F. von Hügel, loc. cit.

outlook has been dominant in the great church from at least the time when that church came to terms with Greek philosophy at the end of the first three centuries of persecution. But over against it there has constantly arisen another, emphasizing an earthly millennium or a bodily resurrection in terms which superficially at least look far more like the biblical conception. Such a view is as alive to-day as ever it was among Fifth Monarchy men in the seventeenth century or among the followers of Joachim of Flora in the twelfth or among the chiliastic Montanists in the second. Whatever the great church theologians may do, this second emphasis keeps on coming back. And as Professor Toynbee says about Russia, 'if this were a sermon, not an essay, the inevitable text would be a famous line of Horace's, Naturam expellas furca, tamen usque recurret: "You may throw Nature out with a pitchfork, but she will keep coming back".' [1]

Before we rule this second view out of order as highly irregular and sectarian, if not downright heresy, we do well to pause. Heresies with no truth in them soon die out. But heresies with at least a grain of truth in them have a knack of reappearing again and again in one form or another. Our suspicion that the sects have truth in their eschatological outlook is heightened by two facts. On the one hand, compared at least with the biblical hope, the great church has in fact so often so little hope to offer, except of the 'pie in the sky when you die' variety, as an alternative to sectarian or materialistic messianic fanaticisms. And on the other hand the course of eschatological theological development in the history of the church looks suspiciously like a self-regarding attempt to secure a selfish heaven for the church rather than a disinterested design offering to supply the genuine needs of a world 'without God and without hope'.[2]

It looks as if the great church either consciously or unconsciously did two things. It transferred the New Testament emphasis upon a future both on earth and in heaven to a future solely in heaven, so leaving this world to go quite literally 'to the devil' and abandoning all expectation of that cosmic redemption, the hope of which is so prominent in the New Testament.[3] It also transferred the New Testament emphasis upon a present and future kingdom of God upon earth to a present church on earth and a distinctly remote future kingdom in heaven.

There is a suspicion of selfishness about the transference of emphasis in both cases. The attempt to call in a new world to redress the balance of the old can be a grand apocalyptic vision of

[1] A. J. Toynbee, Civilization on Trial, p. 164.
[2] Eph. 2, 12, A.V.
[3] Cf. A. D. Galloway, The Cosmic Christ (Nisbet, 1951).

the climax of the triumph of God. But it sounds suspiciously like selfish wishful thinking when it is the defeatist refuge of despair. The invocation of such a *Deus ex machina* is indeed the opium of the people in the most deadly sense. It is a pure narcotic and has no stimulating power whatever. It is utterly selfish and spiritually suicidal. Similarly the equation of the kingdom with the church is thoroughly unscriptural and can so easily involve an apotheosis of an institution,[1] which no amount of camouflaging or verbal special pleading by invoking the high doctrine of the body of Christ can conceal. It is again thoroughly selfish, thoroughly this-worldly and uneschatological and an undoubted distortion of the New Testament perspective. This is a hard saying and yet, unless the distinction between the kingdom of God and the church is made at least as clear as their partial identity and overlap,[2] nonsense is made of the fundamental change of theological vocabulary which is found within the New Testament itself.

This change consists in the substitution by the primitive church of the preaching of 'Jesus Christ and him crucified' for the preaching of the kingdom of God, which is the sum and substance of Jesus' own message. This change of vocabulary is essential to retain identity of meaning. For Jesus himself was the kingdom; the kingdom was manifested in the king. Those therefore who claim New Testament sanction for the identification of the kingdom of God with the church must find not only some way of explaining the still future expectation of the kingdom, for example in the Lord's prayer, but also some other reason than that suggested above for the fundamental change in the theological vocabulary of the New Testament. No one can possibly pretend that it makes no difference to the substance of St Paul's message if we substitute for his claim, 'I determined not to know anything among you save Jesus Christ and him crucified',[3] the counter claim, 'I determined to know nothing among you save the church'. Very high doctrines of the church are only safe from idolatrous pretensions if they are coupled with clear recognition that the church is not in the godhead, whereas Jesus Christ is.

It is the function of the Holy Spirit by his place within the godhead witnessing self-effacingly to Jesus Christ to say 'No' to all such ecclesiastical and other pretensions to a stake within the godhead.[4] But the fact of his self-effacement, which is nothing less than the self-effacement of love itself, should not blind us to the reality of his

---

[1] Cf. A. J. Toynbee, *A Study of History*, vol. iv, pp. 245 ff.
[2] 1 Cor. 10, 11.   [3] 1 Cor. 2, 2.
[4] Cf. J. E. Fison, *The Blessing of the Holy Spirit* (Longmans, 1950), pp. 148 ff.

presence and to the fatal consequence of any attempt to trespass upon his prerogatives.[1] The dethronement of the Holy Spirit from the godhead, in fact if not in theory, is due either to human presumption or to human timidity or to human selfishness. It is especially due to the pride of ecclesiastical man, who desires to possess God with the gained assurance of the logician's mastery of his subject and is not willing to be possessed by him with the given assurance of a lover's confidence in his beloved.

The corrective to such selfishness will not be found by laying greater emphasis upon heaven or hell (with or without purgatory). In fact such an emphasis may only serve to make more rigid a thoroughly selfish attitude towards all religion and so destroy the essence of the Christian religion altogether, if its worship is rightly described as the only real disinfectant from egoism.[2] The terrible sadism of those Christians who have been able to imagine that anyone's sense of the pleasures of heaven could be increased by knowledge and awareness of the pains suffered by others in hell is an indication of how deadly a fruit this root of eschatological selfishness is capable of producing.[3] Nor can this fundamental selfishness be exorcized by the contemplation of a sensual and this-worldly millennium. The fact that it is shared by others does not alter the thoroughly selfish idea behind any offer of bliss along the lines of a Moslem paradise on the improved Damascus model. In fact it must be admitted that all too easily heaven and hell, the prospect of the millennium or of the immortality of the soul or even of the resurrection of the body focus attention on the self rather than upon God. And even if we correct this fundamental self-centredness by concentrating our thoughts about the future not upon ourselves, but upon others, as Professor John Baillie so powerfully insists that we should,[4] it still remains true that the focus of our attention is not upon God, though it has shifted from ourselves to our neighbours. It is a gain to obey the second commandment in our perspective on eschatology, but that perspective will not be biblical unless and until we obey the first commandment too.[5]

[1] If the Hebrew *shaliach* is to be brought into discussions of Christian theology, surely the *shaliach* of Jesus Christ is the Holy Spirit. No other can claim his plenipotentiary powers. For were such claim allowed it would in fact, if not in theory, make the Holy Spirit an irrelevant addendum to an otherwise clear-cut theological system.

[2] Cf. K. E. Kirk, *The Vision of God* (abridged ed., Longmans, 1934), p. xii (quoting Brémond).

[3] Cf. W. Temple, *Nature, Man and God* (Macmillan, 1934): 'Each supposedly damned soul was born into the world as a mother's child, and Paradise cannot be a Paradise for her, if her child is in such a Hell' (p. 454).

[4] Cf. J. Baillie, *And the Life Everlasting* (O.U.P., 1934).

[5] Mark 12, 28 ff.

Perhaps of all the symbols of the end with which the Christian church has pictured the future, the one most calculated to inspire the unselfishness which is the hall-mark not only of all Christian living but also of all Christian thinking as well is the one most prominent in the New Testament and most neglected in church history. That is the parousia or the so-called second coming of Christ. This can only be interpreted selfishly if the note of judgment is omitted and the doctrine of the resurrection of the body whittled down and the fundamental element of surprise eliminated, and attention focused on the experience of the soul in the moment of meeting in a way which is quite foreign to the New Testament and quite out of keeping with any true understanding of the nature of a relationship of love. It is not the experience of the soul, however much that may appear to be the preoccupation of certain mystical ideas of the beatific vision, but the surprise of the soul at the reality confronting it, which fills the New Testament outlook. For in the perspective of the Bible the focus is all the time upon the coming of the Lord to the soul, not upon the going of the soul to the Lord.

It is important to stress this point, which is distinctive of the parousia and singles it out from all other eschatological symbols. For the parousia by stressing a consummation in terms of a movement of God to man can give coherence to the scheme of eschatology, which otherwise inevitably splits asunder according as to whether emphasis is laid upon the future of the individual soul and the end of its transit across the stream of time or upon the future of the collective whole downstream when time flows out into eternity. It is impossible to imagine how such double movements can end in one event. But it is possible to imagine a movement of God, who is not limited as human souls are limited by the conditions of space and time, which terminates in one and the same meeting the transit of the individual soul and the progress of the collective whole. In a figure we can picture the individual soul making its transit from A to

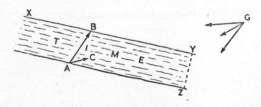

B or making its contribution to the whole from A to C. We can see the frontier of earth for individuals on the other side of the stream of time from X to Y. And we can imagine the end of history as from

Y to Z. But we cannot correlate from our angle of vision the frontiers of the individual soul (XY) and the frontiers of the historical whole (YZ).

But these uncorrelated individual and corporate transits of time as seen from the human angle can be imagined as coming to one single end in the enveloping movement of the divine encirclement (G) which in one single meeting terminates them both. That is the central significance of the symbol of the parousia. Only if it is kept central to the eschatological perspective of the church will the Christian hope be both individual and corporate.

If the end manifests the *telos* or fulfilment of history as well as brings it, at least as we know it, to a full stop and puts *finis* to it, then it is clear that no doctrine of the end entirely unrelated to what has preceded it in the temporal sequence is adequate. If there is at least some truth, if not the whole truth, in the contention that 'real life is meeting' now at the present time, then it will be in some sense meeting at the end, even if then much more will be apparent of its significance than is now clear.

This is additional sanction for the centrality of the parousia in the perspective of the Bible. It gives vivid expression to the grand finale of the historical drama, which consists in the meeting of the Lord Jesus Christ with at least all those that are his and at most the whole creation itself. It is this meeting which opens up the limitless possibilities of the transformation of the 'new heaven and the new earth'.[1] In this final meeting there will be both a movement to God in Christ and a movement of God in Christ. Men and creation will move one way to meet Christ—that at least is one aspect of the truth of the resurrection of the body and one reason why St Paul introduces his most extended treatment of the doctrine.[2] But, far more important, Christ and those who have died and are his will move towards those who are his and are still alive: in other words, he will move towards the stream of time and meet it, just as he has moved towards those souls who have crossed the stream of time and met them. And these two meetings are all part of the single divine encirclement of time, and are one in a way which from our standpoint within time we cannot comprehend.

Spatial and temporal imagery is necessarily symbolic, when applied to an event which marks the full stop as well as the fulfilment of space and time as we know them. But it is not to be explained away even if it is not to be taken literally. And on one point at least its witness is, as we have seen, all the more important for being so signally neglected by the church. It is the coming of the Lord to the

---

[1] Rev 21, 1 reached *via* Rom. 8, 18 ff. [2] 1 Cor. 15, 12 ff.

soul which is the climax of Christian individual hope, not the going
of the soul to the Lord.   It is the climax of the perspective of prevenient grace upon which attention should be fixed eschatologically
rather than upon any interpretation either of life after death for
the soul or of history and its future for the whole, which appears
to deny what is the deepest and the dearest insight of the Christian
gospel.

It is the coming of the new Jerusalem down to man rather than
the raising of the new Jerusalem up by man which is the climax of
the corporate hope of human destiny.[1]   And in both cases it is not a
place or a state or an experience upon which attention is fixed, no
matter whether that place be heaven or that state purgatory or that
experience the beatific vision.   It is not upon any of these that the
New Testament bids us fix our gaze, but upon the meeting, the truly
reciprocal meeting, of those lovers who come to their journey's end
and find it a new beginning when they get there.   That meeting is
the gateway to the unimaginable bliss beyond.   The future fulfils
the present, whether its clue is seen in personal intercourse, Quaker
meeting, or eucharistic communion.[2]

It fulfils not only the insights of the world of grace but also those
of the world of nature too.   For it is as true in nature that no life
is born except through intercourse, as it is in grace that no life is born
again except through intercourse.   Out of the relationship of mutual
love anything may happen, but apart from it nothing creative at all.
At all levels of human experience that is true and in the end it will
be proved true.

Time and space have at least in this meeting eternal significance
for God, even if that significance is not absolute or what we now
individually or collectively imagine it to be.   That is why at the end
Christian hope focuses on the parousia of the man, Christ Jesus.
It is not the unknown with which we are then confronted but with
the at any rate partially known.   And in the meeting is fulfilled the
genuine reciprocity of all true love.   Thus charity is finally redeemed
from its debased meaning of a one-way-traffic street administration
of a condescending dole into its true significance as a two-way-traffic
street exchange of mutual give and take.   Hence the eucharist finds
its end, for which it now waits 'till he come',[3] in the blessing to which
it always points.   This is neither, as with some catholics, in giving,
nor, as with some evangelicals, in taking; it is indefinably in between

---

[1] Rev. 21, 10.
[2] The same clue contains the secret of evangelism and of preaching.   But how
seldom do we remember that the latter is meant to be 'the ordered Hallelujah of the
congregation' (P. T. Forsyth, quoted by J. E. Fison, *op. cit.*, p. 139)!
[3] 1 Cor. 11, 26.

the two at the place of truly sacrificial and therefore fully reciprocal love.[1]

Three symbols, as we have seen, can be said to sum up the Christian perspective on the last things. The first is the parousia, which is the essence of the whole Christian eschatological scheme. It is the meeting to which all life points forward. 'Journeys end in lovers meeting' [2] is not the delusion of romantic love, but the sober essence of Christian eschatology. No wonder the perspective of the apostles focused on the person rather than the thing, upon the king rather than the kingdom! Jesus might himself inevitably and rightly preach the kingdom of God, because he himself gave personal content to his message and indeed was himself the sum and substance of his message. But the apostles did not go about as he did and preach the kingdom. They no less inevitably and rightly went about preaching Jesus Christ and him crucified. This was not a Pauline idiosyncrasy, but the essence of the good news. Once the person ceases to be at the centre of the proclamation the heart has gone out of the gospel.

Undoubtedly there is great gain in the rediscovery of the meaning of the kingdom of God, which is the signal contribution to constructive theology of modern New Testament scholarship. But we shall mistake the meaning of this contribution and make no impact upon the world to-day with any gospel of enough compelling vitality to compete with the Marxist ideology unless the person of our Lord Jesus Christ is right at the centre of both our theological understanding and of our liturgical representation of the Christian religion. Our whole eschatological outlook will be out of perspective unless its focus is on him.

Therefore not heaven nor hell nor purgatory nor the millennium nor the resurrection nor any other eschatological symbol may replace the centrality of the parousia, which alone secures at the end the one essential of Christian living, which is that we can meet our Lord not at the end but at the beginning of our pilgrimage, whether on earth in this life or from earth to heaven in the life to come. It is the failure to think through the eschatological implications of the essential gospel truths of the divine initiative and of prevenient grace which has cut the nerve of Christian hope.

Of course this meeting with our Lord involves judgment, and therefore the second essential of the eschatological perspective of the New Testament is the doctrine of the last judgment, the corollary of the parousia and not an alternative to it. The parables of the

---

[1] Cf. J. E. Fison, *op. cit.*, pp. 196 ff.
[2] W. Shakespeare, *Twelfth Night*, II, iii.

sheep and goats [1] and of Dives and Lazarus [2] suggest that this may well be a total surprise for all. It is bound to be a partial surprise for all, for none will be spiritually perfect then, and spiritual things can only be discerned without surprise by those that are perfect, and even by them only in fellowship with all saints [3] and never by any isolated individual's vision alone.

Certainly the fact that 'every eye shall see him' [4] is no excuse for complacency. It may be doubted whether blatant ostentation is a Christian characteristic even of the parousia if the parousia remains, as it should, the manifestation of the love of God in Christ. For love is never and can never be ostentatious. Jesus was only seen after his resurrection by believers, and how far he will ever be seen except by believers is a moot point. What is clear is that the judgment involves unlimited and inescapable responsibility. At present our responsibility is limited and, as we imagine, all too easily escapable. We all tend to dodge the responsibilities attendant upon a life of real meeting because here is the cross, which no one of us ever wants except in retrospect. This is the cross not of our choice, for which some of us are at times prepared, but the cross of God's appointment, by facing and bearing which alone we can be 'crucified with Christ'.[5]

Willingness to enter into a living and dialectical relationship of love involves facing this issue and being willing for the cross which love's future surprises are always springing upon us. For these surprises, which can never be ruled out of any living relationship of love, constantly appear in prospect to contradict love's past revelations. Only in retrospect is there realized to be no discontinuity, no contradiction, no arbitrariness, no break in the unchanging purpose of love.

Rather than face the fearful future prospect of the peril of such a break, though it is never a present reality as such, men prefer to abide by the past interpretations of love's revelation, and to rely upon them not at signposts to reality, but as reality itself. In this way either the book or the formula or the rite so easily replaces the loving person whom it is meant to mediate and interpret. The means of grace, whether biblical, credal or sacramental, become ends in themselves and at once the most effective insulators from grace. Organic continuity is stressed as the sole criterion of being 'in love', and its security is preferred to the surprising possibilities of dialectical relationship, which are fearfully avoided. Such an attitude may embalm the past: it can never inspire the future. The old must

---

[1] Matt. 25, 31 ff.   [2] Luke 16, 19 ff.   [3] Eph. 3, 18.
[4] Rev. 1, 7.   [5] Gal. 2, 20.

die that the new may be born and there is no other way. We are
not promised for ourselves or for society continuity of life, but
resurrection from the dead. This is a universal law, from which
nothing is exempt.

Modern life is full of devices for escaping the awkward or unexpected surprises of the cross of God's appointment in favour of the
safe certainty of the cross of our own choosing. The offer of
security from the cradle to the grave has the seductive attraction of
providing a way of dodging the unexpected responsibilities with
which the real life of meeting constantly confronts us.[1] But in the
end there is no escape—that is the sober truth, and it is either the
blessed comfort of those who are well content that it should be so
or the dreadful doom of those who are straining every nerve to
prevent it being so.

Freedom is in peril to-day, but not so much from external totalitarian tyranny or from conditions of squalor, hardship or poverty,
grim though these may be, as from the fact that the modern welfare
state makes it so much more easy to-day than it ever used to be
for men to dodge their responsibilities. Nothing can prevent such
responsibilities coming our way every day of our lives. To face
them and not run away from them is the secret of life, no matter
what the external poverty of our livelihood. To dodge them and
escape from them, even into church, is certain death, no matter what
the apparent richness of life.

'Though freedom is not a good thing in itself and absolutely, it
is nevertheless the indispensable condition of all human excellence.' [2]
That is the truth of all vocational living, and the freedom that is
the birthright of every man is the freedom to respond to the call of
God, however mediated, in the humblest duties of every day. It is
the loss of this sense of vocation (= being called), and with it the
loss of all real sense of responsibility (= response to the call), which
is at the heart of so much discontent in our modern world. In the
true sense of vocational responsibility 'now is the judgment'.[3] If
we dodge it now, that is only putting off the evil day, for one
day it will be inescapable and no longer avoidable. That is the
meaning of the last judgment, when we shall be confronted neither
by a vindictive tyrant nor by a sentimental magistrate, but by the
man Christ Jesus. The importance of realizing that Jesus Christ

---

[1] A conspicuously glaring example of this sort of thing is the giving of sex-instruction
in schools. This may be in itself often a good thing. But it is a deadly thing, if it
provides any parent with the excuse that, because instruction is given in school about
questions which are not asked there, therefore he or she has a very good reason for not
answering the questions which are asked in the home.

[2] J. E. Fison, *op. cit.*, p. 191, quoting C. Bigg.   [3] John 12, 31.

is the judge cannot be overemphasized.[1] At the end we shall not approach a distant doomsday, but we shall be confronted by an immediate presence. If only we realized it, it is the presence of a living and loving person, however mediated, with whom we have to deal here and now, and with whom we are bound to deal hereafter.

Such a doctrine of the last judgment is a moral stimulant and not a moral narcotic. Just as a lover will prepare for a date and a rendezvous with his beloved, so we (if we in any way love our Lord Jesus Christ) will prepare for that day of meeting, not as if it would be like the mediæval *Dies iræ, dies illa*, but as if it will be (as indeed it will be) a meeting with one who knows the secrets of all our hearts, not by any external calculation of a *Deus ex machina* but by the natural sympathy of a true lover.

There is thus no slackness in approaching the end, but equally there is no tormenting terror, for it is not the unknown which we go to meet, but someone we know (however dimly) who comes to meet us. The tragedy of the Christian dogma of the last judgment is that so often it has replaced the man Christ Jesus either by the unknown terror or in reaction from that by the wishful thinking of what our baser selves would like him to be. Victorian terrorism has given way to Georgian sentimentality, and the results in our own day in practical antinomianism are not far to seek.

Then there is the third essential in the Christian eschatological perspective of the Bible. This is the doctrine of the resurrection of the body. If the end is genuine meeting, the climax and the transformation of all previous meetings, then it is no meeting of disembodied spirits. For such, the ancient Hebrews offered Sheol and the ancient Greeks Hades and the modern spiritualists seem to be their successors, hoping for a trivial and trifling life in some vague continuance of earthly activity.[2] This may appear desirable to modern spiritualists living in a materialistic age. But to ancient animists living in a non-materialistic age it was anything but desirable. And the desire to escape from the perpetuation of such an immortality was the hope of most, even if only the conviction of a few, in the higher religions of the east.

[1] Cf. R. Niebuhr, *The Nature and Destiny of Man*, vol. ii, p. 302: 'The judgment is upon sin and not upon finiteness', and his quotation from St Augustine, *De civ. Dei*, XIX, 27: 'God the Father will in his personal presence judge no man, but he has given his judgment to his Son who shall show himself *as a man* to judge the world, even as he showed himself as a man to be judged of the world.'

[2] Cf. F. von Hügel, *Essays and Addresses on the Philosophy of Religion*: 'It is certainly, at first sight, very striking that the fantastic abnormality of the form and method, which characterizes all animistic and spiritualist practices, should habitually yield so less than a normal, so shrunken, banal and boring a content' (pp. 196 f.).

The distinctive biblical perspective is focused on no continuance of a psychological something within us, called the soul, but rather on the incomprehensible miracle which affects the whole of us. Resurrection and not immortality is the Christian faith here and now and the Christian hope hereafter. From the beginning of creation to the end of time the Christian faith is a materialistic faith. The eschatological focus of Christian thinking as well as the eucharistic focus of Christian worship is not upon an immaterial state of being or upon some spiritual experience, but upon a meeting of embodied man with embodied God and with embodied fellow men and even with embodied nature. Out of the final meeting will come a transformation affecting not only men but nature.[1] There is no hint of 'pie in the sky when you die'; there is no strategic withdrawal from the body and from the world. On the contrary, in and through the embodied meeting is offered the hope of the transformation of the human body and of the material world.

Such is the glorious prospect of the Christian hope, and whatever such a phrase as 'a new heaven and a new earth'[2] may mean, it certainly promises a final meaning to this world and all that is in it. But this final meaning will inevitably surprise us by opening our eyes to the secrets of another world as well. Just as the church is not the kingdom of God, but has a place either in it or preparing for it, so this earth is not heaven, but has a place in it or preparing for it. With such a prospect before us we need to pay attention not only to von Hügel's warning never to be so enamoured of grace that we despise nature, but also to its antithesis, never to be so wrapped up in nature that we ignore grace.

The secret of the world of relationships and of persons is not found by those who seek to escape from the world of objects and of things, but it is open to all who allow the latter world in all the width of its manifold variety to become to them the medium for the revelation of the former in all the depth of its unfathomable intensity. Thus we live by faith in a world which love transforms, and we live in hope of a world which love will have transformed. 'Journeys end in lovers meeting'[3] puts in a sentence the secret of the eschatological transformation. Love is the turbine or the transformer which converts water into power, objects into persons, and a distant panorama of the last things into an imminent prospect of the person who is coming. That is the perspective of the Bible.

---

[1] Neither such a passage in the Old Testament as Isaiah 11, 1–9, nor such a passage in the New Testament as Romans 8, 18 ff., is meant to be taken literally as prose. But it is meant to be taken seriously as poetry. The hope all such passages inspire is unlimited and it is for this material world.

[2] Rev. 21, 1.   [3] W. Shakespeare, *loc. cit.*

CHAPTER III

THE THEOLOGY OF THE CHURCH

A TRULY Christian eschatology is a vital need at the moment both for the kindling of individual hope and for the assuring of mankind that there is a purpose in history towards which the life of society as a whole as well as of every individual soul is moving. If this is true, then there can be no doubt that the reintegration of a true eschatology into the theological dogmas of the church is a pressing concern for all who are alive both to the opportunities and to the perils of the present position of Christianity in the world.

Dr. J. A. T. Robinson has argued powerfully that the theological issue before the church to-day is as much the problem of the end as one hundred years ago it was the problem of the beginning.[1] What Mr. Davey says of the Epistle to the Romans and the doctrine of justification by faith in the middle of the sixteenth century might be said with something of the same intensity and passion about Genesis and the doctrine of creation in the middle of the nineteenth century and about Revelation and the doctrine of the last things in the middle of the twentieth century. 'It was one of those classical moments of intense theological perception, when one word, one dogma, one cry of repentance, one assurance of reconciliation, appear to contain in themselves the whole truth of God and the whole duty of man.' [2]

The impact of Darwin's *Origin of Species* upon the Christian doctrine of creation was terrific. It is all very well for Dr Raven to dismiss it in retrospect as a 'storm in a Victorian teacup'.[3] Such an attitude is as relevant to the life and death issue with which it seemed to confront its contemporaries as is the dismissal by some catholics to-day of the theological issues of the Reformation as a storm in a Germanic beer-mug. It is easy to be so wise after the event that we fail to realize the meaning of the event at all.

One hundred years ago the fate of Christianity seemed to many to be bound up with the literal accuracy of Genesis. At first the church met Darwin with outright rejection. But gradually the defences of biblical literalism crumbled before the sustained,

[1] J. A. T. Robinson, *In the End, God* (James Clarke, 1950), pp. 15 ff.
[2] E. C. Hoskyns and F. N. Davey, *The Fourth Gospel* (Faber and Faber, 2nd ed. 1947), p. 5.
[3] J. A. T. Robinson, *loc. cit.*

51

courageous and bitterly persecuted criticism of those within the
church, even though it stood firm against the assault of those without.
To-day the battle of Genesis is over.   The old positions on both
sides are seen to be largely if not completely untenable.   The way
is therefore clear, at least so far as the doctrine of creation is concerned, for that *rapprochement* between science and the Christian
religion which has for so long been our most urgent need in days
when overspecialization threatens to cut all lines of intelligible
conversation not only between east and west and black and white
but also between the members of the scientific and the theological
faculties of the same university.

But while all this has been going on about Genesis, what has been
happening to Revelation?   It is scarcely an exaggeration to say that
hardly a shot has been fired in defence of Christian eschatology at
all.   Indeed the dread of incurring the odium of the Marxist slogan,
'Religion is the opium of the people', has caused the church as a
whole to abandon the entire eschatological position so far as its
public utterances are concerned.   Lip-service to the old catholic
dogmas cannot conceal the way in which large sections of Christendom have abandoned not only hell, but heaven as well, except in so
far as sentimental wishful thinking so aptly foreshadows the last
assize with its parody of justice in some juvenile courts.

The western non-Roman church has for too long appeared to let
its whole eschatological position go by default, and has left it to
the extreme sects of protestantism and to the orthodox and Roman
catholic churches to proclaim either a traditional dogma without
vital faith or else a fanatical faith, born not of any certainty in
present experience, but of the conviction that there must somewhere
be a compensation for the lack of it.   The sectarian eschatological
bigot is even more rife in protestant countries than the Marxist.
Only 'a more excellent' theological understanding of the last things
can convert the pagan and the heretic and point the church itself
to the real answer to its need.

It can hardly be denied that for at least a generation the most alive
and the most sensitive of our theologians have been aware of this.
Their task has been greatly helped both by the freedom given them
by criticism in handling the biblical evidence, and also by the gradual
approach (thanks to that freedom) to a clearer understanding of the
nature of revelation than was possible when it seemed tied to propositional expression whether in biblical or ecclesiastical terms.

Now it is clear that it is the present experience of the biblical
writers which gives them the clues and insights they have as to both
creation and eschatology.   Speculative phantasy is as valueless in

both cases as literal information is unobtainable. The view of the beginning in the past and of the future in the end is tied to the understanding of the present, which is really an understanding of the presence, for it depends upon God's self-disclosure of himself either to some individual or to some group sensitive enough to apprehend in some degree his meaning. It is in event and in interpretation, and that means in meeting, that revelation is given. It is in that sense that the biblical record is the revelation of God. And the question for us is: in the light of this new understanding of the nature of any revelation, which is truly a revelation of love, what do the theologians make of the eschatology of the Bible and in what sense do they understand it as relevant to to-day?

The serious consideration of the eschatology of the Bible as a subject of academic and archæological research was given its initial impetus in Great Britain by the work of R. H. Charles. But far more important was the impetus to its study as a living issue in the gospel, given by the revolutionary work of Albert Schweitzer. It was Charles' Jowett Lectures for the last two years of the nineteenth century [1] which opened the eyes of British scholars to a whole range of biblical study, hitherto unilluminated by modern critical scholarship. Despite its drastic reconstructions and at times arbitrary datings, especially of apocryphal and pseudepigraphical books, Charles' work has put all subsequent generations of biblical scholars in his debt.

But it is not to Charles, but to Schweitzer, that at least so far as Great Britain is concerned we owe the revival of the study of eschatology as a living issue, vitally concerned with the permanent relevance of the Christian gospel. It was the translation of his critical study of the lives of Jesus published in the preceding hundred years [2] which cast a bombshell into the midst not only of the humanist liberal interpretation of the gospel but also of the traditional incarnational approach of Anglican theology.

Dealing extremely critically with the rest of the New Testament evidence, Schweitzer managed by handling the mission charge of our Lord in Matthew 10, 5 ff. [3] extremely conservatively, and indeed almost fundamentalistically, to force attention on a grave neglect by liberal scholars of an essential element in the teaching and outlook of Jesus. Schweitzer's critique was an extremely one-sided theological *tour-de-force*, at least as biased in its direction as the liberal lives of Jesus

---

[1] R. H. Charles, *A Critical History of the Doctrine of a Future Life* (A. and C. Black, 1899, subsequently considerably revised).

[2] A. Schweitzer, *The Quest of the Historical Jesus*, E.T. (A. and C. Black, 1910).

[3] Especially Matt. 10, 23.

were in theirs. It would long since have died a natural death but for three factors of the greatest importance.

First of all, though his exegesis was perversely one-sided, no one could deny that Schweitzer had unearthed out of the New Testament an aspect of gospel truth which had been all too easily and conveniently forgotten either because it was difficult to understand, or because it was unacceptable to the mind of much modern Christianity if it was understood. Even though it was an inadequate basis for a positive theology, no one could dispute its value as a negative corrective of an undoubted distortion of the gospel.

Secondly, Schweitzer's own heroic self-immolation in a mission hospital on the Congo only served to throw into higher relief the stature and greatness of a man who could at one and the same time be an authority on Bach and a great performer of his music, an authority on medicine and a great practitioner of its art, and also an authority on the New Testament and a living demonstration of its spiritual power. But personal heroism coupled with intellectual brilliance and æsthetic sensitivity would not have secured for him the continuing theological influence which he undoubtedly wields but for a third and all too easily forgotten factor.

Schweitzer in his greatest strictly theological work, *The Mysticism of Paul the Apostle*,[1] sought to combine eschatology and mysticism and so to safeguard the essential mystical content of the Christian religion, while relieving it of the incubus of an irrelevant and obsolete apocalyptic form. It is only in such a combination of eschatology and mysticism that it is possible to understand the secret of the gospel of the primitive church. Even if Schweitzer's attempted synthesis is profoundly unsatisfactory, it at least points to the need of such a synthesis and so illuminates one of the darkest places of theological uncertainty. For this all his successors must ever be more grateful than they can say.

Perhaps it is possible to sum up his contribution to the cause not only of the Christian church but of civilization itself by saying that as a corrective to liberalism he did permanent service to theology; as a stimulus, not less powerful on the protestant side than von Hügel's on the catholic, towards the rediscovery of the mystical element in religion, he did permanent service to religion; and as a pioneer in music, medicine and missionary work he did permanent service to Christianity and to civilization. But for all his great service and influence, his ultimate dismissal of Jesus himself as in his eschatology at least an heroic but misguided fanatic cannot for one moment be accepted by the Christian church.

[1] A. Schweitzer, *The Mysticism of Paul the Apostle*, E.T. (A. and C. Black, 1931).

Since Schweitzer many theologians have attempted to tackle the eschatological problem of the New Testament.[1] Of Karl Barth it is hard to speak with accuracy, but perhaps it is true to say that the timeless crisis of decision with which he confronts us in his commentary on the Epistle to the Romans [2] has given way to a more serious attempt to grapple with the biblical outlook on time and with the undoubted note of futurity, which no fair exegesis can eliminate from biblical eschatology.

Dr Torrance [3] thinks that Paul Althaus has gone deeper than even the later Karl Barth into the attempt to give full meaning to the process of history and at the same time to relate it to a real end, which is both its judgment and its goal.[4] He makes eschatology thoroughly Christological, and holds that it is 'only when the actuality of the end is placed fully in Christ Jesus that belief in the parousia, and in the parousia as a near-Advent, becomes an essential motion of faith'.[5] It is this loyalty to the Christological basis of eschatology which distinguishes the biblical theologian from the strict idealist.

Karl Heim tried to further the Christian understanding of time by coining two expressions with which to give content to the distinction made by Barth between old time and new time. For Heim old time is static, whereas new time is dynamic, and the use of such terms approaches nearer to something intelligible to any man in terms of his own experience of that mystical lovers' time, which seems to express the secret of eschatology better than anything else. In Karl Heim the relation between time and eternity becomes very vivid as he places the church on the frontier of time and sees it as the place where eternity speaks in time. For in this way we can understand how eternity is not to be conceived of as standing merely at the end of time but also as marching with it all along its frontier.

Dr. Torrance [6] refers to his vivid illustration of the church as a vast iron bridge, which spans the torrent of time with a single arch supported by only two pillars—the cross of Christ which stands on this side of time, and the coming of Christ in power which stands on the other side of time. This is a dramatic illustration, but for its

---

[1] In this and the succeeding paragraphs I am indebted consciously or unconsciously more than I can say to a privately circulated memorandum on eschatology by the Rev. Dr. T. F. Torrance, of which I have now no copy. It is to be published as an article in four instalments in the *Evangelical Quarterly* (James Clarke and Co.) in 1953.

[2] Karl Barth, *The Epistle to the Romans*, E.T. (O.U.P., 1933).

[3] T. F. Torrance, *loc. cit.*

[4] Cf. R. Niebuhr, *The Nature and Destiny of Man*, vol. ii (Nisbet, 1943), p. 297.

[5] T. F. Torrance, *loc. cit.*

[6] *Ibid.*

eschatological significance everything depends upon whether something of the same content is given to the symbol of the parousia as no
Christian can help giving to the event of the crucifixion.   The trouble
with so many theological references to the future parousia is that they
are not vitalized by any present awareness of the mystical presence.
The result inevitably is that, while the first coming of Christ has
reality for faith and love, the second coming has reality only for
reason as a logical counter to complete a theological scheme.

The conclusion of these continental studies of eschatology is to
be found in the work of Dr. Oscar Cullmann.   It is strange that
Barth, Schweitzer and Cullmann all come from the same geographical
area, in or near that political no-man's-land between France and
Germany which perhaps by its territorial peculiarity enables its
citizens to contemplate the eternal with greater ease than either their
French or their German neighbours.   It seems that for both the
latter there is a temptation either to be so involved in time as to give
no thought to eternity, or to be so anxious to escape from time
altogether as to give no reality to history.

Be this as it may, there can be no question about the strenuous
urgency with which Dr. Cullmann,[1] whatever the predisposing
geographical influences upon his work, stresses the reality of time
in the whole Hebraic outlook of the Bible.   He will have nothing
to do with Greek idealism whatever.   For him time is real now and it
always will be real.   He goes so far as to say that the very words
used in the Bible to describe eternity are temporal words.   Both
aion ($a\iota\acute{\omega}\nu$) and aionios ($a\iota\acute{\omega}\nu\iota\sigma\varsigma$) have to do with a limited duration
of time, i.e. an age.   Therefore, Dr. Cullmann maintains, it is quite
wrong to take them as referring to something for which time has no
significance or meaning at all.

He gets over the difficulty of the two kinds of time handled by
Barth in terms of old time and new time and by Heim in terms of
static time and dynamic time by introducing his own distinction,
which is taken up and interpreted by Dr. J. A. T. Robinson.[2]   This
contrasts chronos ($\chi\rho\acute{o}\nu\sigma\varsigma$), which means the mere chronological
duration of clock or calendar time, with kairos ($\kappa a\iota\rho\acute{o}\varsigma$), which has
in secular usage the sense of suitability or convenience, which is
well brought out in Felix' hypocritical promise to St Paul that
he would give him another hearing when he had 'a convenient
season'.[3]   God has his convenient seasons or hours and these are
his secret.[4]

[1] O. Cullmann, *Christ and Time* (S.C.M., 1950) *passim.*
[2] J. A. T. Robinson, *op. cit.*, pp. 44 ff.
[3] Acts 24, 25.   [4] Mark 13, 32.

To confuse God's kairoi (καίροι) with man's chronos (χρόνος) is to make precisely the mistake condemned by 2 Peter.[1] This mistake is not to imagine, as the Greeks did, that God had nothing to do with time at all, but it is to imagine that 'the almanack' has something to do with 'what determines the moment of consummation'.[2] By this distinction between chronos (χρόνος) and kairos (καίρος) Dr. Cullmann is able to maintain the sense of imminence, which is so characteristic of the New Testament eschatological perspective. What is imminent in terms of God's kairoi (καίροι), of the number of which we have no knowledge, may be very far off in terms of man's chronos (χρόνος), which is all our calendars know anything about.

It is a strange commentary upon, but no criticism of Dr. Cullmann's work and the excitement it has caused in theological circles, especially in the Anglo-Saxon world, that many of his arguments and diagrams bear a close resemblance to those of the older fundamentalist dispensationalists.[3] He brings into prominence the old fundamentalist distinction, also emphasized by Dr. C. H. Dodd, between the kingdom of Christ and the kingdom of God,[4] and sees them as successive stages in the realization of the divine purpose of the ages.

His emphasis upon the transposition of the focus of time from its Hebraic emphasis on its future end to its Christian crucial midpoint admirably illustrates and justifies our own calendar reckoning in terms of years B.C. and A.D. By the use of such military symbols as D-day and V-day he is able to make clear the sense in which it can be asserted that the final victory of Christ is an already accomplished fact while at the same time large scale mopping-up operations are still going on.

But the most important thing about Dr. Cullmann's work is that it lays, intellectually at least, its eschatological emphasis upon the point which for the whole New Testament is the focus of Christian hope. The parousia is the key eschatological symbol, and by making it such Dr. Cullmann avoids the twin pitfalls of either a virtual deification of the historical church in Roman catholic 'totalitarian eschatology',[5] or a virtual denial of history in much of that exposition of realized eschatology which dehistoricizes the whole conception of the kingdom of God.

His is a concern, true to the biblical outlook, with the tension between time and time, between time redeemed and time waiting

---

[1] 2 Pet. 3, 8 f.   [2] J. A. T. Robinson, *op. cit.*, p. 49.
[3] Cf., e.g., *The Scofield Reference Bible* (O.U.P., 1909), p. 5 n. and *passim*.
[4] 1 Cor. 15, 24 ff. is the proof text.   [5] T. F. Torrance, *loc. cit.*

to be redeemed. The trouble is that he deals so ruthlessly with any deviation from strictly rectilinear time as not only to cut the nerve of some of the deepest thinking of philosophy and to ignore the deepest experience of mysticism, but also to make havoc of such biblical insights and emphases as in St John most clearly, but everywhere in the New Testament to some degree, point to the present anticipatory foretaste of the future reality as being the secret of all real Christian experience.

The future kingdom of God is a future not of a reality, which is at present unknown, but of a manifestation, which is at present veiled. The reality is present here and now, though partly hidden. There is no question of strictly consecutive and often contradictory phases of revelation, as in the old fundamentalist dispensationalism, but of overlapping realities, always but dimly experienced and even more uncertainly interpreted, to do justice to which a merely rectilinear conception of time is quite inadequate.

Before leaving the continent and turning back to survey the British theological perspective on the last things, it is worth while pausing to consider the work of Rudolf Otto, who introduces the mystical [1] element in religion into all his work and so manages to give more reality to his 'modified futurist' or 'anticipated eschatology' [2] than the more arid purely intellectualist conceptions of the future are usually able to convey. Far too dependent though he is on the Book of Enoch for his interpretation of the Synoptic outlook, he nevertheless manages to orientate thought in an exciting way upon a future which is both imminent and already partially realized. The tragedy of his death suggests the possibility that what he so clearly understood intellectually he never experienced mystically himself, a fact which is perhaps pathetically supported by the nature of his efforts at Marburg to work out his own idea of the liturgy in practice. [3]

But whatever the truth of such suggestions, there is no doubt that Otto rendered a signal service to Christian theology as a whole, and not least in respect of its eschatological thinking. The conclusion of his great book, *The Kingdom of God and the Son of Man*, is a splendid criticism of the barren aridities of any theological dogma and speculation, which is unaware in actual experience and life of

[1] R. Otto, *The Idea of the Holy*, E.T. (O.U.P., 1928): 'Essentially, mysticism is the stressing to a very high degree, indeed the overstressing, of the non-rational or suprarational elements in religion: and it is only intelligible when it is so understood' (p. 22).
[2] So described by H. E. W. Turner (*Central Society of Sacred Study Leaflet 201*, April 1950), p. 14.
[3] Cf. R. Otto, *Religious Essays* (O.U.P., 1931), pp. 53 ff.

that reality of contact with the *mysterium tremendum ac fascinans*, which is the heart of all real religion everywhere.[1]

Otto may have been a spectator in his own experience of the truth he saw, but he saw more clearly than most theologians both the necessity of relating the Christian religion to all other comparative religions, and also the imperative need to take into account the mystical element of religion as alone able to give in present experience any real content to future eschatological symbols. Otherwise these symbols inevitably degenerate into counters used by jugglers in theological abstractions, which have lost all contact with reality whatever.

When we turn to Great Britain from the continent of Europe we become aware of a difference in the approach to eschatology and in the treatment of it. There is far less consideration of the problems aroused by philosophic thought about time and eternity, and far more realization of the practical and pastoral implications of the biblical evidence. Whereas some modern continental theologians, like the fundamentalists they in this respect so strikingly resemble, are at home in the Pauline epistles but are apparently to some extent out of their depth in parts of the Synoptic Gospels and in the whole of

---

[1] R. Otto, *The Kingdom of God and the Son of Man*, E.T. (Lutterworth Press, 1938): 'For the theologian,' he writes, 'the charisma, together with the pneuma, as an anticipation of the eschatological order is an essential element of a community which is intended to be a church of the Nazarene. That this church has lost its charisma, that men look back to it as a thing of past times, that men make it and the inbreaking Kingdom belonging to it trivial by allegories, does not show that this church is now on a higher level, but is a sign of its decay' (pp. 275 f.). Cf. A. G. Hogg, *Redemption from this World* (T. and T. Clark, 1924): 'Christianity essentially is, and must remain, a religion of redemption from this world, and, moreover, of a redemption which we begin to experience here and now. But the world from which it offers this present redemption is neither nature, in any absolute sense, nor yet exactly " the present age" of apocalyptical conception. In Christianity the redemption of which we already have experience is from the world of the worldly-wise into the world of the childlike: it is from the world of the delimited and manageable into a world of inexhaustible possibilities, a world in which many terrible and all good things are possible; it is from a world of prose into a world of poetry. But never is it redemption from the world of fact into a world of fairy-tale. When the poetry of prophetic messianism developed into the fairy-tale of apocalypse with its fatally rigid division of this world from the next, God brought it back to poetry again, but to a poetry lived and acted. He brought it back to lived and acted poetry, first of all in the herald-consciousness of John the Baptist, and then perfectly in the miracle-working of Jesus Christ. I cannot better express my conception of the new world into which the Christian should find himself here and now redeemed than in the words of a beautiful quotation I have met with from a writer with whose work I have no other acquaintance: "There is a kingdom into which none enter but children, in which the children play with infinite forces, where the child's little finger becomes stronger than the giant world: a wide kingdom where the world exists only by sufferance; to which the world's laws and developments are for ever subjected; in which the world lies like a foolish, wilful dream in the solid truth of the day." A description such as this may read like poetry rather than solid fact; but it is a poetry which Jesus lived and acted out' (pp. 25 f.).

St John, their British contemporaries tend to be dominated in their eschatological thinking by the 'Platonic tradition in English religious thought', [1] approached by way of an Hellenistically interpreted St John.

There have been of course scholars like Dr. T. R. Glover,[2] who have continued the liberal tradition of ignoring eschatology even after the dropping of the Schweitzerian bombshell. There have been others who, like the distinguished authors of *The Lord of Thought* [3] at the beginning of the post-Schweitzerian era and like Dr. T. F. Glasson [4] at the end of it, have excised eschatology if not from the New Testament itself at least from all its effective relevance to the twentieth century. For them as for Schweitzer, however the New Testament evidence is evaluated for its own day, its eschatological mythology is hopelessly out of date so far as our day is concerned. If anything of the kernel is to be left as part of the Christian gospel, it must be a kernel from which a very large husk has been removed.

Dr. Glasson's main point deserves much more attention than it has so far been given. And though he stands somewhat apart from the main stream of eschatological thought, his contribution is important. At least he sees that it is the parousia which is at the heart of the problem. He does not try to excise eschatology from the teaching of Jesus, though he has been so misinterpreted in some quarters. In this respect he differs from earlier liberal thinkers. But what he does do is to question very seriously whether any specific doctrine of a second coming or parousia was part of the teaching of Jesus himself.

In doing this Dr. Glasson has undoubtedly corrected a bias, established by von Hügel's 'luminous' texts,[5] in favour of leaving the second coming as an integral part of our Lord's teaching, while attempting to belittle its importance either on grounds of its misinterpretation by the early church or on the theory of its fulfilment by the coming of the Holy Spirit at Pentecost. Dr. Glasson takes explicit teaching about the parousia out of the dominically authenticated gospel and attributes its prevalence in the New Testament more to the attitude of the early church in interpreting all the messianic proof texts, which were unfulfilled by Christ's first coming, as referring to his second coming.

[1] Of which Dr W. R. Inge remains in our day the most notable, but by no means the only exponent.

[2] T. R. Glover, *The Jesus of History* (S.C.M., 1917).

[3] L. Dougall and C. W. Emmet, *The Lord of Thought* (1922), referred to in *Essays on the Trinity and the Incarnation*, ed. A. E. J. Rawlinson (Longmans, 1928), p. 32.

[4] T. F. Glasson, *The Second Advent* (Epworth Press, 1945).

[5] F. von Hügel, *Essays and Addresses on the Philosophy of Religion* (Dent, 1921), p. 123.

In so far as Dr. Glasson cuts the nerve of its real relevance for to-day and so takes the heart out of the eschatological gospel of the New Testament, it will be a main point of this book to disprove his thesis. But in so far as he claims that our Lord himself hardly ever, if ever, spoke of his own parousia, he should be given credit for emphasizing a most important point. It is a fact that our Lord neither spoke clearly of the parousia nor of the Paraclete [1] until the very end of his earthly ministry. That neither proves nor disproves the parousia or the Paraclete, but it is a piece of the biblical evidence, which ought to be faced.

Dr. Glasson however is on the periphery of eschatological thought in Great Britain. At the centre of it the two names that instantly suggest themselves are those of Dr. C. H. Dodd and Professor T. W. Manson. It is possible to distinguish between their views and to characterize Dr. Dodd's eschatology as being 'realized' and Professor Manson's as 'graded'.[2] The distinction is rather forced, though Manson makes more of the difference between Jesus' outlook before Simon Peter's confession of his messiahship at Cæsarea Philippi [3] and his outlook after it than Dodd does.

The main emphasis of each writer is designed to focus attention on the fact that if a Christian means what he says when he confesses that Jesus is the Christ, then he must mean that in Jesus Christ the end, to which the Old Testament looked forward, has arrived. This is the point that, as we have already seen, Niebuhr [4] impressively emphasizes by driving home the application of the great Pauline apologia, 'Seeing that Jews ask for signs and Greeks seek after wisdom; but we preach Christ crucified, unto Jews a stumblingblock and unto Gentiles foolishness; but unto them that are called, both Jews and Greeks, Christ the power of God and the wisdom of God'.[5]

The claim that Jesus was the Christ was 'absurd' [6] to the Jews because, though they believed history had a meaning, the disclosure of that meaning in Jesus was neither what they expected nor what they wanted. Jesus had taken what was to all intents and purposes a prophetic aside [7] and seen in it the clue to the whole meaning of prophetic messianism. The Jews themselves had never seen any messianic significance in it at all, for the idea of the Messiah triumphing through suffering was to them as inconceivable as the

---

[1] Cf. J. E. Fison, *The Blessing of The Holy Spirit* (Longmans, 1950), pp. 81 ff.; C. K. Barrett, *The Holy Spirit and the Gospel Tradition* (S.P.C.K., 1947), *passim*.
[2] H. E. W. Turner, *loc. cit.*   [3] Mark 8, 27 ff.
[4] R. Niebuhr, *The Nature and Destiny of Man*, vol. ii, pp. 36, 56 ff.
[5] 1 Cor. 1, 22–24.   [6] R. Niebuhr, *op. cit.*, p. 36 n.
[7] The Servant Songs of Isaiah 40–55; cf. C. R. North, *The Suffering Servant of Deutero-Isaiah* (O.U.P., 1948).

idea of God being in any way involved in suffering was incredible to the Greeks with their emphasis upon the divine impassibility. To the Greeks of course any idea of a messianic purpose in history at all was nonsensical, for if time is conceived of in no sense as rectilinear but solely as cyclical, there is nothing more to be said than Lucretius' endorsement of the Preacher [1] in his most pessimistic mood: 'Everything is always the same.' [2]

But if unlike the Greeks the Christians assert a meaning in history, and if unlike the Jews they see in Jesus that meaning disclosed, what sense can be made of any history at all since the crucifixion and of church history in particular? How can the Christian church have in any intelligible sense a future hope if all that was lacking in the incarnation and atonement of Jesus Christ was the element of sheer finality? This is the question to which realized eschatology has so far given no adequate answer. For without the insights of mysticism it is impossible for any theology which is securely based upon the finality of Jesus Christ to give adequate content to the future hope of the church in terms of any eschatology which is more than an unrelated appendage to the rest of its outlook.

The realized eschatologists certainly make the teaching of Jesus and especially his parables [3] live in an existential way, which has redeemed so much of the New Testament from the trivial allegorizing sermon illustrations to which pious devotional exegesis had tended to reduce it. But with all this to their credit it still remains true that to illuminate the Johannine perspective upon eternal life without adequately facing the Synoptic presuppositions, which underlie its whole approach and to which it is so often providing a corrective, is to make the same mistake as to interpret the earlier Karl Barth, writing a corrective note [4] in the margin of theology in terms of the later Barth writing his own dogmatic theology.

[1] Eccles. 1, 9; 3, 15.
[2] Lucretius, *De Rerum Natura*, Bk. III, 945: 'Eadem sunt omnia semper.'
[3] Cf. C. H. Dodd, *The Parables of the Kingdom* (Nisbet, 1935).
[4] Cf. K. Barth, *The Word of God and the Word of Man*, E.T. (Hodder and Stoughton, 1928): 'Do not think that I make my contribution to theological discussion, to-day or any day, in rivalry with the fundamentalist, liberal, Ritschlian or history-of-religion type of theology. Take it rather as a kind of *marginal note*, a gloss which in its way agrees and yet does not agree with all these types—and which, I am convinced, loses its meaning the moment it becomes more than a note and takes up space as a new theology next to the others. So far as Thurneysen, Gogarten and I really may be said to form a "school" in the familiar sense of the word, our work is superfluous. I think that every one, however important may be the contents of his marginal note, may well *remain* in his own school and with his own masters, if only as a *corrective*, as the "pinch of spice (biszchen Zimt) in the food", as Kierkegaard says. "My theology" is related to the theologies proper somewhat as the Community of Moravian Brethren is related to the communions and churches proper: it has no wish whatever to form a new type of its own' (p. 98). In the light of subsequent events, *verb. sap.*!

From this point of view realized eschatology reads St John into St Mark and is frankly and flatly heretical by the standards of a considerable portion of the New Testament evidence. 'I beg you, brothers,' says St Paul for example, 'not to let your minds get easily unsettled or excited by any spirit of prophecy or any declaration or any letter purporting to come from me, to the effect that the Day of the Lord is already here.' [1] The school of realized eschatology has grasped the essential New Testament fact that a fulfilment of the Old Testament hope must involve both the realization of the kingdom of God 'in the same sphere of reality' as that 'in which men now live and suffer', and also its manifestation as 'something that will not arise out of history but will supervene upon history from God'.[2] But it has failed to give full weight [3] to the double-sidedness both of the Synoptic outlook and even of the Johannine formula, 'The hour cometh and now is'.[4] Convinced of the present presence it ignores the future parousia.

This is to do less than justice to the essential faith of the New Testament and to cut the nerve of the theological virtue of hope which is in such sorely short supply among us in consequence. In the conviction that we have all we need in Jesus Christ, the hope of the wonder that lies ahead for the church and for the world as well as for the individual soul is lost either in a vague or unfounded optimism about better things to come for the world as a whole and for the redeemed community within it, or else in some highly individualized conception of the beatific vision. The parousia may be retained as a theological proposition, but it has long since ceased to be a living symbol of hope for any save the literal Adventists. The inevitable result has been the excision of 'Maran atha' [5] and all that it stands for not only from theology but from liturgy as well, with consequences even more disastrous for worship than for doctrine.

It is important to say this quite frankly, or else the blessings which we undoubtedly owe to realized eschatology will blind us to the fatal legacy with which it has so far left us. Of the blessings there can be no doubt. Whereas for Schweitzer it was Jesus who was terribly mistaken, for Dodd perhaps and for Glasson certainly the major mistake was that of the early church. Whereas for Schweitzer there is no final judgment at all, for Dodd history itself is the judgment. Admittedly Dodd with his realized eschatology has the advantage over Schweitzer with his consistently futurist eschatology in that he frees our Lord from bondage to late Jewish apocalyptic ideas. But this is no gain if it

---

[1] 2 Thess. 2, 2 (Moffatt). [2] T. F. Torrance, *loc. cit.*
[3] Heb. 4, 12, 'two-edged'. [4] John 5, 25. [5] 1 Cor. 16, 22.

lands us in such a radical reconstruction of the New Testament evidence as forces us to a very dubious interpretation of its meaning.[1]

It is all very well for Dr. Dodd[2] to say that 'the time-scale is irrelevant to the ultimate significance of history' and to buttress that assertion by quoting 'One day is with the Lord as a thousand years, and a thousand years as one day', and by claiming this telescoping of time as the legitimate prerogative not only of the Lord but also of the 'philosophical historian' as well. Such an attitude is a distortion of the true significance of 2 Peter[3] if it in fact denies the reality of the time scale altogether instead of merely transposing it from the key of chronos ($\chi\rho\acute{o}\nu os$) to that of kairos ($\kappa a\iota\rho os$).[4]

It is hardly an exaggeration to say[5] that in giving up a teleological view of contemporary history Dr. Dodd has in fact gone to the other extreme and abandoned an eschatological view as well, for he has left us with no eschatological expectation in a situation in which everything that really matters has happened already. This is to destroy the original meaning of the word, eschaton ($\check{\epsilon}\sigma\chi a\tau o\nu$), altogether. Certainly it is true that it gives the life, death and resurrection of Jesus Christ their rightful all-important emphasis in a sense in which Schweitzer's futurist eschatology can never claim to do. But on the other hand, to refer the meaning of the parables solely to the coming of the kingdom of God up to the moment of the crucifixion and not to the progress of the kingdom in the history of the church at all, is to leave the actual realization of the kingdom completely in the air in sharpest contrast to the historical future orientation of the whole Bible.

Certainly the last thing, to eschaton ($\tau\grave{o}\ \check{\epsilon}\sigma\chi a\tau o\nu$), confronted men in Jesus Christ, so that it would be much better to speak of the last one, ho eschatos ($\acute{o}\ \check{\epsilon}\sigma\chi a\tau os$), or even to abandon the term altogether in favour of the biblical usage, which speaks of the coming one, ho erchomenos ($\acute{o}\ \check{\epsilon}\rho\chi\acute{o}\mu\epsilon\nu os$).[6] But in 'the coming one', the 'last' or the eschatological 'Adam',[7] what confronted man was a veiled mystery which left man with freedom and opportunity for decision. The last judgment may be a present fact, but it is certainly not a

---

[1] The controversy, e.g., over the interpretation of Matthew 12, 28 and Mark 1, 15 is by no means settled and the ruthless excision of futurist references from the parables is most questionable; cf. T. F. Torrance, loc. cit. To free our Lord from the intellectual limitations of his contemporaries does not serve a true Christology if it lands us in Apollinarianism.

[2] C. H. Dodd, The Parables of the Kingdom, p. 71.   [3] 2 Pet. 3, 8.
[4] J. A. T. Robinson, op. cit., p. 49.   [5] Cf. T. F. Torrance, loc. cit.
[6] E.g. Matt. 11, 3; Rev. 4, 8.   [7] 1 Cor. 15, 45.

present fact of which we are now fully aware. If it is here, it is not fully operative. The unveiled eschaton of love would be a sight so terrible to sinful men that they could not for one moment bear its 'consuming fire'.[1] It would probably mean damnation on the spot if it were fully in operation, but mercifully it is not.

The meaning of history is the mercy of God,[2] and still to-day there is a continuing and purposeful historical process at work. The coming of Jesus Christ into the world has not divested time of its meaning but has invested every moment of time with an hitherto undreamt-of meaning. History itself is unfolding before our eyes 'the story of an ever-increasing cosmos creating ever-increasing possibilities of chaos'.[3] For this continual and mounting tension between Christ and anti-Christ realized eschatology leaves no room. It can speak no word of teleological hope to those now grappling with the historical dilemmas of our time.

Over against the school of realized eschatology stands one other very influential group of thinkers. These are the catholically minded incarnationists, whose thinking centres round a community conceived of as organized on an organic rather than a dialectical pattern. This leads at times to a virtual deification of the church and to a transubstantiation of its earthly realities into realities of grace. For such an outlook lip-service to a traditional future eschatology may be genuine in so far as individual hopes of immortality are concerned, but it can hardly have any meaning in the biblical sense for any corporate hope either for the world or for the church.

It leaves no room for real surprise at the end, and no eschatology which eliminates such surprise can claim for one moment to be biblical. All issues are already settled and known and there is no longer any genuine eschatological tension between having and hoping.[4] Salvation is secured in a continuity of possessiveness, which is itself a contradiction of the very nature of love. Whether the realized teleology of the incarnationists is achieved by the transubstantiation of the realities of nature into those of grace, as with the Roman catholic tendency, or by the reverse process of the transubstantiation of the realities of grace into those of nature, as in the implication of Dr. G. F. MacLeod's striking metaphor, 'God is earthed', the result in both cases is an over-simplification of the true biblical outlook, of which eschatology is the key.

Spiritual healing and pacifism, taken out of the context of biblical faith, can so easily be symptomatic of a point of view which believes

---

[1] Heb. 12, 29.   [2] 2 Pet. 3, 9.
[3] Cf. T. F. Torrance, *loc. cit.*, quoting R. Niebuhr, *An Interpretation of Christian Ethics*, p. 108.   [4] 2 Cor. 6, 10.

5

that humanly perfectly healthy individuals in a humanly perfectly ·
ordered society together comprise an ideal which, if it could be
realized, would mean the coming of the kingdom of God upon earth.
To believe in such a realization is only to believe one side, and that
the optimistic side, of biblical eschatology. To believe that such
a realization would mean the coming of the kingdom of God is to
eliminate the very heart of any eschatology which is true to the
essential biblical faith in the living and the loving God.

In its assurance of the consummation of all things in Christ such
an attitude loses sight of the dreadful reality of the abiding consequences of heaven and hell, which will be with us not only up to
the end but in the end as well.[1] It knows only an organic interpretation of society and understands the working out of God's
purpose in the world only in terms of an organism, forgetful of the
even more fundamental dialectical relationship involved in any
thoroughgoing application of the principles on which alone a God
of love can be conceived to operate. It looks to a *telos*, but has
no inkling of a *finis*, especially of a *finis* which is a surprise. It
has got such a hold on the presence that it leaves no room for the
parousia.

This is theologically a distortion of the biblical evidence. Ethically
it runs the risk of losing the reality of love altogether. It results
in the transformation of the personal and therefore unpossessible
living God into a propositional and therefore possessible dead god—
a god safe from the perils of psychological investigation in his stark
objectivity, but impotent for the salvation of any soul or of society
as a whole.

Whatever the verdict upon all these varying approaches to the
problem of eschatology, the conclusion of this portion of our study
is that of all the living issues in theology to-day none is more search-
ingly relevant to our needs than is the attempt to come to grips with
the biblical doctrine of the last things. We are being forced back
to a re-examination of the biblical evidence in no spirit of idle
curiosity but in a life-and-death search for an expression of our faith
adequate both to meet the challenges of the world and the claims of
the church. A revitalized eschatology would transform the prospects
of reunion, rejuvenate the cause of missions, revive the reality of
worship and reinvigorate the whole life of the church. The spur of
the moment to tackle the eschatological problem comes not only from
the outside pressure of the world but also and even more from the
inside need of the church.

---

[1] Dr. J. A. T. Robinson's otherwise profoundly searching eschatological study falls
into this error at the end after avoiding it right up to the end (*op. cit.*, pp. 108 ff.).

Inside the church there is hardly a single live contemporary issue from marriage to reunion which would not be immeasurably helped towards a solution by a deeper understanding of the eschatological hope of the Bible. As far as ethical questions are concerned, if Christian standards are to be upheld and seen in their right perspective and in their contemporary relevance to human needs, there is an imperative demand for a realistic appreciation of the present church situation. What are we to do with the Sermon on the Mount? Is it the heart of the gospel, as traditional liberalism used to affirm? Or is it an interim ethic, valid only for the infinitesimal interval before the end of the world, as futurist eschatology used to affirm? And if the latter, is it now irrelevant in view of the time-lag of nearly two thousand years since Jesus first taught it?

Surely it is neither the heart of the gospel, for the mount of the beatitudes is not the mount of Calvary and never can be; nor is it irrelevant to to-day in view of the time-lag of two thousand years. It is what is expected of those who are 'in love' or 'in Christ' (the phrases for our immediate purpose might be interchanged). People 'in love' are neither expected to behave like other people nor do they themselves see why they should. Their love, if genuine, has lifted them above the normal standards of human conduct and community behaviour, so that they often appear to others to be living in a dangerously antinomian manner. So it appears in every real romance and so it appeared in the first romantic days of the Christian faith. The behaviour of Jesus and the early Christians appeared scandalous to many of their most seriously minded contemporaries.[1]

Lovers cannot avoid giving this impression, but they can avoid going out of their way to seek to give it.[2] They live in a different world from other people, a mystical world not of timelessness, but of time so speeded up that it is an apt colloquialism to say that it flies. For them the ethic by which they live is an interim ethic. but the interim is measured not by clock time but by lovers' time. The ethics of Jesus are inconceivable out of such a relationship: they are natural within it. They are rooted in mystical awareness of the presence and in eschatological expectation of the parousia. And when either root is cut, the fruit [3] soon withers away.

Thus the morality of Jesus cannot be divorced from his religion.

[1] Cf. H. R. Mackintosh, *The Christian Experience of Forgiveness* (Nisbet, 1927): 'We need have no hesitation in conceding that the Judaists at first sight had something to say for themselves, for St Paul's gospel does have an antinomian look. But must it not always be so, where gospel is really present? Did not the Pharisees bring a charge of antinomianism against Jesus, who received sinners and ate with them?' (p. 119).

[2] This is a good criterion for distinguishing what is a stunt and what is not.

[3] Gal. 5, 22.

His behaviour expressed in outward terms the inner principle of his holy communion with his Father. He practised on the mount of Calvary what he preached on the mount of the beatitudes. He lived, in the Barthian phrase, 'between the times', but the measure of the interim cannot be expressed in terms of a ministry of three or any other number of calendar years. It belongs to time, but to another dimension than that of clock time.

It is thus only those for whom, because their eschatology is matched by their mysticism, the imminence of the end is no less a reality than it was for the first-century Christians, who can understand and rightly apply among themselves the standard of the interim ethic of the Sermon on the Mount. Attempts to ignore Sinai and to apply the beatitudes direct to the world situation to-day are rightly deplored in Niebuhr's powerful arraignment of those who take upon themselves the name of Christ, but forget their master's warning that 'the sons of this world are for their own generation wiser than the sons of the light'.[1] It is so very tempting to find in the words of Jesus sanction for taking a short-cut out of our present ethical perplexities and to fail to realize the complexities of the actual situation in which we are all of us, whether we like it or not, so profoundly involved.

The trouble about Niebuhr [2] is that his intellectual awareness does not seem to be matched by any mystical comprehension of the eschatological realities about which he speaks. At the level of the mind he speaks of our condition, as few others succeed in doing: at the level of the soul he somehow fails us, just at the very point at which very significantly Thomas Merton [3] picks us up. The fact is that ethics, eschatology and mysticism must come together for any true solution of the church's problems to-day.

And they will not come together unless the impact of eschatology upon worship is allowed full weight in the church. Realized eschatology has done much to correct the 'mere memorialism' of the protestant Lord's supper, stigmatized by P. T. Forsyth as not only æsthetically but also spiritually far less satisfying to the human soul than the Roman catholic mass.[4] In countless evangelical

---

[1] Luke 16, 8.

[2] Niebuhr's strength and his weakness on the whole question of eschatology were brought out with verbatim records of his own words in a broadcast on the B.B.C. Third Programme, February 29, 1952, by Rev. E. H. Robertson, entitled 'The Christian Hope.'

[3] A Trappist monk, now in America, whose written works, *Elected Silence, Waters of Silence, Seeds of Contemplation, The Ascent of Truth* (Hollis and Carter, 1949 ff.), have achieved an astonishing circulation.

[4] P. T. Forsyth, *The Church and the Sacraments* (Independent Press, 2nd ed. 1947): 'As to the sacraments it may be surmised that the writer holds a mere memorialism to be a more fatal error than the Mass, and a far less lovely' (p. xvi).

statements of recent years we have been reminded that though any repetition of Calvary is unthinkable, a re-presentation of it is the heart of every eucharist, where worshippers and communicants find themselves at Calvary and in the Upper Room not by the forced effort of memory and imagination to go back two thousand years, but in the free response of the soul to the contemporary impact of that eternal drama to-day.

At the eucharist we are 'there'—that is the teaching both of Dix and of Dodd. And it is identical with the mission preaching of D. L. Moody and, still more, of the mission singing of I. D. Sankey. In word as well as in sacrament, by the simplest undenominational evangelicalism as well as by the highest denominational sacramentalism, it is eschatology which lies at the heart of Christian worship and is the secret of its converting and its sanctifying power. In fact the eucharistic presence and the eschatological parousia are bound up in indissoluble unity. The tragedy is that the eucharistic sacramentalist is so often so assured of the real presence that he feels no need for the real parousia, while the apocalyptic evangelist can be so convinced of the real parousia as to fail completely to relate his future hope in any except a compensatory way to the real presence. Whenever either of these things happens, the presence of personal love has been replaced by the presence of propositional logic, whether guaranteed by verbal formula or ritual act.

True eschatology cannot be relegated to the final chapter of a *Summa*. It must interpenetrate the outlook of theology at every point of doctrine. That is the New Testament way unless its last and most disputed book is allowed to determine and dominate the outlook of all the others. 'Maran atha'[1] must come right into the middle of doctrine and permeate the whole of worship if we are to rediscover not only the faith but also the hope of the early church. And we cannot do this unless the secret of love, which eludes any and every attempt to possess it and honours any and every expression of willingness to lose it, is at the heart of the worship of the church.

Reliance on a presence guaranteed in the visible continuity of time might be all right if God were not a God whose very nature is love. But for the God of love it is a tragic distortion of the eschatologically guaranteed presence, which can only be understood by those who have entered into the Pauline secret, and know what it means 'as having nothing' yet 'to possess all things'.[2] It is the fear of being surprised by the unknown which so completely paralyses any real relationship of love, for in such a relationship there can be no limit to the surprises which lie in store for those who are willing

[1] 1 Cor. 16, 22.   [2] 2 Cor. 6, 10.

to pursue the pilgrims' and the lovers' way which ends inevitably, as every genuine strand of Christian eschatology is bound grudgingly or rejoicingly to confess, in a surprise for every one.

Any reliance on any device, however holy its sanction or its guarantee, which is designed to eliminate the possibility of surprise or to safeguard against its consequences is evidence of complete misapprehension of the nature of love itself and therefore of the nature of God himself. Claims as of human right on the divine presence are invalid unless matched by confidence as of divine grace in the divine parousia, and if they are so matched they will not be made. And on the other hand confidence as of human right in the parousia is mere delusion unless it is matched by certainty as of divine grace in the presence.

Only those who know the presence can hope for the parousia. Only those who hope for the parousia can know the presence. No amount of theological verbal juggling can obscure this basic fact of love. And this basic reality of the presence necessitating the parousia and of the parousia presupposing the presence is significantly very seldom spoken of as such in the Bible. The use of abstract terms like presence or parousia is avoided wherever possible in the Bible for the simple reason that such terms inevitably tend to objectify a reality, which if it is love, can only be known in the dangerous reciprocity of mutual meeting and never in either the safe objectivity of rite or formula or the safe subjectivity of feeling or experience.

The Church of England retains at the centre of its eucharistic liturgy the specific eschatological reference [1] which so many other churches have completely lost. This would be a far greater gain if it were matched throughout the Book of Common Prayer with a similar eschatological awareness. Unfortunately this is so far from being the case that the most explicit reference to the second coming in the whole book is in the collect for the third sunday in Advent on which the eschatological emphasis usually gets as much subordinated to the ministerial as it is on the preceding sunday to the biblical. In this way the season of Advent has been largely deprived of the chance of providing year by year the eschatological corrective that Anglican incarnational emphasis so badly needs.[2]

---

[1] '. . . a perpetual memory of that his precious death, until his coming again' (Prayer of Consecration): cf. 1 Cor. 11, 26.

[2] For the Anglican distortion of Advent, cf. *Theology*, December 1951 (S.P.C.K.). For the lop-sidedness of Anglican incarnational emphasis, cf. D. M. Baillie, *God was in Christ* (Faber and Faber, 1948): 'Modern Anglican theology has tended to be intolerant of paradox, smoothing out contradictions, sometimes almost turning itself into a commonsense Christian philosophy, semi-Pelagian rather than Augustinian or

As far as hymns are concerned, Professor John Baillie's [1] reference to Principal Cairns is supported by the evidence of Canon M. A. C. Warren. [2] The note of triumph and confident expectation, such as is expressed in Isaac Watts' familiar hymn, 'Jesus shall reign', is typical of the authentic missionary evangel. It expresses the mystical confidence of faith rather than the reasoned confidence of intellect. But it must be admitted that this authentic eschatological note is often distorted by either an over-pessimistic emphasis or a compensatory over-optimistic corrective of it. In fact modern hymn-books come out in almost monotonous regularity to provide the corrective, each reacting from its predecessor and seeking to counterbalance it. Nothing sounds more unlike the authentic New Testament hope than the pitiful dirge of the introverted self-pity of some evangelical pietists unless it be the forced optimism of a modernist extrovert, seeking by conscious effort to bolster his own and his fellows' inward lack of assurance by the use of hymn-books full of exhortatory heartiness.

From worship it is but a step to missionary endeavour and to evangelism, both at home and overseas. Here again the need for a true eschatology is evident on every hand. The missionary societies are increasingly alive to a situation in which the limitations of all those who do not accept the eschatological hope of a fundamental biblicism are more and more apparent. The World Council of Churches is preparing to deal with this very subject at its next conference at Evanston, Illinois, U.S.A., in 1954. And its preliminary conference at Rolle in Switzerland in 1951 brought out the need for a message of hope, first to be given to the churches and then by the churches to the world. [3]

At this conference it was significant that Niebuhr's brilliant analysis of the four groups of peoples now living in the world and of their different attitudes in the present situation, though it served to expose the strikingly divergent outlooks of contemporary humanity in face of the issues confronting them, did not do much to provide any unifying

---

Calvinistic in its mood (is this the proverbial semi-Pelagianism of British thought?)—until it comes to the doctrine of the Incarnation. Then it becomes quite different, treating the *mysterium Christi* as a solitary exception, a hard kernel which is never soluble in any howsoever powerful solvent of theological thought. The result is to make the theological system as a whole too "rational" and by contrast to make the Christological dogma too "irrational", too little connected with the rest of our theology, too much a sheer mystery, whose meaning we do not know. Paradox may then become a mere *asylum ignorantiæ*, instead of being a truly religious mystery, close to experience and to faith' (p. 107).

[1] J. Baillie, *Belief in Progress* (O.U.P., 1950), pp. 215 ff.
[2] M. A. C. Warren, *The Truth of Vision* (Canterbury Press, 1948), p. 45.
[3] Cf. E. H. Robertson, B.B.C. Third Programme, February 29, 1952.

message of hope, applicable to them all and understandable by them all. The most considerable contribution made at the conference to such a message was provided by the simple meditation of Professor Edmund Schlink of Heidelburg.

He made it very clear that the biblical faith in the coming of Christ, which is too often considered as a somewhat superfluous appendix to the main body of Christian truth, becomes in a really critical situation a great dynamic reality in the life of the church.[1] His testimony is worth quoting, for it bears witness to the central conviction of this book. 'This expectancy of the coming Lord', he said, 'liberates us from anxiety and makes us truly realistic in our judgment of the world. Such an attitude is the strongest possible impetus to be watchful, to hurry, to lose no time, and to see that no man gets lost. It releases the strongest possible zeal, because it keeps us from worrying about ourselves.'

It is the breakdown of western political imperialism which has forced a re-thinking of the objectives and hopes of all missionary work in so far as the latter has been so often unconsciously based upon the presupposition of the supremacy of western white civilization. If the missionary cause of a hundred years ago demanded the heroism of going to the physical certainty of 'the white man's grave', there is no reason why in our own day it should not demand the equivalent heroism in a spiritual, if not a material certainty. The heroism of the real cross is very different from the heroics of adventure story books and by comparison often seems humdrum.

The attempt of western protestantism to continue to force a one-way-traffic operation of the gospel is suicidal, and even more disastrously so when that operation is conducted upon spiritual rather than material lines. The embodied reciprocity of love, which finds its hall-mark in marriage, is the *punctum stantis aut cadentis ecclesiæ* to-day of every missionary-minded body. But it is hard for western protestantism, and indeed for much catholicism as well, to put into reverse a machine which has been so manifestly blessed of God in the past few hundred years. Yet it is as true in missionary as in military operations that the weapons that won the last war are always sure to lose the next.

From the Maccabees, who saved Israel by their exclusiveness in the second century B.C., it is but a step to their successors who destroyed Israel by their exclusiveness in the first century A.D. The emphasis of the gospel needed for salvation in one generation may, if repeated as a talisman in the next, be the surest way of ensuring damnation. So futile is it to copy even the greatest saints to the

[1] Cf. E. H. Robertson, B.B.C. Third Programme, February 29, 1952.

ignoring of the essential originality of every work of the Holy Spirit. No merely imitative endeavour, conceived on lines that necessitate a slavish copying of an original, can fully serve the creative purpose of God himself.

Dr. Warren [1] has sought to purge the memory of the missionary societies and so to restore to them the living hope of their founders. But opinions as to the importance of the idea of hastening the second coming in giving urgency to the missionary cause differ widely, from those who, like Dr. Warren, tend in this respect to minimize its influence, to those who, like the later Inter-Varsity Fellowship if not the earlier Student Volunteers, make it all-important. It is interesting to see how exclusively in terms of the fulfilment of the Matthæan prophecy, 'This gospel of the kingdom shall be preached in the whole world for a testimony unto all the nations: and then shall the end come',[2] Dr. Cullmann [3] interprets the meaning of the delayed parousia in a manner strikingly reminiscent of the old-fashioned and one-sided emphasis of the protestant fundamentalists.

By his intellectualist distinction between God's kairos ($\kappa\alpha\iota\rho\sigma$) and man's chronos ($\chi\rho\acute{o}\nu\sigma$), and by his emphatic rejection of any non-temporal significance in the conception of eternity, he shows himself blind to that mystical corrective which might have been an invaluable contribution to his undoubtedly stimulating eschatological survey. It is Dr. Warren's merit that he is by no means blind to this factor, and he seeks to give the future parousia the weight it ought to have in tipping the scales against any merely optimistic scheme of missionary progress, whether conceived in a straight line of direct upward evolutionary advance or in an up-and-down movement of greater rise and lesser fall after the pattern of Professor Latourette's monumental study.[4]

But it is doubtful whether even Dr. Warren's missionary argument avoids completely the temptation to improve upon the essential limitations of any truly apostolic witness. For these limitations involve above all else that self-limitation which is willing to stop trying to prove the gospel and is content to bear witness to it. If the gospel is a gospel of love, this limitation must be gladly accepted, for the attempt to prove love courts inevitable failure and catastrophic consequences for the *hybris* of such trespassing.

[1] M. A. C. Warren, ed., *The Triumph of God* (Longmans, 1948), pp. 350 ff; *The Truth of Vision, passim.*
[2] Matt. 24, 14.
[3] O. Cullmann, *Christ and Time* (S.C.M., 1950), pp. 157 ff.
[4] K. S. Latourette, *A History of the Expansion of Christianity*, vols. i–vii (Eyre and Spottiswoode, 1947).

The trouble about so much even missionary-minded Christianity is that it shares the belief that the second coming cannot be preached because it cannot be proved, whereas the first coming can be preached because, up to a point at least, it can be proved. Nothing could be more erroneous. All honour to the apologists who have in every age a vital work to do! But the ranking list of the ministry in the Christian church puts apostles and not apologists in the top place. If we were aware of our apostolic limitations as we proclaim the first coming of our Lord we should recover our apostolic confidence to proclaim his second coming, as the secret of the eschatology of hope which the whole missionary cause so badly needs.

And what is true of the missionary church overseas is even more true of the evangelistic church at home. In face of bleak prospects for the future on the one hand and of vague and unconvincing sentimentality and wishful thinking on the other, there is the deepest need for the bracing and invigorating tonic of a healthy and not a morbid eschatology. If this is lacking, then real religion is bound either to claim too much for the present or to claim too little for the present and too much for the future to make up for what is at present lacking. In face of the latter danger, to which it is to-day usually alive, much evangelism and also much of the seeking after holiness, whether in evangelical conventions or in catholic retreats, is liable to fall into the former error. A certainty is claimed either in evangelistic experience or in sacramental reality which, not being interpreted with an eschatological awareness of the relativity with which the whole present is bound to be characterized in the light of what the future holds, all too easily degenerates into cocksureness or even bigotry. The secret of love is lost in the claim to possess it here and now. The presence without the parousia becomes an idol, and not less an idol for being enshrined in holiness and beauty too.

This is bound to be the case where evangelistic witness preaches personal experience and tries to communicate its secret direct. Proof from experience is no more valid than proof from history as a substitute for apostolic testimony. It has its value for apologetics, but not elsewhere. Nothing could be further from the truth than to imagine that St Paul went around as a missionary and an evangelist telling the story of his own conversion and using it as a lever with which to convert his hearers. In fact of course, so far as we know, he never gave his testimony, in the sense of telling the story of his own experience on the Damascus road, except when he was challenged and called upon to give an account of himself. Then and then only the apostle became the apologist and gave his apologia.[1]

---

[1] Acts 22, 6 ff.; 26, 12 ff.; cf. 1 Cor. 15, 8.

Otherwise he almost invariably stuck to his apostolic witness. When he deviates from it to give a brief excursus in spiritual auto-biography,[1] he apologizes for doing so. And perhaps the self-conscious assertion of his apostolic credentials and of his apostolic message which we come across now and again in his epistles shows the temptation to which he knew himself subject and to which he sometimes succumbed. It looks as if the stress he laid on preaching only 'Christ crucified'[2] at Corinth was due to his sense of failure when he tried a tentative approach to apologetics at Athens just before.[3]

If even an apostle could fall into the temptation of trying to claim too much for the present by way of proof, how essential it is to balance the true doctrine of the presence with the true doctrine of the parousia! Failure to do this leads time and again either to a low doctrine of the presence or to a high doctrine based not upon apostolic testimony but upon apologetic evidence. The idea of a gospel with nothing in the future save the notion of sheer finality has only to be stated in the light of Romans 8 to be realized to be a farcical travesty of the apostolic message. What is needed is not a low doctrine of the present presence to save us from idolatry, but a high doctrine of the future parousia able to match a high doctrine of the present presence and so save us both from idolatry and apostasy.

Salvation is in jeopardy the moment the focus of our evangelistic witness is transferred from God and his love in Christ to ourselves and our real or imaginary experience of him. It is equally imperilled the moment our sacramental conviction leads us to such certainty of present possession as to leave no room for the related realization of our lack of any present possession at all in comparison with the immeasurable future possibilities of love. The doctrine of the present real presence is only a legitimate Christian conviction when it is combined with such a parallel doctrine of real absence as allows effectively and not merely theoretically for a future real parousia. If we are speaking of a relationship of love, then withdrawal is the prerequisite for return and the Ascension is the indispensable pre-condition both of Pentecost and the parousia. Security by virtue of any temporal continuity, whether couched in terms of ecclesiastical sacramentalism or of psychological experience, is no substitute for the only legitimate Christian security, which whether mediated sacramentally or experimentally is first and last an eschatological security.

At this point the positive protest of the Reformation on behalf of the doctrine of justification by faith is as valuable to-day as it was when Luther first made it. The occasion of the Reformation was an

---

[1] 2 Cor. 12, 1 ff.   [2] 1 Cor. 1, 23; 2, 2.   [3] Acts 17, 22 ff.

eschatological question. The scandal of the sale of indulgences raised
the far deeper issue of the whole nature of the soul's relationship with
God. Should the spiritual life be thought of as a long progress on
earth and in purgatory towards God as its goal? Or should it be
regarded as in some mysterious way a response both in its beginning
and all along the way to a prior movement of God to the soul?
Theoretically the whole catholic mediæval sacramental system safeguarded the priority of the divine initiative. But in fact what was
sacramentally interpreted in one way was experimentally lived in
another and precisely opposite way. Indulgences focused the issue
on the eschatological question. Was the future to be conceived
of as an almost endless pilgrimage to God or as an immediate
response to God?

If the post-Reformation protestant churches dropped out
purgatory from their eschatological perspective on the alleged
grounds of the lack of any biblical evidence for it, the real justification for dropping it went much deeper. Anyone who had caught a
glimpse of the gracious divine initiative as the secret not only of the
beginning of the Christian life but also of its continuation and end as
well could not countenance for one moment a doctrine of justification by faith which applied at the beginning only to be reversed by
a doctrine of sanctification by works, in purgatory if not on earth,
which applied at the end.

To drop purgatory and to put nothing in its place was a fatal
error. But to insist on the unity of the purpose of love and of the
nature of its working amongst men was a vital necessity. It was
this that at their best the Reformers were out to secure. It was
this that lay behind Calvin's rediscovery [1] of the covenant as a
scriptural witness to the oneness of God's purpose both in the
history of society as a whole and in the life of every individual soul.
God did not work in one way without Christ at Sinai and in another
way with him on Calvary. 'Always it is the same God who redeems.
Always it is the same Christ who mediates the redemption. Always it
is the same covenant which constitutes the instrument of redemption.' [2]

In the light of this rediscovery we can understand the deeper
reason for the rejection of purgatory at the Reformation. It seemed
to the reformers to be a complete reversal in the hereafter of the
rediscovered secret of the ways of God with man here and now. For
Calvin at least, if not for Luther, eschatology had to be an integral
part of theology and not a mere appendage to it. It had to fall in
line with the whole and could not remain in contradiction to the rest.

[1] F. W. Dillistone, *The Structure of the Divine Society* (Lutterworth Press, 1951)
pp. 117 ff.   [2] *Ibid.*, p. 119.

The over-confident claims of the mediæval church to possess a present security, to which it knew it was not entitled in terms of any real relationship with a God of love, had led to an inevitable timidity and loss of confidence in face of an eschatological prospect, which offered God compensation in full hereafter for the exaggerated claims made upon him here. There were two ways of dealing with this situation: either to reduce confidence to the same level here and now as it had been reduced for the hereafter, or else to raise confidence to the same level for the hereafter as it might rightly be raised here.

The first way would be sheer apostasy: it would overthrow the gospel altogether. The second could avoid both idolatry and apostasy, but it was only possible with such a combination of mystical awareness of the presence and eschatological expectation of the parousia as would balance the one against the other in that genuine personal relationship, in which justification by faith becomes a reality of love rather than a fiction of law.[1] Whatever the church may claim, and it may claim much, it may not claim to possess now as a temporal security, however holy its guarantee, that which is only possible as an eschatological security. That is the real significance of the Reformation protest on behalf of justification by faith, for to trespass here is to trespass on the holy ground of love itself, and that is blasphemy against the Holy Spirit.[2] It carries with it the inevitable corollary of his dethronement from the godhead and his replacement by some thing, which (however holy it may be) can only be regarded in such a place as an idol, 'standing where he ought not'.[3] It may seem to safeguard faith, but it means the destruction of hope, and by claiming to possess love now it rules out the possibility of being possessed by love hereafter.

This grievous and fatal twist to Christian conviction is not in any way straightened out by any lip-service adherence to a traditional future eschatology which is unrelated to present experience. No living hope can exist except through the purging of memory.[4] This is vital for any true understanding of the eschatological nature of the sacrament of holy communion. To 'do this in remembrance of' Jesus without understanding the eschatological significance of what you are doing is to be in danger of trying to cling to the past, which is deadly to the growth of a living hope, as every mourner knows

[1] C. A. Anderson Scott, *Living Issues in the New Testament* (C.U.P., 1933), pp. 62 ff.
[2] Cf. J. E. Fison, *op. cit.*, pp. 148–177.
[3] Mark 13, 14.
[4] Cf. St John of the Cross, *The Ascent of Mount Carmel*, Bk. III, ch. 1 ff. (*The Complete Works of St John of the Cross*, ed. E. Allison Peers (Burns Oates and Washbourne, 1934), vol. i, pp. 225 ff.).

and even every schoolboy when he leaves his *alma mater*.   It is only
as we are willing to lose the past and all its memories that we find
it given back to us with all its hopes.

A living and genuine eschatological hope must spring out of the
present.   It cannot be something unrelated to it as fulfilment or
merely related to it as compensation.   It must be something integrally bound up with it at every point.   It involves an outlook on
the future which springs inevitably from the present, and it also
involves an outlook on the present which leads inevitably to the
future.   The disjunction of past, present and future, which is
inevitable in logic but impossible in love, means the destruction of
all genuine Christian faith and hope, for that is bound to assert
that the future end is in some way vitally related to the past finality
of the revelation of God in Jesus Christ.

It is no unknown reality to which Christians look forward.   It is
no phantasy without any point of contact with present experience or
past history.   It arises out of present experience both with the inevitability of indestructible love and also with its unpredictability.
With certainty must go surprise right to the very end.   Between the
cocksureness of those who think they so possess the presence that
they leave no real room for the parousia, and the timidity of those
who in fear and trembling before the parousia dare make no claim
upon the presence, the way of Christian assurance is very narrow
indeed.   Where eschatology has gone astray either by being strictly
realized or rigorously futurist, love has disappeared, and assurance
which is grounded in love cannot exist.[1]

Such a critique of present church tendencies and emphases inevitably opens up the question of reunion.   Seen in their true eschatological light, how many of the wounds of our divisions would be
healed at once!   Over against the ecclesiastical *hybris*, which is the
besetting sin as much of the smallest modern sect as of the mediæval
papacy itself, there stands one certain corrective and one sure safeguard.   The end will be a surprise to all.   No one can read that
conviction out of the New Testament and no lover would want to.
Any church which lives in the light of the eschatological hope has
a chance of experiencing the truth of Marcus Aurelius' great saying
that ' just to look at things from another angle than that from which
we have seen them hitherto may actually mean the beginning of a

[1] Cf. H. R. Mackintosh, *The Christian Experience of Forgiveness* (Nisbet, 1927),
quoting James Denney, 'Nothing is more characteristic of churches than their attitude
to assurance and the place they give it in their preaching and their systems of doctrine.
Speaking broadly we may say that in the Romish church it is regarded as essentially
akin to presumption; in the Protestant churches it is a privilege or a duty; but in the
New Testament religion it is simply a fact' (p. 247).

new life'.[1] Any individual who takes seriously the fact that it is only 'with all the saints' that he can hope to understand 'what is the breadth and length and height and depth, and to know the love of Christ which passeth knowledge'[2] will see the denominational frontiers which separate him from his brethren in Christ in a different light from those who either genuinely think or try to force themselves to believe that within their own little circle only are the elect of God.

No ontological claims for the church as if it were the kingdom of God can stand for one moment against the eschatological challenge of the kingdom itself. How many of the ecclesiastical absolutes of to-day will appear relatives at the parousia? How dare we claim as absolute now what will appear relative then! The genuine humility of every Christian individual and of every Christian church living in the light of the eschatological hope is the precondition of any advance along the road to reunion and the surest guarantee of reaching its end. The hypocritical pride which is found consciously or unconsciously to characterize the outlook of every ecclesiastical body and indeed of every ecclesiastical soul, which has lost that hope, is the greatest hindrance to reunion and the surest barrier to all progress towards its achievement.

Of the church, as of so many of her members and of her ministers, it could so often be said with tragic truth 'The lady doth protest too much, methinks!'[3] And the tragedy is that the protest is loudest where the certainty is least. Christians can only become aware of their true security in God if they live in the light of a genuine Christian eschatology. No wonder our divisions persist when we have largely lost our true eschatological hope and see the future either as in some sense a continuation of and a ratification of our present ecclesiastical set-up, or else as something so unrelated to it that it has no effect whatever on our present thinking about it!

When it comes down to practical and pastoral matters we can see in every parish the way in which the sects and the spiritualists are making havoc of the church of Christ, the former by an emphasis upon an apocalyptic future climax to history, which has no relation except that of compensation to its present reality, and the latter by a stress upon the certainty of a kind of future life for individuals, which had no attraction whatever either for the ancient Israelites or for the ancient Greeks, and which has nothing in common with the authentic Hebræo-Christian biblical doctrine except the mere fact of the continuation of an existence of some sort after this life.

There can be no lasting corrective of a positive and salutary

[1] Quoted by F. W. Dillistone, *op. cit.*, p. 246.
[2] Eph. 3, 18 f.   [3] W. Shakespeare, *Hamlet*, III, ii.

kind to these heresies unless the church discovers a more adequate
doctrine of the future both for society and for individuals than the
rival heretical alternatives offer. The early church outlived the
pagan world, it out-thought it and it out-hoped it. That world
could not fairly be characterized as being without life or without
thought, but it could be described as being without hope.[1] The
corollary of its godlessness was its hopelessness.

If the pagan world to-day is in a similar plight—and it undoubtedly
is, whether it knows it or not—then the answer to those who fill the
vacuum with a partial, if not a false god, and with a fantastic, if not
a futile hope, is the proclamation of the true God and the true hope.
In fact what is perhaps the earliest extant epistle of St Paul may
provide us with the perspective that we need, providing the interval
of waiting, to which it refers, is not interpreted as sanctioning a
most unapostolic passivity or inactivity. In writing a description
of what conversion meant to his Thessalonian converts, he says
that they 'turned to God from idols to serve the living and true God
and to wait for his Son from heaven, whom he raised from the dead,
even Jesus'.[2] That is conversion not only from the past but towards
the future, and it is precisely that kind of conversion which the
church as well as the world needs to-day, and which only the
rediscovery of a living eschatological hope can produce.

It is not without significance that the massive interpretation of
history offered us by Professor Toynbee[3] should see in the religion
of the internal proletariat of a dying civilization the secret of the
birth of the civilization which is to succeed it. Starting out to prove
that the world's religions were the epiphenomena of the world's
civilizations, Professor Toynbee has been driven to see their relations
in the opposite light. And it is significantly the religion of an
oppressed internal proletariat, if it reacts in a peaceful and not
in a warlike way against its oppressors, on which he pins his faith.

Whether his universal scheme of comparative civilizations will
prove acceptable to historians only time can show, and whether his
universal scheme of comparative religions will prove compatible
with the uniqueness of the claim of the Christian church for Jesus
Christ only the publication of the remaining volumes of his *A Study
of History* can show. But surely he has already done enough by
focusing attention on the pattern of withdrawal and return as the
secret of new life and vitality to correct the one-sided teleological
and organic conception of the working of God's purpose through
the church in history. In the light of Toynbee's work we should at

[1] Eph. 2, 12.   [2] 1 Thess. 1, 9 f.
[3] A. J. Toynbee, *A Study of History*, vols. i–vi (O.U.P., 1934 and 1939).

least pause before we are swept off our feet by the modern stress upon the one single triumphant divine movement of resurrection, Pentecost, parousia and consummation, and let go too easily the traditional and at least superficially transparently clear evidence of the New Testament in favour of an eschatological 'return' as being at the very heart of the original Christian hope.

Furthermore, the very fact that the expected locus of all creative religions is on Toynbee's view to be found in principle in the internal proletariat of a dying civilization, and may be in practice to-day (so Toynbee hazards a prophecy) among the oppressed internal Negro proletariat of the U.S.A., suggests that the most characteristic feature of any such religion will be its future hope. Of course this hope may be just the refuge of despair, the compensation in the future for all that is lacking in the present, but it may also be the fulfilment in the future of the deepest reality in the present, if that reality is love. And if it is this, then it is true to the heart of the New Testament gospel.

In trying to interpret this hope, it is all very well for the dominant church of the dominant governing class in the dying civilization to proclaim a realized eschatology. From the point of view of such a church and such a class such an attitude is very satisfactory. But it is likely to seem nonsensical from the point of view of the depressed masses of the internal proletariat. If they are not allowed to hope for the genuine future fulfilment of their genuine present experience of love, then they will turn inevitably to the frightful future fulfilment of their present experience of hate. The Zealots will try to force the pace of the coming of the kingdom of their hope, if the only alternative offered them appears to involve the acceptance of the kingdom which they loathe.

It is a genuine futurist eschatology of love which alone can save the internal proletariat of those parts of the world, now ruled by the colonizers or by the descendants of the western civilization of Christendom, from the rival futurist eschatology of hate, which is consuming the energies of those who from our point of view might be considered to be as much the external proletariat of our civilization to-day as were the barbarian bands who brought about the collapse of the Græco-Roman civilization in St Augustine's day.[1]

[1] But there is one vital difference. The barbarians of the fifth century A.D. were in every way an external foe, even though the fall of the Græco-Roman civilization was far more due to decadence within than to opposition without. But the external proletariat of our day owe their inspiration to the religion of Karl Marx, which emanated from within our civilization. To-day the enemies without have their sympathizers within to a degree the Græco-Roman civilization never knew. Indeed it may be that the tidal wave of communism is better seen as the war-like religious reaction of the oppressed internal proletariat of the western civilization than as an external foe.

British partiality for realized eschatology to-day may be quite as much conditioned by our imperial, social, economic and ecclesiastical set-up (without our being conscious of it) as may be continental partiality for either a merely futurist or a timeless eschatology. Each emphasis in its different way looks suspiciously like a possible refuge of an unconscious selfish escapism.

In one other particular the need of the church for a true eschatology is pressing. There is apparently a complete divorce and a complete inability to communicate intelligibly between those trained to think in terms of the relatively impersonal categories both of patristic and scholastic doctrine, and those whose theological categories of understanding have been exclusively confined to the terms of the biblical tradition and of personal evangelism. It is very difficult for these two groups of Christians to enter into any living conversation at all.

This is a problem which touches the heart of our religion,[1] for it is hard to get intelligible agreement, except in terms of lip-service to traditional formulæ, about even the personality and deity of our Lord Jesus Christ himself, as the modernist controversies both inside and outside the Roman catholic church have made perfectly plain. On the one hand traditional orthodoxy repeats the ancient formulæ and seldom tries to relate them to or give them significance for the vital issues of contemporary thought in such a way as would make their vocabulary come alive. On the other hand modernism ventures with new categories of thought to probe the interior life of our Lord and to consider his cosmic significance with all the apparatus of the modern techniques of psychology and the modern vocabularies of science and philosophy. This sometimes succeeds in making the Christ of the church come alive, but in such a way as to leave an uncomfortable suspicion that he is not the real Jesus at all.

Attempts to settle these differences of thinking about the central dogma of the Christian faith, or even to establish enough real confidence for genuine dialogue between the two outlooks, such as, if it took place, might transform the depth of understanding of both, have proved extremely difficult. It is very easy to brand your opponents by some heretical label used in the great Christological controversies of the fourth and fifth centuries. But though the heresies constantly reappear in church history they never reappear in exactly the same forms. So it is easy for the modernist to deny with truth that he is an Arian, and it is easy for his opponent

---

[1] For a very sensitive and acutely penetrating reconnaissance of the problem, cf. W. R. Matthews, *The Problem of Christ in the Twentieth Century* (O.U.P., 1950).

to deny with equal truth that he is an Apollinarian. Yet each of them may be guilty of what in our day is the equivalent of what were in other days the Arian and the Apollinarian heresies. For unless the Christological controversies of the fourth and fifth centuries were 'much ado about nothing' they are likely to be much ado about something, which under another form is very much with us still.

Under present circumstances it would be invaluable to be able to check Christological doctrine by eschatological, just as it is always essential to check eschatological by Christological. If we could refer the Christological dispute, whether between orthodox and modernist or between scholastic and biblical thinkers, to the end (and the future end at that), then the touchstone of faith might be clarified, according as to whether or not it was Jesus Christ with whom the disputants then expected they would be confronted. If it were he and not some other person or idea or state of affairs or condition of living, then that very conviction would go far to establish mutual confidence that each disputant shared the essential faith of the church that Jesus was genuinely 'the Christ, the Son of the living God'.[1] This would be far more convincing evidence than continual hair-splitting about either the Synoptic record or the Chalcedonian definition, for it is a fact that almost any meaning can be read into the biblical or the credal formulæ, and lip-service to those formulæ is no guarantee of heartfelt allegiance to the faith they enshrine. The propositions may be identical, but their meaning can be so twisted as to refer to different persons.

The situation is transformed if the scene is transposed from history to eschatology. The historical evidence of the Bible can always be disputed, and the propositional formulæ of the creeds and the councils can even more calamitously be made to prove the unprovable and so to reduce the living and the loving personal God to the dead abstraction of the conclusion of a logical argument. But once the argument is transferred to the future, Christian belief has a chance to come clear of its propositional arguments and to disclose whether it is genuine trust in Jesus as 'the Christ, the Son of the living God',[2] or a spurious substitute for it.

Furthermore, transpose proofs about historic events and make them pointers to the reality behind those events, which is all we can do about the future, and at once the whole attitude of the church towards the historic events of the past becomes sensitive enough to appreciate the revelation of God's love in those events. It is impossible to prove from history that Jesus was either the Messiah or the Son of God. It would be gain indeed if constant reference to

[1] Matt. 16, 16.   [2] *Ibid.*

his future coming (where it is in the nature of the case impossible even to pretend to offer proof) could be used to check the arrogance of attempts at proof in connection with his past coming.

What is needed is a real integration of the thinking of the early Fathers and of the great scholastics both with the modern understanding of the Bible and with the personalist emphasis of so much modern Christian thinking. There is no short-cut out of our difficulties. So much of the popular modern presentation of the Christian gospel allows for an intimacy of relationship between man and God conceived of in terms of conscious individual experience, but tends to belittle or obscure the reverent awe inherent not only in any true understanding of the nature of the holy God of the holy scriptures and of the holy symbols and the holy images of the holy church, but also in any deep awareness of the range of unconscious and subconscious relatedness involved in any truly personal relationship.

Modern psychology may be still very much in its infancy and therefore still quite inadequate as an intellectual instrument to replace the tools of patristic or scholastic philosophy. But if the church had once to venture out of its biblicism into metaphysical definitions of its faith—and it is hard to claim any guidance of the Holy Spirit unless this is agreed—then there is no reason in principle why it should not have to do the same again, only this time perhaps using psychological rather than metaphysical terms. The perils of such a course were great in the third and fourth centuries. They are no less great to-day. The inadequacy of the result even of so great a venture of faith cannot be denied by any serious student of the patristic age. But the probability of inadequacy is no excuse for the timidity of the intellectual cowardice which refuses to make the attempt to give intelligible expression to its faith in terms of contemporary thought. How great would be the gain in such a perilous venture if both the traditions we have referred to could take their full and reciprocal share in it! How great would be the chance of mutual understanding if both those who speak in terms of personal and mainly conscious experience and those who speak in terms of relatively impersonal and often subconscious realities could see themselves and see their attempts to interpret the Christian faith in the light of a true eschatology!

If anything like such a vision could dawn, genuine dialogue between scholastics and evangelicals would become possible in a way which without it is inconceivable. A genuinely held biblical eschatology would shatter the over-confidence both of scholastics in their propositions and of evangelicals in their experiences. And who can exaggerate the gain that would result to both?

The tragedy is that, without a rediscovery by both of the wonder of the eschatological revelation of the Bible, there is little chance of this happening. And such a rediscovery is out of the question on the basis of a reinvestigation of the New Testament by itself. Present prejudices, due to factors in church history by which we are all conditioned, so easily colour the interpretations which we give to the New Testament evidence, that modern differences would harden into an absolute divorce between rival dogmas read back into the New Testament rather than find themselves being composed and harmonized by reaching a new understanding of the New Testament and by reading a new interpretation out of it.

The only way to advance is to adopt the French proverb, *Il se recule pour mieux sauter*, and to go far back and rediscover the Old Testament roots of New Testament religion. Any church or individual in danger of losing those roots is in danger of missing the heart of the gospel of reciprocal love by becoming incapable of entering into genuine dialogue or conversation with anybody else at all. Therefore it is to the Old Testament that we must first turn for that re-examination of the evidence for the eschatological hope of the Bible, on the rediscovery of which as a living reality in our own day and generation so much depends.

CHAPTER IV

THE DAY OF THE LORD

THE Old Testament is interested in life, not in death, and in life here on this earth rather than life hereafter in heaven—or anywhere else. It is this which throws it into such sharp contrast with the outlook both of Babylonia and Egypt. Babylonia with its Aralu [1] had an equivalent to the Hebrew Sheol. But the Babylonians were interested in Aralu in a way in which the Hebrews were never really interested in Sheol. Egypt also with its Book of the Dead shows a concern with the details of the hereafter which may find parallels in Tibet but certainly not in Palestine.

To be taken round Cairo Museum in 1929 by the famous missionary and Islamic scholar, Dr. S. M. Zwemer, and to be given for a text the words from Ecclesiastes, 'He hath set eternity in their heart',[2] was an experience never to be forgotten. Everything in that museum, with its unsurpassable material memorials of the great Egyptian civilization, seemed to be concerned with religion and death, and nothing at all with ordinary secular life, except the monuments of the Pharaohs and the inscriptions of their campaigns and the famous squatting scribe [3] of the very early dynastic era.

To live in Cairo and to see along the whole line of the western desert from north of Mena to the Fayyoum the evidences of memorials to the dead was to have the same unforgettable impression deepened. The tombs in the valley of the kings at Thebes, with their elaborate precautions to prevent the disturbance or the discovery of their mummified bodies, witness to the same preoccupation of the ancient Egyptians with life after death. And the western horizon of the setting sun, with its tremendous memorials to the dead at Sakkara and at Gizeh, speaks even more eloquently than all the details of the Book of the Dead of the constant eschatological outlook of the most ancient and far and away the most long-lived civilization the world has ever known.

[1] Cf. H. W. Robinson, *Inspiration and Revelation in the Old Testament* (O.U.P., 1946), pp. 96, 99. W. L. Wardle, *Israel and Babylon* (Holborn Publishing House, 1925), pp. 94 ff.

[2] Eccles. 3, 11, R.V. margin.

[3] S. A. Morrison, *Cairo* (C.M.S. Bookshop, Cairo, n.d.), pp. 27 f.

It was out of this country that the ancient Hebrews emigrated to Palestine and it was in such a geographical context that the whole of the Old Testament was written.   In the light of the close proximity of Palestine to Egypt and of the close relations always existing between the two countries, the most remarkable thing in the whole literature of the Old Testament is its relative lack of any interest in the hereafter at all, its depreciation of Sheol [1] as an undesirable inevitability if not something worse, and its failure to give any concrete individual hope for life after death until the eve of the closing of the canon of the Hebrew scriptures.[2]

How much Sheol or something comparable to it ever meant to the Hebrews as an effective and positive article of faith it is difficult to say.   There may have been much more in the popular pre-prophetic eschatology than we know,[3] and those who have seen the great Hebron mosque built over the traditional site of the cave of Machpelah will be less likely to be negatively dogmatic on the subject than the arm-chair student of Sheol who has never visited Palestine.[4] But the fact remains that the silence of the Old Testament about a life after death will be impressed upon the mind even more by the absence of material remains for the archæologist to investigate than by the absence of textual evidence for the literary critic to examine.

Almost everything remaining of the ancient Egyptian civilization is connected with religion or death, with temples or tombs.   And even making every allowance for the geographical and geological reasons for the permanence of what was built on the edge of the desert as opposed to the inevitably temporary character of most buildings on the mud either of the Nile valley or of the Delta, nevertheless the solid body of religious and eschatological evidence dug up by the archæologists in Egypt remains in striking contrast to the absence of anything comparable so far discovered in Palestine.

This contrast must not be overdrawn in the interests of any particular eschatological thesis.   It is part and parcel of the general

---

[1] A depreciation shared, of course, by others; e.g. the Babylonians (cf. W. L. Wardle, *op. cit.*), the Romans (e.g. Horace, *Odes*, IV, vii, 15, *pulvis et umbra*) and the Greeks, whose early outlook is summarized as follows: 'The Homeric picture of the shadow life of the disembodied soul is the work of resignation, not of hope.   Hope would never have beguiled itself with the anticipation of a state of things which neither afforded men the chance of further activity after death nor, on the other hand, gave them rest from the toil of life; one which promised them only a restless, purposeless fluttering to and fro, an existence, indeed, but without any of the content which might have made it worthy of the name of life' (E. Rohde, *Psyche*, E.T., 1925, 5th ed., p. 55, quoted by J. Baillie, *And the Life Everlasting* (O.U.P., 1934), p. 70).

[2] Isa. 26, 19; Dan. 12, 2; cf. H. W. Robinson, *Inspiration and Revelation*, p. 101.

[3] Cf. H. H. Rowley, ed. *The Old Testament and Modern Study* (O.U.P., 1951), pp. 303 f.

[4] Cf. Gen. 49, 33.

contrast immediately suggested to anyone who has visited the Cairo and the Jerusalem museums. Starting with the ancient prehistoric remains of Galilee and of Carmel man, the galleries of the Jerusalem museum carry the visitor right down to the later Arab and Turkish periods of occupation. In the whole of this beautifully set-out demonstration of the successive epochs of Palestinian history, the most significant single fact that instantly strikes every visitor is the paucity of remains from the biblical period. Alike in quality and in quantity the disparity between the biblical and both the pre-biblical and the post-biblical periods is obvious.

The failure of the Jews to develop any nationally characteristic architectural and artistic culture is as striking in its negative evidence as are their positive religious and spiritual achievements and the literature which records them. The parables of the talents [1] and of the pounds [2] sanction consideration for a theory of the rights of property and ownership which is based much more upon the mutual productivity of the relationship between the owner or steward and his possessions than upon any legal or hereditary title-deeds. On this ground Martin Buber is well entitled to put forward a claim for the rights of the Jews in Palestine, based not upon any legal title-deeds of ownership which they may possess in the form of a divine promise to Abraham, but upon the overwhelmingly more fruitful relationship between them and the land than anything that could be suggested either of the pre-Jewish Canaanite or of the post-Jewish Arab and Turkish occupants. But the creativity of the relationship between the Jews and Palestine lies solely in their spiritual achievements and in the literary record which enshrines them. Otherwise the evidence of archæology is decisive and overwhelming that on the artistic and secular cultural level the Jews have no claim at all.

Yet when this contrast between Egypt and Palestine has been emphasized as it should be, there still remains the abiding eschatological contrast not wholly explained by it. For a rocky and mountainous country like Palestine finds its geographical and geological parallel in Egypt not in the mud of the Nile Valley and the Delta with its transitory remains, but in the rocky edge of the western desert with its imperishable memorials. Even the difference in climate and rainfall cannot obscure this comparison.

Failure to find remains of eschatological or other significance upon the plains of Sharon, Philistia or Esdraelon might be explicable on geographical grounds, though as a matter of fact the mound of Gezer in the Shephelah on the edge of the Philistine plain has proved one of the richest Palestinian finds for evidence of religious ritual

[1] Matt. 25, 14 ff.   [2] Luke 19, 12 ff.

and burial practice.[1]   (Even this Gezer exception however turns out
to be no exception, for the finds date to the time of the Canaanite and
not of the Jewish occupation.)   But the failure to find any impressive
evidence of memorials to the Jewish kings in Jerusalem is something
hard to explain away, even when all allowance has been made for
the vicissitudes of Jerusalem's history.   Anyone who has seen the
so-called 'Tombs of the Kings'[2] behind St George's Anglican
cathedral can realize the possibilities of permanent memorials in the
limestone rock on which Jerusalem is built.   And even more provoca-
tive of inquiry is the so-called 'Tomb of David'[3] in its unhistorical
setting in the midst of the strange amalgam of a Moslem mosque
built upon and into the remains of a Christian Crusader church.

Why is there such total absence of authentic funeral or burial
remains of any real importance or significance from the period of
Jewish and biblical Palestine?   If Solomon took such trouble to
build the Temple and his own palace he might have been expected
to have made some memorial worthy of his father.   And if filial
piety was not one of his outstanding characteristics, what we know
of him suggests that ostentation certainly was, at any rate in the
latter part of his reign, if not at the beginning of it.   We should
have expected that he would have made some large scale prepara-
tions for his own memorial, even if not on the scale or with the
grandeur of a Tutankhamen or a Cheops.   But there is no evidence
that he did.   And this dangerous *argumentum e silentio* carries
weight when the paucity of archæological evidence for any developed
Hebrew eschatology of the individual is backed by the similar paucity
of the literary evidence.

The positive evidence for the after-life of the individual in anything other than the highly undesirable shadowy existence of Sheol
comes very late indeed in the Old Testament, and though the positive
evidence for the future hopes of national and corporate eschatology
in this life begins much earlier, it begins with a resounding 'No'
to the popular outlook and only considerably later develops the
positive prophetic eschatology.   Amos' words are indubitably
authentic and set the tone for all that follows.

> Woe unto you that desire the day of the Lord!   Wherefore would ye have
> the day of the Lord?   It is darkness and not light.   As if a man did
> flee from a lion and a bear met him; or went into the house and leaned
> his hand on the wall, and a serpent bit him.   Shall not the day of the
> Lord be darkness and not light? even very dark and no brightness in it?[4]

---

[1] Cf. H. W. Robinson, ed., *Record and Revelation* (O.U.P., 1938), p. 422.
[2] These tombs date from the first century A.D. (B. Meistermann, *Guide de la Terre
Sainte* (Paris, n.d.), 3rd ed., pp. 265 ff.).   [3] *Ibid.*, pp. 179 ff.   [4] Amos 5, 18 ff.

The popular eschatology which Amos was ridiculing in language inconceivable except from a roamer of the wilderness of Judæa (for where else in the world could anyone meet a lion and a bear in one day?) was national, not individual. It had to do with this life, not the next. The nationalism which Amos had to contend with in the reign of Jeroboam II was becoming more jingoistic as the artificial prosperity of Israel increased at precisely the same time as the threat from Assyria increased. Whether the eschatological triumph of Israel was ritually and dramatically focused in a New Year's festival [1] or not, and whether in Jerusalem there was a ceremony of royal enthronement to symbolize the enthronement of Yahweh in his Temple or not, there can be no doubt that for the people as a whole the day of the Lord, or the day of Yahweh, was not really Yahweh's day at all, but Israel's. It was the national trump card which would then be played even though Yahweh might be the player. And the spirit of popular expectation had the same vivid sense of being on the eve of wonderful events as has sustained the Jewish Passover hope of 'Next year in Jerusalem' throughout the ages. 'Perhaps the very next New Year's day would be the day of Yahweh!' [2]

Against the whole idea of the nature of this day, though not at all against its imminence, the prophet thundered his terrific 'No', which he amplified with a denial of any presumption or privilege on the basis of a most-favoured-nation treaty clause in the covenant between Yahweh and Israel.[3] The prophetic eschatology therefore comes on the scene as an eschatology of woe. The future is black: Amos can see nothing but judgment ahead, and for him as for all the prophets there is no getting round the fact that 'judgment' must 'begin at the house of God'.[4] The dramatic nature of the implications of such an ethical eschatology appears in the entirely unexpected conclusion of inevitable judgment for sin which Amos draws from the conviction which he shared with his audience of Yahweh's unique interest in Israel. 'You only have I known of all the families of the earth: therefore I will visit upon you all your iniquities.' [5]

It is not clear how far the earlier pre-exilic prophets were prepared to offer any future hope at all. Everything depends upon the extent to which their books have been subsequently edited in order to provide them with a happy ending. There is, for example, clearly

---

[1] A highly disputed point; cf. the summary of the evidence and the literature referred to in H. H. Rowley, *op. cit.*, pp. 303 ff., and H. W. Robinson, *Inspiration and Revelation*, pp. 135 ff.

[2] H. H. Rowley, *op. cit.*, p. 305.

[3] Amos 1, 3 ff., and the totally unexpected 2, 6 ff.

[4] 1 Pet. 4, 17.   [5] Amos 3, 2.

hope at the end of Amos, but it comes after the sweeping condemnation which appears to leave no room for it. 'Behold, the eyes of the Lord God are upon the sinful kingdom and I will destroy it from off the face of the earth.'[1] At what point does the authentic prophecy stop? Does it go right on to the end of the book? Most critics would argue that it does not, because there seems to be a clear reference to the destruction of the Temple at Jerusalem over a hundred years later as an event which has already occurred.[2]

Yet it may well be that Amos himself did not stand by his unconditional denunciations as if they were inflexible items of a systematic theology. Promise as well as doom may be unconditional in verbal form, but conditional in moral obligation. Indeed any regard for the inevitability of a proportion between a revelation received and the mental and spiritual and social state of the receiver must necessitate a conditional character for all such promises or threats. In the last resort it is the acts of God which 'are his speech', for 'the words which interpret' his action 'are a human contribution' to revelation.[3]

Whatever we may think of the authenticity of the end of the Book of Amos, no one but the herdsman of Tekoa could possibly have said that 'as the shepherd rescueth out of the mouth of the lion two legs or a piece of an ear, so shall the children of Israel be rescued that sit in Samaria in the corner of a couch and on the silken cushions of a bed'.[4] Amos had probably himself never sat upon anything we should call a couch anywhere in his life and certainly not in Samaria: and he had probably never seen a silken cushion. But though he had not the inside knowledge of Hosea to heal the sicknesses and reform the abuses of which he was conscious, he had perhaps all the clearer diagnosis of the evil for being a spectator of it rather than an actor in it.

Certainly his diagnosis was deadly, but it did not prevent his herdsman's simile suggesting some hope even for Samaria. There is a chance of rescue, even if it is only of something of which the whole or at least the greater part is already dead. There is no suggestion of individual hope after death in the passage, so we are left to draw our own conclusions as to its implications for the historical prospects of the nation. Perhaps we should be wisest to draw the same conclusion about the attack of the pre-exilic prophets upon the popular eschatology of their day as upon their similar attitude to the popular sacrificial cultus.

[1] Amos 9, 8. [2] Amos 9, 11.
[3] H. W. Robinson, *Inspiration and Revelation*, p. 144.
[4] Amos 3, 12.

When Amos asks in the name of Yahweh the rhetorical question, 'Did ye bring unto me sacrifices and offerings in the wilderness forty years, O house of Israel?',[1] grammatically and prophetically he clearly expects the answer 'No'. But it is one thing for a prophet or a preacher speaking in a concrete and particular situation to make such an unqualified negative pronouncement. It is quite another thing for a systematic theologian to transfer the prophet's particular application of truth into a generalization of universal application. St Paul, for example, in dealing with 'things sacrificed to idols',[2] could say categorically as a theologian that idols simply did not exist,[3] but at the same time as a missionary he well understood that they could be a real peril not only to idolaters but to newly converted Christians as well.[4] Therefore as an apostle he was extremely careful about his behaviour.[5]

As a prophet Amos said 'No' to the popular sacrificial system and to the popular eschatology of hope. In each case he was speaking 'to the condition of' his hearers about the actual ritual and dogma which he saw affecting their daily lives. We may well hesitate before we turn his prophecy into systematic theology without qualification. And this goes for all the prophets, whether we are dealing with Jeremiah's denunciation of sacrifice [6] or with Zephaniah's description of doomsday.[7] It was all very well for Jeremiah to thunder against the very system upon the maintenance of which his parents may have depended for their bread and butter.[8] It can be argued that without that system he would not have enjoyed either spiritual or physical life at all. And in the case of Zephaniah the book that inspired the mediæval Dies iræ, dies illa can open up vistas of hope before it closes.[9]

But if not as systematic theology, certainly as prophecy the unequivocal and unrelenting universality of the doom of Zephaniah's great day of the Lord deserves to stand in the centre of the eschatology of the prophets. His vision starts in a vivid awareness of the terrors of the Jerusalem souks [10] when the enemy have breached the walls of the city: but it ends in a picture which it is difficult to limit

---

[1] Amos 5, 25.   [2] 1 Cor. 8, 1.   [3] 1 Cor. 8, 4.   [4] 1 Cor. 10, 20 f.
[5] 1 Cor. 9, 19; 16, 14. A striking modern commentary was provided in the Russian Orthodox cathedral in Jerusalem during the war. An Anglican priest, a first-generation convert from East Africa, said he could not worship God in a building so full of ikons and paintings. It was for him too near his idolatrous pagan background. The fact that he came from an evangelical diocese of the Anglican communion obviously affected his judgment, but it did not in the least alter the significance of his commentary upon 1 Corinthians.
[6] Jer. 7, 22 f.   [7] Zeph. 1, 14 ff.   [8] Jer. 1, 1.
[9] Zeph. 3, 9 ff., though of course this is very probably an editorial 'happy ending'.
[10] Zeph. 1, 10 f.

to any one merely historical event, however catastrophic. The prophet has brought us to the end of history so far at least as the historical era of which we are aware is concerned.[1]

Other previous 'days' have not been Yahweh's in the sense that this last day is his. Those responsible for their alienation from him will inevitably suffer on the day that is truly his, just as certainly as a later prophet was able to say that the God-fearers would be rewarded.[2] In a very vivid phrase the secret of God's *kairos* ($\kappa\alpha\iota\rho\acute{o}\varsigma$) is put in a nutshell: 'They shall be mine, saith Yahweh of hosts, on the day when I act.'[3] It is the day on which God strikes, D-Day even more than V-Day. It is not so much a duration of abstract time as a moment of concrete time, packed full of the meaning of God.

With such an eschatological prospect in view, the prophetic message aimed at presenting as vividly as possible the challenge of an inescapable and irrevocable and immediate choice, which there was no possibility whatever of avoiding. 'Because I will do this unto thee, prepare to meet thy God, O Israel,'[4] puts the whole issue in a sentence. In the Old Testament as in the New it is the imminence of judgment which is part of the lever used to awaken the people to the urgency of the need to face its reality. But in neither Testament is the inescapability of judgment based upon its imminence. It is based upon the nature of God. It is not from any calculation based either upon political sagacity or on meteorological or medical information of the secondary means God may use to carry out his judgment, whether those secondary means are Assyrian tyrants or climatic disturbances or plague, pestilence and famine, that the prophet deduces his messages of imminent doom. It is from his knowledge of God in the present that he derives his certainty of the future. Biblical eschatology is always based upon biblical theology.

And so far as eschatology goes, this derivation provides the moral urgency which is primary, but it also provides the sense of imminence which because it is secondary is not to be ruled out as unimportant or as having no validity in its own right at all. Imminence is not to be ignored because inevitability does not depend upon it. Both imminence and inevitability are vital elements of prophetic eschatology. To understand how this can be, it is important to examine the conception of the day of Yahweh a little more closely.

If we rule out the idea that it is simply identical with or merely derived from the much disputed New Year's festival or the enthronement of the Israelite king as a symbolic way of demonstrating and

---

[1] Zeph. 1, 14 ff.   [2] Mal. 3, 17.
[3] H. W. Robinson, *Inspiration and Revelation*, p. 144.   [4] Amos 4, 12.

perhaps of effecting the kingship of Yahweh in Israel,[1] we are left with the option of either deriving it from the distinctly hypothetical general eschatological conception of world catastrophe said to be widespread all over the Middle East long before the rise of the Hebrew prophets,[2] or from the much simpler origin suggested by 'the Hebrew characterization of time by its concrete content'.[3]

This latter explanation, as we have already seen, is by far the most obvious solution to a problem, which it largely, if not exhaustively, solves without forcing us to look any further than the name and meaning of Yahweh himself for its significance. The Hebrews did not think of time as an abstract idea. They thought of it as something concrete and definite, getting its meaning from the content which filled it. So much is this the case that Wheeler Robinson can sum up its meaning in a simple definition on lines so strikingly suggestive of Martin Buber's personalist philosophy of meeting that it is of no mere archæological interest to grasp its significance. ' "Time" ', he says, 'is that which meets you on your path through life.' [4]

The content given therefore to the day of the Lord at any particular period of Jewish history or by any particular prophet or by the common people of any particular age depended essentially on what it was believed Yahweh would be doing on that day. It depended on his character. But ideas of his character differed profoundly, first between the earlier and later periods of the Old Testament, and secondly between those who had some first-hand awareness of him and those who had none. The popular view which the prophets denounced was based on no first-hand awareness of him; it had no roots in present experience whatever. It was largely the product of wishful thinking or of some psychological mechanism of compensation. Over against this popular view stood the prophetic view, always viewing the future from the standpoint of the present and always interpreting the future in the light of such understanding of the present as the prophets possessed. It was as the prophets' awareness of the presence deepened and widened that their interpretation of the parousia of God developed.

To speak of 'the day' is not so much to delimit a period of durational time (as we understand it by our clocks and by our calendars) as to indicate an activity. The day of Yahweh was therefore the day of Yahweh's activity, or, as we might say, his

---

[1] Cf. H. W. Robinson, *Inspiration and Revelation*, pp. 139 ff., and on the derivative theory, 'Whereas Gressmann derived the day from the eschatology, Mowinckel derives the eschatology from the day' (p. 140).
[2] *Ibid.*   [3] *Ibid.*, p. 138.   [4] *Ibid.*, p. 109.

D-Day. His activity determined its character, and his activity was always conceived by the Hebrews as swift, sudden and complete in a moment. It was so in the beginning when he finished each day's work of creation in plenty of time to contemplate the success of each creative experiment before proceeding to the next. It would be so at the end. His intervention could not in the nature of the case be a long-drawn-out affair, however long-drawn-out might be its consequences.

Therefore the eschatological focus of the Old Testament is not upon a period of weal or woe for man and for nature too, but upon a short sharp decisive action, often conceived of in a military sense, leaving behind it incalculable consequences of weal and woe for man and for nature too. At first this action was limited in its effect to a particular part of the world and to a particular people living in it. Gradually, as the knowledge of Yahweh in the present deepened and widened, these restrictions and limitations were lifted, first to include gradually other nations besides Israel until finally all nations and the whole earth came within its scope, and then secondly to reach out and deal with those who had already died as well as those who were alive on 'the day'. Yahweh's activity in the distant regions of Sheol was at first conceived of after the manner of a rescue commando raid on Dieppe. It was enemy-occupied country, even though Yahweh might temporarily invade it.[1] But later on all limits were removed:[2] it was no longer a case of an experimental raid on Dieppe: it was D-Day on the Normandy beaches leading on with lightning rapidity to V-Day itself. The conquest of Sheol meant the resurrection of the dead.[3]

If the popular pre-prophetic view thought of 'the day' solely in terms of Israel's triumph and her enemies' defeat, the prophets had to pay for the vast extension of their horizons of Yahweh's activity by the recognition that victory on such a scale might involve the destruction of little Israel herself, if her behaviour left Yahweh with no other alternative. On the very lowest estimate, if she would not include others he was bound to exclude her, for in fact by so doing she excluded herself.

Such an eschatological prospect reveals very clearly that the authentic Jewish hope for the future was centred always in the sphere in which Yahweh was then conceived of as being active. The lack of interest in Sheol was due to the fact that it was out of

[1] Ps. 6, 5; 30, 9; Isa. 38, 18; Amos 9, 2; and H. W. Robinson, *Inspiration and Revelation*, p. 100.
[2] Job 26, 6; Ps. 139, 8; and H. W. Robinson, *ibid.*
[3] Isa. 26, 19; Dan. 12, 2; and H. W. Robinson, *ibid.*, p. 101.

Yahweh's sphere of interest and operations. Other nations might find its prospect equally distasteful, but they were interested in it nevertheless because their gods were interested in it and active in it too. But for the ancient Hebrews it had no interest because at first they thought that it had nothing to do with Yahweh at all.

Genuine future hope is always based by the Jews upon present faith. It is their present understanding of the nature of God and of his ways of working which determines their thinking about the future. Only if in the present God is known to act in any particular way can he be rightly believed to act in this particular way in the future. As long therefore as prophecy was regarded as a kind of dictaphonic record or a cinematographic pre-view of the shape of things to come, with no necessary connection with present realities at all, there was no hope of any clear understanding of the true nature of genuine eschatological conviction. And the situation became even more fatal to any eschatological conviction at all when in reaction from the dictaphonic conception of inspiration the pendulum swung in favour of an interpretation of prophecy conceived of almost entirely in terms of social sagacity and political statesmanship.

Only when some such interpretation of the meeting of Yahweh with Moses at the Burning Bush, as Martin Buber offers,[1] opens our eyes to the true meaning of meeting in the present can we rightly conceive of its significance in the future. 'I shall be there as he who I there shall be'[2] is the secret of the presence promised at Sinai as much as it will be the secret of the parousia at the end. If it cannot be engineered now, neither can it be engineered then. Any attempt at manipulation by ritual or formula or ascetic discipline is as futile in the former case as by gnosis or prophetic spell in the later. If it is a surprise now, it will be a surprise then. If it evokes an exclamation[3] in the first place now and only sanctions an interpretation afterwards, it will do the same then. If personal encounter between man and man and *a fortiori* between man and God is incapable of transcription into adequate propositional terms now, how much more will it be incapable then!

We are here at the heart of one of the deepest problems of the Old Testament, the true nature of the distinction between Yahweh and the false gods, worshipped inside Israel as well as outside it in the surrounding nations. The true God of Israel was in the last

---

[1] M. Buber, *Moses* (East and West Library, 1946), pp. 39 ff.; *The Prophetic Faith* (Macmillan, 1949), pp. 24 ff.

[2] M. Buber, *Mamre* (Melbourne U.P. and O.U.P., 1946), p. 12.

[3] Cf. M. Buber, *Moses*, p. 50. The word YHVH is derived from the same root as the Arabic third person singular masculine pronoun *huwa*, he. It was originally an exclamatory sound, meaning 'O He!' or 'He!'

resort not organically but covenantally related to his people. The
Baals on the other hand, no matter whether they went by the name of
Melkart in Phœnicia or of Yahweh himself in Ahab's reign in Israel,
were regarded as being in an organic relationship with their people.
If the people were destroyed, their god was destroyed with them.

It was not so with the true God. The Israelites had not always been
the people of Yahweh. There was no security that they would always
remain his people other than his covenanted promise not to desert
them. Even that promise, though often understood in terms of
an unconditional contract, was in fact like every other biblical
promise made conditional for the enjoyment of its blessings upon
the continuing faithfulness of the people to their responsible vocation
of loyalty to the will and purpose of Yahweh so far as they knew
him and understood him.

The characteristic prophetic insight of Hosea into the secret of
the origin of the relationship between Yahweh and Israel was
expressed in terms of a romance. 'When Israel was a child, then
I loved him, and called my son out of Egypt.' [1] Theology interprets
the relationship in terms of election,[2] but such a theological technical
term serves to obscure the essentially personal character of the
relationship unless after the manner of the prophet it is interpreted
in terms of the romance of the deepest human experience of falling
in love.

This of course was as utterly different from the relationship
conceived to exist between the surrounding peoples and their gods
as love is utterly different from lust and yet to an outside observer
so very akin to it. The relations of a Baal with his people had no
historical beginning. The god and the people were bound up
together in one organic and indestructible whole. As long as they
existed, he did: but their disappearance from the earth necessarily
involved his too. In Israel the prophets could conceive of a true
Israel within a false or a nominal Israel. The distinction would
have been inconceivable in Phœnicia or Moab. It was the attempt
in fact, if not in theory, to degrade Yahweh to the status of a Baal
which evoked the terrific protest of Elijah on Mount Carmel [3] and
of all the great prophets who followed him.

If then there was this vital difference between Yahweh and the
Baals, and if Yahweh, unlike the Baals, had not always been so
organically bound up with his people as to be indissolubly linked
with their history, how did he come into relation with them? What
was the origin of the religion of Israel? There can be no doubt

---

[1] Hos. 11, 1.   [2] Cf. H. W. Robinson, *Inspiration and Revelation*, pp. 148 ff.
[3] 1 Kings 18, 1 ff.

7

about the answer which the Old Testament gives. The origin of the
religion of Israel lay in a covenant made between Yahweh and Israel
through an individual Israelite, no matter whether he be thought of
as Abraham [1] or as Moses [2] or even later as Joshua [3] or Josiah.[4]

Moses' experience was typical. It was what happened to him
at the Burning Bush [5] which started the whole train of events which
culminated in the covenant of Sinai. It was through an encounter
with an individual that Yahweh made his covenant with the people.
And if we try to look more closely at the nature of that encounter,
all we can say is that Yahweh met Moses. That is the sober biblical
testimony, for which no proof can be given, and beyond which we
cannot go. All we can do is to examine the sequel.

Moses knew that, when he reported on his meeting with Yahweh
to the Israelites and tried to get them to join him in the adventure
of pilgrimage to which he believed Yahweh had called him, he would
at once have to face the question as to who this god was who had
met him and as to what were his credentials. To have given the
metaphysical reply, 'I am that I am', even with the purposive
intention, 'I will be that I will be',[6] was hardly the way to go about
stirring up the Israelite slaves in Egypt to make a revolutionary
break-away from their present masters. Yet that was what it had
to do. And metaphysics was no more the way to do it than the
suggestion of some interpretative explanation of God along the
lines of his connection with the wind or with a volcano.[7]

Much more likely than any of these interpretations of the name
Moses gave to the God who had met him is the view that it was
originally not an interpretation at all, but an exclamation. When
Moses was asked who had met him at the Bush he just exclaimed
'He!' [8] That was all he could say. It was 'He' who had met him
and it was 'He' who wanted the Israelites out in the desert so that
he could meet them too.[9]

[1] Gen. 15, 18.   [2] Exod. 24, 7 f.   [3] Josh. 24, 25.
[4] 2 Kings 23, 3.   [5] Exod. 3, 1 ff.   [6] Exod. 3, 14.
[7] Cf. W. O. E. Oesterley and T. H. Robinson, *Hebrew Religion: Its Origin and
Development* (S.P.C.K., 1930), pp. 136 ff.
[8] Cf. M. Buber, *Moses*, p. 50.
[9] For a commentary on this whole conception of the significance of Yahweh's
meeting with Moses and our interpretation of it, cf. D. L. Sayers, *The Mind of the
Maker* (Methuen, 1941), p. 35: 'Suppose that I suddenly say "ouch". That will
convey to you exactly what was meant to be conveyed by the former statement "I feel
pain". It has the great advantage that it does not hint at any psychological theory
of what has happened; it does not drag in knowledge not wholly derived from direct
awareness, as any attempt at precise definition would do. Normally, it is an in-
voluntary remark; but it is a pity not to use deliberately an expression which conveys
exactly what we mean to convey and no more. A typical element of knowledge
acquired by direct awareness is that which we convey to another person by the ejaculation "ouch".' (Quotation from Eddington, *Philosophy of Physical Science*.)

If this is true of the origin of the Sinai covenant then it is in essence true of all the prophetic recalls to the spirit of that covenant. It was out of some such meeting with God that each prophet received his vocation and the clue to its interpretation. He could never prove to others the reality of what had happened to him. He could only point to Him who had met him. To contract out of that world of meeting with Yahweh and to lull yourself into a false security on the basis of possessing Yahweh was precisely the peril of the idolatry to which the Israelites were so exceedingly prone. They were constantly trying to turn the living God, Yahweh, into the dead idol, Baal. This was as suicidal if the Baal was called Yahweh as if he was called Melkart or Chemosh.

No one who had caught a glimpse of the new dimension of life opening out of real meeting could ever dream of offering any hope but death to those who refused on principle the only gateway into enduring life. Understanding of the nature of the new dimension deepened and widened as each prophet added his insights to those of his predecessors. But even a very imperfect understanding at first hand was better than a much more perfect interpretation at second hand, behind which there was no contact in personal experience with the reality spoken about.

It was doom to be outside the world of meeting by your own deliberate choice (and there was no other way of being outside it, for it was not a world closed to all except the few, but a world open to all who were willing to recognize and enter it). This was true of the individual and so it was true for the community too. The corollary of prophetic monotheism was the universal judgment of prophetic eschatology. It was not that the theory of monotheism demanded it, though it did. It was that the one God made it inevitable. Monotheism as a theory [1] never interested the Hebrews in the creative prophetic period of their history. It was one God and only one as an inescapable fact to be reckoned with by everyone which concerned them.

---

[1] Cf. M. Buber, *Moses*, pp. 7 f.: 'It is a fundamental error to register the faith with which I deal as simple "Monotheism". Here may be applied what was written half a century ago by Paul Yorck von Wartenberg to the philosopher Wilhelm Dilthey, his friend and my master: "I should consider it desirable for an attempt to be made to disregard all these categories, Pantheism, Monotheism, Theism, Panentheism. In themselves they have no religious value whatsoever, being only formal and of quantitative character. They reflect views of the world and not views of God, and constitute only the outline of an intellectual attitude; and only a formal projection even for this." It is not so decisive whether the existence of a Unity exalted over all is assumed in one's consideration, but the way in which this Unity is viewed and experienced, and whether one stands to it in an exclusive relationship which shapes all other relations and thereby the whole order of life.'

That was why universal judgment was the direct corollary of prophetic monotheism. On the day of Yahweh everyone would be inescapably confronted with Yahweh. Theoretically, considerations of the scope of that day did not interest the Hebrew prophets. What interested them was its effect upon all within its scope, and in the end that meant all the dead as well as all the living, though to begin with its boundaries were both temporally and territorially extremely circumscribed. Thus monotheism, as we understand it, was only relevant to the outlook of Israel when anything less than a mono-thestic faith meant no faith at all. It may have been relevant for Moses, confronted with the world empire of Egypt. Whether it was so or not, it certainly only came unmistakably upon the scene again with the rise of the great writing prophets. For only with the rise of those prophets, synchronizing with, but just anticipating the rise of the great world empires of Assyria, Babylon and Persia after the manner of the working of God 'in the nick of time',[1] was it again a matter of life or death to the Hebrews to have such a faith. For Isaiah it was the end of faith if Sennacherib could not be included in the purposes of God.[2] But the issue of world imperialism which faced him had been largely [3] irrelevant to Israel between the period of the Exodus from Egypt and the indecisive battle of the Syro-Palestinian coalition against Assyria at Karkar in 853 B.C.[4]

Much of the manner of modern writing about the rise of ethical monotheism in Palestine is as profoundly misleading as is the modern manner of substituting a propositional interpretation of the meaning of Yahweh for the original ejaculatory exclamation at the Burning Bush. Certainly any attempt at an evaluation of the significance of prophetic eschatology must start with a true under-standing of prophetic theology and see this as the product not of abstract reasoning about the universe but of concrete reaction to God. It is out of personal encounter with God and a life of meeting with him, however varied the manner of its mediation, that the prophets get their clue as to the meaning of the particular historical events of their own day and so of history as a whole. The world event may be a revelation of God, but it will be only

---

[1] The reason for the apparently little margin of time God appears to leave himself is due not only to the difference between his time-scale and ours but also to the inevit-able proportion between a revelation received and the mental and spiritual state of the receiver. A sense of imminent necessity is often an important, if unconscious, spur to increased sensitivity.

[2] Isa. 10, 5.

[3] Though Shishak's (Sheshonk's) raid on Jerusalem was perhaps not so exceptional an event as we imagine (1 Kings 14, 25; cf. W. O. E. Oesterley and T. H. Robinson, *A History of Israel* (O.U.P., 1932), vol. i, pp. 274 ff.).

[4] *Ibid*, pp. 295 f.

recognized by a man who sees it as such either by recognizing its personal impact upon himself as a medium of God's revelation, or by realizing its meaning by the light thrown upon it by some other personal meeting with God.

It is quite possible that others besides the great prophets might have expanded their doctrine of the scope of the day of Yahweh from the near neighbours of Israel [1] to the great empires [2] and so to the whole world [3] and even to the borders of another world beyond this.[4] Indeed this would be an example of a favourite form of the psychological mechanism of compensation, which dogs all theology and eschatology in particular. By this a persecuted or oppressed individual or group manages to secure a kind of vicarious satisfaction in the future miseries of others, and this future compensation offers a *modus vivendi* which makes endurable the present abject conditions of life. At its vicious worst this psychological mechanism can be seen in the gloating of those, who think themselves sure of heaven, over their unfortunate contemporaries whom they have destined to hell. At its comparatively harmless best it can be seen in the satisfaction Pharaoh gets from finding that he is not alone in his misery, but that all his enemies share his fate.[5]

What is distinctive in the prophetic understanding of the day of Yahweh is not its range and scope, though in the end this is very impressive indeed, but its impartiality. It is not in the first chapter of Amos with its doom on Israel's neighbours, but in his second chapter with its doom upon Israel. The temptation of all privileged peoples, and not least of those spiritually privileged, to rely upon their privileges and not to see them as responsibilities finds here its most striking rejection and refutation. It is a warning, which runs right through the prophetic writings,[6] and is as relevant to-day as when it was first uttered against all ecclesiastical, racial or political presumption. The *de profundis* of doomsday rings like a knell from Amos to Malachi, and it is in the fall of Jerusalem, not the fall of Nineveh, that it finds its dramatic expression and realization. 'Is it nothing to you', cries Jerusalem, 'all ye that pass by? Behold and see if there is any sorrow like unto my sorrow, which is done unto me, wherewith the Lord hath afflicted me in the day of his fierce anger.' [7] And as if one such terrible manifestation of God's judgment upon the holy city was not enough—and Deutero-Isaiah at any rate

[1] Amos 1, 1–2, 3; Isa. 34, 5 ff.; 63, 1 ff.
[2] Isa. 13, 6; Jer. 46, 10; Ezek. 30, 3.
[3] Isa. 61, 2; Joel 3, 14 ff.; Obad. 15.
[4] Ezek. 39, 8 ff.   [5] Ezek. 32, 31.
[6] Isa. 2, 12 ff.; Zeph. 1, 7–14; 2, 2 f.; Joel 1, 5; 2, 1–11; Mal. 4, 1–5.
[7] Lam. 1, 12.

thought it and the exile that followed it were more than enough [1]—
Zechariah prophesied another.[2]

There is thus no question but that the first eschatological corollary
of the ethical monotheism of the writing prophets is the doctrine
of a universal and utterly impartial judgment upon all peoples,
including the chosen people itself. This judgment is conceived of
on a gradually widening scale, but it is to begin with an historical
event rather than an eschatological one. Any attempt to draw a
hard-and-fast distinction between the two would be to impose on
the prophets something which would have been regarded by them as
an arbitrary and artificial contrast. The vindication of Yahweh
on his day had to be conceived of as an historical event. In the
absence of any clear conception of a life after death there was no
other way in which it could be regarded. And even when the
resurrection doctrine won a place in late Jewish thought it was not as
a substitute for the day of Yahweh, but as a corollary to it. It was
the extension of the range of Yahweh's activity that made it not only
a conceivable possibility but a glorious hope. For the rest, all that
can be said of the day of Yahweh as an historical event is that it was
through an historical event that the prophets conceived of the operation of the eschatological deed. Had they been writing systematic
theology it might have been possible to mark off Zephaniah's
Dies iræ, dies illa as the point of transition from history to eschatology, but as they were not, it is unfair to deduce from the
increasingly supernatural character of the manner of the operation
of Yahweh any sharp transition from a strictly historical end in
view. In fact, though the manner of operation becomes increasingly
supernatural, its setting remains always for the prophets natural and
historical.

The day of Yahweh will demonstrate that he is 'up and doing'.[3]
It will be a day of great divine activity, and if the part of vengeance
in that activity seems to us disproportionately large, it is well to
remember that the vengeance envisaged depends for its interpretation
upon the character of the avenger. The key to his character is
found in the summary statement that 'The Lord of Hosts is exalted
in judgment and God the holy one is sanctified in righteousness'.[4]
That is at least as great an advance upon the pre-prophetic outlook
as is our Lord's own reinterpretation of the prophetic view.[5]

---

[1] Isa. 40, 2.
[2] Zech. 14, 1 ff. (of course not written by the author of Zech. 1–8).
[3] Mal. 3, 17; cf. G. A. Smith, *The Book of the Twelve Prophets* (Hodder and
Stoughton, 1928), vol. ii, p. 363 n.   [4] Isa. 5, 16.
[5] As evidenced, e.g., by his omission of the note of vengeance (Isa. 61, 2) in the
summary of his message (Luke 4, 18 f.).

The winding up of national and perhaps universal history will inevitably bring doom upon the wicked who are alive at the time, and it is difficult to see how the righteous can be imagined as exempt from the terrible upheavals and devastations of the earth [1] which together with disturbances in the heavens [2] go to make up the prophetic description of doomsday.   But the imagery and its details, whatever their character, are not the important point.   They are part of the prophetic attempt to put no top limit or ceiling to the powers that in the day of Yahweh will be operative and loose in the world. D-Day would see armaments in operation which had been hitherto undreamed of.   It was a true insight of the prophets derived from their present experience of Yahweh to suggest by the imagery they chose the surprising and indeed the staggering power at his disposal. It remained for Jesus to make plain that the nature of that power was love in a demonstration of it in fact even more staggering than any prophetic image could have conceived.

Whatever, therefore, are the instruments he uses, whether the hosts of locusts,[3] for example, or the hosts of men [4] or even the hosts of heaven,[5] the day of Yahweh gets its name from the fact that then it will be his activity which will be unmistakably evident and completely adequate to effect the object he has in view, whatever means he uses to achieve it.   Prophetic passages which we often interpret in retrospect from a Christian standpoint in a saving and consoling way have a terrible moral astringency as originally uttered.   The Battle Hymn of the American Republic is not a syllable too strong for the tremendous energy and drive with which the prophets invested Yahweh on the day of doom.[6]   We do a grave disservice to the truth of God if because we find sanction in Jesus Christ for changing the emphasis of doomsday we deprive it of the tremendous drive and energy which the prophets imputed to it.   The terror of the meek is more than a match for the terror of the military.

When we turn from a consideration of the nature of the day to its imminence, we have to admit at once that as long as Yahweh's D-Day had no effect in Sheol, imminence was the only way of expressing relevance.   Unless it came in the lifetime of those living or at least might come within it, there was no point in its proclamation.   It might be part of the stock-in-trade of an astrologer or a soothsayer, but certainly never of a prophet.   The prophets preached it as inevitable because of their own experience of God.   They preached it as imminent, because both of that same experience,

---

[1] Isa. 2, 10 ff.;   32, 5 ff.;   Amos 8, 3 f.;   Zech. 14, 4 ff.
[2] Isa. 13, 9 f.;   Joel 3, 15;   Zech. 14, 7.
[3] Joel 1, 4 ff.   [4] Isa. 13, 17.   [5] Isa. 13, 10.   [6] Isa. 63, 1 ff.

which gave them a foretaste of the ultimate transcendence of successiveness by simultaneity, and also because they had no grounds for safely postponing it to a later date. It might happen at any time; therefore it might happen now.

It is fashionable to-day to say that in all their talk about imminence the prophets are stressing the urgency of a moral inevitability by emphasizing its chronological immediacy.[1] It is certainly true that future temporal imminence is always in the Old Testament prophets and in the New Testament evangelists and apostles as well as by our Lord himself subordinate to present moral urgency. If eschatology springs out of theology in any integral way, and if revelation is by event and interpretation rather than by proposition or prognostication, this must be the case. But the notion of imminence is not, therefore, to be dismissed as of no significance in its own right.

In the Hebrew notion of filled rather than abstract time and in the biblical use of God's kairoi ($\kappa\alpha\iota\rho o\iota$) to check man's chronos ($\chi\rho\acute{o}\nu o\varsigma$), as well as in the experience of a simultaneity in love which overcomes the sense of successiveness outside it, we have clear indications of the way in which imminence may be seen to have significance of its own, which is not in the least invalidated by a time-lag in clock or calendar time. It is our clock and calendar time which is the abstraction needing correction from God's point of view, not by a timeless eternity such as a trance might suggest (as if God lived in a trance!), but by an eternity packed chock-a-block with time, in which time may be imagined as compressed after the manner of an accordion in use. This latter is the time that lovers know, and to be in love may be to be in God, for 'God is love'.[2]

It is in terms of this sort of lovers' time that the prophetic note of eschatological imminence can be seen to have a permanent validity of its own. And it is not the apocalyptic conception of chronologically datable eras and dispensations but the prophetic conception of imminent events which expresses the moral inevitability of the abiding future consequences of present and, as we might say, existential decision. This was the burden of the prophetic eschatology, and it was a true insight of Arthur Burroughs, later Bishop of Ripon, to take an eschatological text, 'Multitudes, multitudes in the

---

[1] It is true that specific forecasts of dates are sometimes wrong and are then re-interpreted in the light of their proved error. But the stock proof of this is an exceedingly dubious example. Jeremiah prophesied an exile of seventy years (25, 11 f.; 29, 10). Politically this is an exaggeration. Jerusalem fell in 586 B.C. Sheshbazzar is said to have returned in 536 and Zerubbabel was certainly in Jerusalem in 520. But what of the religious calendar? The temple of Solomon was destroyed in 586 and the temple of Zerubbabel was dedicated in 516. Seventy years exactly!

[2] 1 John 4, 8.

valley of decision',[1] to summarize his attempt to bring home the
eternal significance of this central prophetic message to Britain
during the 1914–18 war.[2]

The immediacy of doomsday sounds like a knell throughout
prophecy with its grim and reiterated refrain, 'The day of the Lord
is at hand.'[3]   It was this message that John the Baptist picked up
and which in his mouth sounded no longer as an echo of the past,
but as a voice in the present.[4] And it was with the same form of
words, though with a far deeper content, that our Lord himself
started his mission.[5] If we ask for a reason for its nearness we are
thrown back upon the fact that it is already 'in the heart' of God,[6]
and therefore it cannot be far away.[7] And if this should seem a
surprise,[8] then that is what it always must be, though it should
be a surprise that is welcome and not unwelcome.[9] It is a surprise
in the Old Testament from Amos [10] to Malachi.[11] It is a surprise in
the New Testament, and the surprising fulfilment of it in the first
coming of our Lord does not eliminate the still surprising *dénouement*
which awaits us at the end.   To eliminate the element of surprise
from the end is to eliminate it all the way through.   It is in fact
to turn the living Yahweh into a dead Baal and to transform the
love of meeting into the lust for possession.

If the climax of the Old Testament revelation as to its nature is
given all unwittingly to his hearers and perhaps even to the prophet
himself in the Servant Songs of Deutero-Isaiah,[12] it is perhaps in the
same prophecy or in its appendage that we should look for that sense
of the transmutation of eschatology into mysticism, which is the
so very much misunderstood crown of both the Old Testament [13]
revelation and the New.   Judgment is already a fact, for it is already
in the heart and purpose of God.   It is a complete mistake to read
this either in Deutero-Isaiah or in St John as an assertion of a
timeless reality after the manner of Greek thought.   It is in each
case the climax of an essentially Hebraic conception of time and a
corrective of a distortion of that conception, not by reference to
some other reality but by reference to the true criterion for understanding that same reality itself.   And that true criterion is in fact
God himself.

[1] Joel 3, 14.
[2] E. A. Burroughs, *The Valley of Decision* (Longmans, 1918).
[3] Isa. 13, 6; Ezek. 30, 3; Joel 1, 15; Obad. 15.
[4] Matt. 3, 2 f.   [5] Matt. 4, 17.
[6] Isa. 63, 4; cf. H. W. Robinson, *Inspiration and Revelation*, p. 137.
[7] Deut. 30, 14.   [8] Isa. 55, 8 f.
[9] Isa. 59, 9.   [10] Amos 5, 18 ff.   [11] Mal. 3, 1 f.
[12] Isa. 42, 1–4; 49, 1–6; 50, 4–9; 52, 13–53, 12.
[13] Cf. J. E. Fison, *The Blessing of the Holy Spirit* (Longmans, 1950), pp. 77, 84 f.

It is because the Old Testament steadfastly rejects all attempts to reduce the holy God who prosecutes trespassers and the loving God who defies any presumptuous human possessiveness to the status of an idol which can be manipulated to suit man's convenience or even conjured to meet man's need that it constantly points forward to the day of Yahweh as something quite unique and therefore quite incapable of adequate verbal interpretation.   There is a standing protest against all idolatrous verbalism, however sacrosanct its biblical or ecclesiastical sanction, in the eschatological clarification in deed of all words: 'Therefore my people shall know my name: therefore they shall know in that day that I am he that doth speak; behold, it is I.' [1]

And as for the scene of this clarification, it is the triumphant conviction of the prophets that it will be on earth.   This is not merely because faith in a worthwhile life after death is so very late in coming upon the biblical scene, but far more because such a faith in the hereafter, when it does come on the scene, is not born of despair of the present existing order of life upon the earth but of awareness of some reality revealed within and through this present order, which is more real than anything else in this order and which is therefore bound to outlast this order, for it does not share its limitations.   In other words, prophetic eschatology is born of faith in God in the present and, in so far as it is genuine prophecy and not theoretical apocalyptic, never of mere speculation about the future, uncontrolled by reference to the present.   True eschatology always has reference to something really present and is never merely an inference from what is really absent.

The poetic prophecies [2] of Yahweh's vindication on earth are more in danger of being spiritualized away in the alleged interests of his vindication in 'a new heaven and a new earth' than of being misinterpreted as being literal prose descriptions of the shape of things to come.   Whatever may be the case with the later apocalyptic developments of prophecy, there is no doubt that the magnificence of the authentic vision of the prophets was due to their refusal to abandon faith in the real and actual ability of Yahweh to deal with everything which opposed his purpose on earth and to achieve that purpose by his own act, however improbable such a vindication might appear, from the actual conditions, both internal and external, under which each prophet laboured.

'Though he slay me, yet will I trust in him', [3] is the spirit out of which genuine eschatology is born.   The wider prospects of apocalyptic vision could only be entrusted to a people which both

---

[1] Isa. 52, 6; cf. Mal. 3, 17.   [2] E.g. Isa. 24, 21.   [3] Job 13, 15.

individually and corporately had learnt the lesson of such total dereliction as is envisaged in the first beatitude [1] and expressed in unforgettable Aramaic in the cry from the cross itself.[2] Even when such a vision did eventually appear after the experience of the exile and in the persecution of Antiochus Epiphanes, it proved too much for many Jews and turned their heads to such a consideration of rewards in the hereafter as is quite incompatible with any awareness of love here and now. For Job himself there was no such hope. Whatever may be the intention of the Burial service it seems certain that for him the scene of Yahweh's vindication had to be earth itself, even though that meant that in order to see it he had to be 'brought up from the underworld as a ghost, like the spirit of Samuel brought up before Saul' [3] by the witch of Endor.[4]

It is out of the anguish of the clash between the apparently irrefutable evidence of all contemporary events, whether of totalitarian tyranny or of gross individual injustice and undeserved suffering, that the final Hebrew resurrection faith emerged to triumph over the shadowy and undesirable continuation of a ghostly existence in the underworld of Sheol. And to this extent it is true that the apocalyptists, who developed that resurrection hope, 'called the New World into existence, to redress the balance of the Old'.[5] But before this is dismissed as some psychological projection or compensation or as simply wishful thinking, it is important to grasp clearly the significance of the prophets' reticence on the whole subject and their confidence (without any reference to any sort of life after death) that, despite all the evidence to the contrary, the day of Yahweh would come and come on earth, so that all then living would see the Lord

> Vindicated and enthroned,
> Unto earth's remotest end
> Glorified, adored, and owned.[6]

When the resurrection faith dawned, it dawned not as a substitute for the expectation of the day of Yahweh, but as a corollary of it. It was born of a realization that Yahweh's sphere of influence and of effective intervention was not limited to this earth, but extended far beyond it. If the positive conception of the effects of that day was in the end the precise opposite in prophetic eschatology from what popular eschatology imagined, then and then only

---

[1] Matt. 5, 3.   [2] Mark 15, 34.
[3] H. W. Robinson, *The Cross of Job* (S.C.M., 1938), p. 37.
[4] 1 Sam. 28, 3 ff.
[5] George Canning, Speech, December 12, 1826.
[6] F. R. Havergal.

could its scope be extended to include the dead as well as the
living. For them too, as well as for the living, there was offered
as the fulfilment of the better things, open to all who entered
the covenant between Yahweh and his people, an election not to
privilege but to responsibility, not to self-aggrandizement but to
service, understood not in a nationalist but in an ecclesiastical
sense.[1] Responsibility did not cease with death as privilege did:
opportunities for service did not come to an end then, though
opportunities for self-aggrandizement did: membership of the church
did not lapse at that point, though membership of the nation did.

It is only when faith in Yahweh for his own sake, with no thought
of ulterior motive in any doctrine of rewards or punishments, is
established on the unshakable foundation of the covenant and of
communion with God within it that the Old Testament opens the
door to an eschatology of the individual as well as of the nation.
We may pronounce the religion of the writers of the wisdom literature
to be 'religion at a very low temperature',[2] but the last word upon
them is not in them.   It is in the writers of the apocalyptic literature
who succeeded them, and on the apocalyptists no one has written
more finely than Edwyn Bevan, who sums up the message of Ben-
Sira in Ecclesiasticus in these words:

> There is in his book, one might perhaps say, a breath from the sea.
> And if there is a want of passion, of conflict, in this type of Judaism, if
> you must pronounce it too smoothly accommodating to the world,
> wait a little and you will see a fierce enough trial cause another temper
> to be manifested in Israel, an anguish going down to the deep places
> of the soul, and evoking there not only a bitter cry, but with the cry, a
> vaster, a more radiant hope.[3]

The 'anguish' Bevan refers to is the Maccabean struggle, and the
'vaster, more radiant hope' is the developed doctrine of a future
life after death, which was the apocalyptic reply to Antiochus'
challenge. It is quite true that the tendency was to replace 'the
poetry of prophetic messianism' in A. G. Hogg's graphic phrase,[4]
with 'the fairy-tale of apocalypse', but the New Testament endorses
the substance of the apocalyptic hope as a true corollary of the
substance of the prophetic day of Yahweh, even if it is remarkably
reticent about the details of apocalyptic speculation, which often
owed their origin more to the popular than to the prophetic conception of the day of Yahweh.

---

[1] H. W. Robinson, *Inspiration and Revelation*, pp. 156 f.
[2] W. L. Sperry, *Religion in America* (C.U.P., 1945), p. 55, quoting Professor
Whitehead.
[3] E. Bevan, *Jerusalem under the High Priests* (E. Arnold, 1904), p. 68.
[4] A. G. Hogg, *Redemption from this World* (T. and T. Clark, 1924), p. 25.

The essence of the doctrine of the resurrection is quite clear: 'many of them that sleep in the dust of the earth shall awake, some to everlasting life, and some to shame and everlasting contempt.'[1] The resurrection is thus incidental to the judgment, and as for the scope and significance of judgment day the apocalyptists have no unanimous dogma. The rival eschatologies which appear in the prophets continue throughout the writings of the apocalyptists. Is the basis of any claim to be included in the kingdom of God, whether for the living or for the dead, to be primarily racial or moral and spiritual?[2] This is the prophetic question-mark and challenge to all eschatological thinking from the days of Amos to the appearance of John the Baptist. On the whole it is true to say that 'when the perfect kingdom is being considered the question with regard to Israelites is: Who, if any, will be excluded? while with regard to the Gentiles it is: Who, if any, will be admitted'?[3]

St Paul is faithfully transcribing the attitude of a typical Pharisee when he describes the Gentiles as being not only 'alienated from the commonwealth of Israel, and strangers from the covenants of the promise', but also without 'hope and without God in the world'.[4] There were always differences between the wider and the narrower views. The tradition of the narrower Ezekiel was made more rigid by the work of Ezra and Nehemiah, and the vision of Deutero-Isaiah was reinforced by the protests against racialism enshrined in the books of Ruth and of Jonah. It is impossible to exclude all particularism if there is to be true universalism.[5] Love is exclusive in order to be inclusive, but all history shows how easy it is either to forget or to deny the eschatological word of the Lord: 'Whosoever shall seek to gain his life shall lose it: but whosoever shall lose his life shall preserve it.'[6] The early church had the most acute controversy over the question of maintaining or destroying the racial barriers between Jews and Gentiles, and the apostles even after the resurrection seem to have been completely unaware of any eschatological hope except on a national basis.[7] It was the better elements in Judaism, and not the worse, who were desperately anxious not to betray what they considered to be the 'entrenched clauses' in the basic privileges of the chosen people.

As for the manner in which the apocalyptists believed the future they hoped for would be realized, its classical expression comes from Daniel in the immediate context of the quotation which our Lord

[1] Dan. 12, 2.
[2] Cf. T. W. Manson, *The Teaching of Jesus* (C.U.P., 1931), pp. 256 ff.
[3] *Ibid.*, p. 257.   [4] Eph. 2, 12.
[5] Cf. H. H. Rowley, *Israel's Mission to the World* (S.C.M., 1939), pp. 39 ff.
[6] Luke 17, 33.   [7] Acts 1, 6.

employed to express his own messiahship to Caiaphas.[1] Here in
one tremendous vision we see the judgment with the books and the
fire and the throne and the court and the king himself.

> I beheld till thrones were placed and one that was ancient of days did
> sit; his raiment was white as snow, and the hair of his head like pure
> wool; his throne was fiery flames and the wheels thereof burning fire.
> A fiery stream issued and came forth from him: thousand thousands
> ministered unto him, and ten thousand times ten thousand stood before
> him; the judgment was set and the books were opened.[2]

The value of such a description lies not in its details, except in so
far as these reflect present realities and not mere future imaginings.
The great conflagration of Persian eschatological speculation appears
in the classical description of the day of Yahweh, where the mediæval
hymn, *Dies iræ, dies illa: solvet saeclum in favilla*,[3] emphasizes in
grim earnestness the prophetic refrain about 'the fire of his jealousy'.[4]
It has its New Testament sanction in 2 Peter,[5] which is the final term
of the whole biblical conception of the day of Yahweh. Whatever
its speculative significance, its use as an eschatological concept is
rooted in the present experience of meeting with God, which is so
often described in terms of burning or fire by prophets and mystics
alike. Again and again from Moses [6] to Pascal [7] the same image
occurs, and it is even brought by St Cyril of Alexandria into the
heart of Christological dogma with the simile of the iron in the fire
used to illustrate the union of the two natures of Christ in a 'true
Gestalt'.[8]

Whatever is made of this suggestive simile of the effect of the
meeting of two in one, there can be no doubt it is on such a meeting
that the conclusion of the vision is focused, with its image of 'a son
of man' drawing near to 'the ancient of days'.[9] In this great
messianic passage there is no doubt that the kingdom which is
envisaged is something which is itself the sequel to or the legacy of
the meeting between the 'son of man', whether he be an individual
or merely a synonym for 'the saints of the Most High' [10] on the one
hand, and God himself, or 'the ancient of days', on the other. The
indestructible kingdom of God emerges from that final meeting,
and it is the significance of the whole messianic hope of Israel to
make plain that without such a meeting no final kingdom is conceivable. It does not so much matter whether the movement of

---

[1] Mark 14, 62.   [2] Dan. 7, 9 f.
[3] Thomas of Celano, *Analecta Hymnica* liv, p. 269.
[4] Zeph. 1, 18; 3, 8.   [5] 2 Pet. 3, 10.   [6] Exod. 3, 2 ff.
[7] J. Chevalier, *Pascal* (Sheed and Ward, 1930), pp. 94 f.
[8] M. Gregory, *Psychotherapy, Scientific and Religious* (Macmillan, 1939), p. 133.
[9] Dan. 7, 13.   [10] Dan. 7, 18.

the drama is from earth to heaven or from heaven to earth. What matters is that there should be a meeting between God and some other, however that other be conceived. That is the secret of all the possibilities of transformation which the day of Yahweh does not so much close as inaugurate. For hope as much as faith and love abides [1] till the very end, and guarantees that there can be no end which does not itself look forward beyond itself to a new beginning.

For the Old Testament as a whole the figure of the Messiah is an incidental extra to the main drama of the messianic age, which will be 'the sequel to that "Day of Yahweh" when evil will be judged and good vindicated' [2] and not a substitute for it. On that day God will be at work in a sense and to a degree at present inconceivable, and the manner of his working will take the form of a confrontation of men, and of nature too, with his presence and with the unavoidable necessity of meeting him. From time to time the conviction dawns that this means that he will work through some person, i.e. the Messiah, and at moments of crisis hopes arise that he is actually at the beginning of his eschatological work in some figure of contemporary history. [3] In so far as the latter more strictly and narrowly messianic hope is conceived, if it is tied to some present reality and not allowed free speculative rein, the only way the Jews could envisage the realization and fulfilment by anyone of a messianic vocation was through some meeting with the living God, however directly or indirectly that might be mediated. Nothing in Hebrew past or present experience justified any hopes of either absorption into the divine after the manner of some non-biblical mystical theories of human deification, [4] or of projection from the divine after the manner of the Greek contraption of the *deus ex machina* let down upon the stage of the theatre. [5]

In so far as the messianic age had no Messiah it was the sequel to the day of Yahweh, and the essence of the conception of the day of Yahweh was the coming of Yahweh to men where they were, meeting them on earth and eventually in Sheol too, and through that meeting opening up to them incalculable consequences of weal or woe. Everything that followed (whether we call it heaven or hell) was the result of that meeting. In so far as the Jews perhaps and

---

[1] 1 Cor. 13, 13.

[2] T. W. Manson, ed. *A Companion to the Bible* (T. and T. Clark, 1939), p. 310.

[3] E.g. Zerubbabel (Hag, 2, 23, and probably Zech. 3, 8 and 6, 12 also).

[4] Though some interpretations of Immanuel (Isa. 7, 14; 8, 8), as a God-embodied nation or generation or individual, suggest it.

[5] Though some apocalyptic interpretations of the son of man or the heavenly man suggest it.

Christians certainly conceived of the messianic age as being in-
augurated by a personal Messiah, he had first to meet God before
he could be the mediator through whom God could meet with the
rest of men and through his meeting with them open up endless
vistas of transformation involving nature as well as man. It was
not the actual vocation of the servant of Yahweh in Deutero-Isaiah
which prevented the Jews from recognizing his messianic significance:
it was the suffering entailed in the fulfilment of that vocation which
repelled them. However the call, and the meeting with God involved
in it, is mediated, it is this which lies at the heart of the whole Old
Testament conception of the relationship first between the community
and God, then between the remnant within the community and God,
and finally between every individual within the community and God.
That relationship is a covenant relationship and it is out of such
a meeting or coming together that entirely new possibilities for
the future emerge.

Apart from the conception of such a meeting accompanied by
fire, the apocalyptists added two other important notes to the
dominant prophetic eschatology. They brought in the idea that in
the end things would look very much as they had at the beginning.[1]
This can be interpreted in two ways: either it is an importation of
alien and cyclical views of time, which otherwise, except in
Ecclesiastes, have no place in Hebrew thought, or it may be an
attempt to check the tendency of all apocalyptic writing to run away
from the world of fact into the world of fancy by stressing the
connection of what would be at the end if not with what was in the
present at least with what had been at the beginning. As such it
has a value, which as a mere reflection of a cyclical view of time
it has not.

The other contribution of the apocalyptists towards our understanding of the day of Yahweh was that they were the first to provide
the Jews with some conception of the unity of all history and with
some rationale of its significance. They had what might be described
as a *weltanschauung* in a sense the prophets never had. They had
a plan, and they mapped out space and time to fit into it. Such a
plan can do great good, but if it replaces the prophetic insistence
upon the personal immediacy of judgment by a rational theory of
the impersonal inevitability of judgment, then it does irreparable
harm. And it was to guard against what had in fact begun to prove
a fatal tendency in apocalyptic that first John the Baptist and then
Jesus himself brought back its fairy-tale to a 'lived and acted poetry'.[2]
With them the last judgment became again, as it had been with

[1] 2 Esd. 7, 30 ff.   [2] A. G. Hogg, *op. cit.*

the great prophets, a moral stimulus and not, as it tended to be with the apocalyptists, a moral narcotic. And the measure of the advance of the eschatology of our Lord upon even the greatest of the Old Testament prophets is that he succeeded, as they never did, both in doing this and also in combining with their conception of the day of Yahweh the vivid apocalyptic expectation of life after death, of which they had hardly an inkling.

There is thus an incomparably richer and more coherent eschatology in the New Testament than in the Old. For both, the day of the Lord is central, but in most of the Old Testament its moral leverage is corporate rather than individual, because its effective sphere of action is confined to this world. In the New Testament, on the other hand, its horizon is infinitely extended: its leverage is even more individual than corporate: and its character is entirely transformed by the conviction that its secret lay with some known person rather than in some unknown event. This is not to deny that the Old Testament might have realized much of the significance of this had the meaning of the day been radically ruled by the character of Yahweh, who would then be operating to make it his day, and had the clues as to his nature provided by the greatest prophets been fearlessly followed up. But they were not, and the Old Testament leaves us at best with something which can only be described as a grim prospect in comparison with the thrilling and the tingling expectation of the New.

The apocalyptists certainly 'brought the New World into existence', but they had to pay a heavy price for their daring lengthening of the prospects and the horizons of the individual in a loss of ethical stringency and rigour in their eschatological teaching. Nevertheless they prepared the way for the fully developed doctrine of the New Testament, and enabled it to span both this world of corporate hope and the next world of individual hope with an eschatology, not merely of a speculative future interest but of an immediate present relevance. They enabled man to feel at home in a world that might not be very evidently God's, but was very evidently planned.[1] Modern man is homeless, and Buber[2] is right in seeing this as perhaps the most tragic element in our contemporary situation. If apocalyptic eschatology could again enable him to feel at home, then the perfected prophetic eschatology of the New Testament might provide him with the bracing atmosphere of high and hopeful moral adventure which he so badly needs if he is to live in his home as he ought to live and make his home what it ought to be.

[1] Dan. 2, 36 ff.; 7, 1 ff.; cf. H. W. Robinson, *Inspiration and Revelation*, p. 131.
[2] M. Buber, *Between Man and Man* (Kegan Paul, 1947), pp. 126 ff.

8

But this is to anticipate.   So far as the Old Testament is concerned, the danger of all apocalyptic eschatology is the danger of all scholastic theology.   It seems to make man at home in the world, but the world in which it makes him at home is so often not the real world. Nevertheless it was 'apocalyptic and not prophecy that was the first to grasp the great idea that all history, human, cosmological and spiritual is a unity and a unity that follows inevitably as a corollary to the unity of God as enforced by the Old Testament prophets', [1] though perhaps it would be more true to say that in this respect apocalyptic was the first to make 'explicit what was already implicit in prophecy'.[2]

It was great gain for those involved in the immediate Maccabean struggle for existence to be able to 'see the working out of the divine purpose in a series of stages, diversely pictured, yet always culminating in the final victory of God'.[3]   But to have a clear pattern of the tangled web of history, whether it is offered by Daniel or by Professor Toynbee, is gain only in so far as it interprets a living present awareness of its secret.   It is deadly if it becomes a substitute for it, and that is what it is always in danger of doing, whether in the fanciful development of apocalyptic imagery or in the logical arguments of scholastic propositions.   No human scheme or pattern, however holy its sanction, is ever proof against the shattering impact of the mercy and love of the living God.   Were it otherwise, it would insulate us from all contact with and awareness of him. We should have made our home secure, but in so doing we should have inevitably shut him out of it and so have lost the only eschatological security we can ever hope to have.

The old safe world of Aristotle and Ptolemy broke up in face of the new comprehension of the depths of sin, plumbed first by St Augustine and later by Luther, and the new comprehension of the universe opened up by Copernicus,[4] and so left man homeless and in his homelessness either afraid or cocksure.   In a strikingly similar manner Jesus Christ broke up the imagined future security offered by the apocalyptists in the next world, just as the great prophets before him broke up the imagined future security offered by popular nationalism in this world.   They did the latter by outright negative condemnation : he did the former by indirect positive reorientation.

The prophets knew from their personal encounters with God, of which Moses' experience at the Burning Bush is a typical representative illustration, that the real world was not the safe world

---

[1] H. W. Robinson, *Inspiration and Revelation*, p. 132, quoting R. H. Charles.
[2] *Ibid.*   [3] *Ibid.*
[4] M. Buber, *Between Man and Man*, pp. 126 ff.

run by the Baals, but the very unsafe world in which alone Yahweh could be met.   Right from the start it was to that unsafe world of meeting that they bore their witness by wholesale denunciation of all the safety devices, whether ecclesiastical or national, on which those who refused to risk their lives in the unsafe world relied as a protection against any chance of ever being forced to enter it.

Therefore the prophetic eschatology was very largely an eschatology of doom, and only after the severest purging of selfish nationalistic hopes did the prophets offer hope at all.   If hope were encouraged, the greatest prophets knew that it must be for all.   Thereby even the proclamation of hope shattered one more defence in the exclusive safety-first precautions of the popular eschatology, which confined its hopes to Israel alone.

First, then, the prophets interpreted the significance of their own experience of the unsafe world in which alone Yahweh could be met (though he might use any or all of the paraphernalia of the safe world of the ecclesiastics or the politicians as his meeting-places) as meaning doom for all who relied for their security, either in the present or in the future, on any of the protections offered by the safe world of no encounter.   Secondly, as they progressively realized more and more of the significance of the real world of meeting in which they lived and so understood more and more the manner of its final realization and manifestation, they came to the conclusion that they could only prophesy hope for men at all if they prophesied it for all.   In this way they shattered the future hopes of those who thought either that these were secured for them in this life or that they were reserved exclusively for them in the next.

Thirdly, they retained the concept of the day of Yahweh even though they utterly transformed its meaning.   It was as much the centre of their eschatology as it had been of the popular eschatology which preceded theirs.   This is very important in view of Christian tendencies to displace it by some other eschatological symbol or concept.   To put the eschatological emphasis on the resurrection of the body is not to do justice to the main weight of Old Testament evidence, which is overwhelmingly weighted down on the side of the day of Yahweh.   Far more serious is the fact that emphasis on the resurrection puts man back at the centre of the eschatological scene, which was the very thing the prophets were out to avoid.   They knew God well enough in the present to realize that it was his activity in the future that was really significant.   If that involved resurrection, so much the better for the good and so much the worse for the bad. But in either case the resurrection was a corollary to the activity of God on the day when he would make that activity unmistakably plain.

To switch the emphasis on to any other eschatological symbol than the day of Yahweh is to give a fatal twist not only to the actual evidence of the Old Testament but also to its interpretation in the light of the New Testament sequel. '"Time" is that which meets you on your path through life',[1] and that means in the end both for the Old Testament and for the New none other than God himself. This is the Old Testament key to the New Testament lock, for it is the doctrine of the parousia which is the clue to Christian eschatology.

Jesus fulfilled the prophetic protest against reliance on the false securities of the world of safety first not so much by condemning them, for so far as eschatological doctrine was concerned he did not go in for condemnation on the prophetic scale. (There was no need, for the prophets had done it all before him.) But he did what they had not been able to do. He pointed positively to the possibility of entering into a world of unlimited meeting in the present and offered this as the only sure guarantee of ever entering it in the future. In other words, he gave a positive content to future hope and drew it from present experience in a way the prophets had never been able to do.

They could not bear witness to themselves. Being sinful men any attempt to do so was bound to smack of self-advertisement and so do the opposite of what they desired to do. But Jesus being sinless could bear witness to himself and such witness had no taint of self-advertisement. His unbroken communion with his Father made evident the only grounds of present confidence having any eschatological validity whatever. The prophets' broken communion with Yahweh justified their negative destruction of all confidence which had no eschatological validity. It did not enable them to make explicit the positive content of their own present conviction and confidence, which had eschatological validity.

It is easy to exaggerate the contrast between the prophets and our Lord in order to make a case for Christianity against Judaism. But nevertheless it remains on the whole true that so far as eschatology was concerned they could only say, 'Thus saith the Lord',[2] whereas he could say, 'Verily, verily I say unto you'. They could only utter the word which smashed the false securities. He was the Word who proclaimed himself as the way to the only true security. They confronted men with judgment, while he offered men salvation; and both terms are essentially eschatological if they express more than either venomous hate or pious sentimentality.

---

[1] H. W. Robinson, *Inspiration and Revelation*, p. 109.
[2] Though the mystical element in Deutero-Isaiah (parallel to St John) is most important.

Finally, Jesus transformed the conception of the day of Yahweh, or the day of the Lord, for (as the early church realized) he was the Lord. By such a transformation the fear of the largely unknown was turned into the expectation of the at least partly known. Grimness gave way to glory and the threats of judgment to the thrill of love. To see how this came about we must examine the evidence of the New Testament. But we cannot leave the Old without glad acknowledgment of an infinite indebtedness to it for making plain beyond all possible shadow of doubt that the only reality here and now, besides which all else in our experience pales into insignificance, is that God meets man. That is what he is continually doing now, and that is what he is going to do at the end in a way that we cannot possibly at present understand. The prophetic tradition of the Old Testament never attempts to prove this, but it never ceases to bear witness to it and it stakes everything upon it. Its eschatological message is as badly needed to-day as it ever was both for its own intrinsic truth and as an indispensable preparation for the fullness of that truth, which the New Testament reveals.

CHAPTER V

THE PAROUSIA OF OUR LORD

THE New Testament bursts upon us with 'the voice' [1] of John the Baptist after the long silence of prophecy, broken only by the echoes of the past. As if this was not a startling enough revelation, there follows the gradual unfolding of the meaning of the eschatological secret of the Old Testament. It turns out that what had been a prophetic aside, itself set within the context of an aside, is the centre and core of the whole eschatological prospect. For the Old Testament the whole idea of any Messiah is very much an aside. In some form or other, spiritual or national, prophetic or popular, the day of Yahweh would usher in the kingdom of God—that was the outlook of the Jews. But in that outlook the figure of the king is on the whole quite incidental, though it dominates the scene in some form or another at occasional moments of national or religious crisis. Christian exegesis has read much more back into the prophetic oracles of strictly messianic significance than the prophets probably ever intended should be read out of them.

But as if the placing of the Messiah in the centre of the eschatological prospect was not enough, the New Testament proceeds to take its clue as to the meaning of messiahship not from the heart of the Old Testament messianism, the concept of a Davidic king, but from a complete aside which, until Jesus took it and applied it to himself as Messiah, no one had ever thought of as being messianic. Who the prophet who wrote the Servant Songs [2] had in mind is the subject of an endless debate which is still going on.[3] Most probably his figure may be imagined as a pyramid, starting at its base with the hope that the whole nation of Israel will fulfil the vocation of the servant and proceeding via the hope in the remnant to the hope in a single individual. If so, the figure of the pyramid with its apex clear in view needs correcting from the standpoint of the Old Testament by the figure of a mountain with its summit perhaps glimpsed by the prophet but on the whole hidden in mists and clouds. Even if opinion is veering towards a recognition that in original intention

---

[1] Mark 1, 3.
[2] Isa. 42, 1–4; 49, 1–6; 50, 4–9; 52, 13–53, 12.
[3] Cf. C. R. North, *The Suffering Servant of Deutero-Isaiah* (O.U.P., 1948).

the Servant Songs had a messianic significance, it is certainly hardening against allowing the claim of anyone before Jesus to have seen such a meaning in them.

It is the old story of love's self-disclosure of itself. The fulfilment of the past is never what is expected in advance. In prospect it looks like complete contradiction: only in retrospect is it realized to be perfect completion. The attempt to live in the safety-first world of no surprises is suicidal, for it rules out all possibility of entering the dangerous world of love, which is full of surprises. That is the meaning in human experience of taking up the cross daily. In prospect this has no appeal at all: only in retrospect is it seen to be the only way to fulfil the purpose of life. The New Testament fulfils the Old, but how different is the fulfilment from the expectation of it!

So it must always be; but it is one thing to see it written as large as life on every page of the New Testament: it is quite another thing to follow out its implications in contemporary life. It is the one thing the Christian church is constantly in danger of relegating to an academic issue of the past and always refusing to face up to as an existential issue in the present. It would be the merit of the rediscovery of the authentic eschatological outlook of the New Testament that, by bringing back this note of surprise into our expectation of the future right to the very end as the final term of a reality which is always with us, it might give us courage to face the perils involved in living in the light of it in the present. The real world, in which 'journeys end in lovers meeting',[1] is only to be entered by those who risk the perils of abandoning the unreal world of a security guaranteed in terms of economic materialism or of apocalyptic spirituality, of racial isolationism or of ecclesiastical departmentalism.

Only so can the world of 'the holy' and of holy love be seen, let alone entered. The little child may have an inkling of it and see it filled with witches as well as fairies and with wolves as well as Red Riding-hoods. But adults have lost the innocence of little children and there is only one way in which they can get it back. It is the magic of tribulation to bring innocence with experience.[2] Nothing else can do it, and even tribulation can only do it when it is something we cannot dodge rather than something for which we volunteer. It meant for Jesus the cross. It cannot in principle mean less for us, for by the measure of our falling short of his self-sacrificing love we fail now to see the dimension of love which one day we are

---

[1] W. Shakespeare, *Twelfth Night*, II, iii, 44.
[2] G. A. Smith, *The Book of Isaiah* (Hodder and Stoughton, 1927).

bound to see. To be 'crucified with Christ'[1] is the secret, as the apostle learnt it: it was so completely different from being crucified alone that it needed his conversion on the Damascus road[2] to get him to see its significance at all. For hardship of his own choice he was prepared before that experience: for hardship that was laid upon him and that he did not choose he was only ready after it.

If we are not ready, it is some comfort but no excuse to know that notwithstanding all the great expectations of the poor, the Jews as a whole and sooner or later every single apostle in particular were also found unready. That is why the New Testament opens with an appeal to get ready. John the Baptist's mission was a final reaffirmation of the prophetic day of Yahweh and an appeal after the manner of Amos and almost in his very words, 'Prepare to meet thy God, O Israel'.[3] Both geographically in the scene of their life and work and theologically in the rigour of their ethical diagnosis and denunciation, and also vocationally in the sense not only of the grandeur of their call but also of its limitations, Amos and John the Baptist have much in common. And if the former paved the way for Hosea, so did the latter for Jesus.

How much concrete and positive hope either of them offered is not clear. In the case of Amos, as we have seen, much depends on the textual evidence, which is in dispute. So likewise in the case of John the Baptist it is not certain whether he offered more than an insurance against the doomsday, which he felt was so inescapably imminent. If indeed he held out hopes of a messianic baptism 'with the Holy Ghost',[4] then he raised high hopes. But there is a strong possibility that this is no part of his message, but rather a later Christian interpretation of it and consequent interpolation into it.[5]

Be this as it may, whether John the Baptist's eschatology was one of unrelieved doom or not, there is no doubt about the moral stringency of his message and of his determination to stop the presumption, which appears to have been as common in his day as it had been in the time of Amos, that national privilege exempted Jews from the most elementary moral obligations. John the Baptist knew enough of God in the present to know that such presumption at any time was complete folly and if persisted in till the day of Yahweh simply suicidal. He is the last of the great prophetic succession which at least from Elijah to Elijah *redivivus*[6] prepared

---

[1] Gal. 2, 20.   [2] Acts 9, 1 ff.   [3] Amos 4, 12.   [4] Luke 3, 16.
[5] There is no positive manuscript evidence for deleting the phrase. But the entire context, except 'gather the wheat into his garner', speaks only of judgment. Even if the word 'spirit' is retained, its meaning may be 'wind' and refer to winnowing, just as 'fire' refers to purification or destruction.
[6] Mark 9, 11 ff.

the way of the Lord for over eight hundred years. This great succession is completely misinterpreted if the prophets, who were under no illusions [1] about their own limitations, are transformed into systematic theologians, claiming to be competent to map out a complete theological universe. The last of them was more aware than any of his predecessors of his limitations, perhaps because of his spiritual sensitivity or because of his contemporaneity and kinship with Jesus, and it was significantly said of him by Jesus with all possible emphasis that 'among them that are born of women there hath not arisen a greater than John the Baptist'.[2]

John's message of the day of Yahweh therefore has Jesus' *imprimatur* both by word and by deed in his complete and ultimately inexplicable [3] identification with him by accepting baptism at his hands. But it only has his *imprimatur* as a preparation for something incomparably greater and grander, of which John himself had at first no inkling and which left him in the end completely mystified.[4] There can be no doubt about this startling contrast between John's conception of what he was preparing for and Jesus' realization of it, whatever interpretation is given to the enigmatical word of the Lord which after giving him absolute pre-eminence over all his predecessors proceeds to put him firmly in his place with the reminder that 'he that is but little in the kingdom of heaven is greater than he'.[5] If our Lord started no new movement but rather joined up with his cousin's, if he first accepted what John had to offer rather than started off by making his own offer, if he allied himself with John not out of patronage but because of his vocation, and if finally he was baptized by John because he felt it his duty and not because he felt that through it he could secure some spiritual benefit, it is impossible to exaggerate the care with which he linked himself with the prophetic succession and thereby (as we may well surmise) with the prophetic eschatology.[6] If 'creative life is always on the yonder side of convention', as Professor Jung insists,[7] then so far as the specific religious conventions of the Jews were concerned it was the prophetic rather than the priestly or the scribal or the apocalyptic with which Jesus chose to identify himself at the outset of his ministry.

[1] Mark 1, 7 f.; Matt. 3, 11 f.; Luke 3, 16 f. The Fourth Gospel goes out of its way to emphasize John the Baptist's subordination and his limitations, probably for dogmatic and apologetic reasons (John 1, 19 ff.; 3, 22, ff.).
[2] Matt. 11, 11.   [3] Matt. 3, 15.
[4] Matt. 11, 2 ff.; Luke 7, 18 ff.   [5] Matt. 11, 11.
[6] After all, when it comes to eschatology, except for the apocalyptists who else had anything to offer? Let the priests and the scribes be given their place, but let them keep to it! It is not their place to speak on eschatology. This was to all intents and purposes a prophetic preserve. Trespassers are in danger of prosecution.
[7] C. G. Jung, *The Integration of the Personality* (Kegan Paul, 1940), p. 295.

But it was not long before he found himself on its yonder side. If he joined John the Baptist, he soon left him: this was as true of his eschatology as of his morality. According to St Matthew's Gospel Jesus started his ministry after leaving John the Baptist with a message which was identical in verbal form with John's. It was an eschatological message: 'Repent ye, for the kingdom of heaven is at hand.'[1] But how different it sounded on Jesus' lips! As with his simplest parables of morality, so with his deepest utterances on eschatology, he coined no new phrase but he gave a new meaning to every old phrase he used. On his lips the imminence of the day of Yahweh meant a prospect of thrilling hope rather than of terrible disaster. It had something of the fascination of a lover wooing rather than the awe-inspiring terror of an avenger threatening.[2] It appealed to men either to enter the kingdom or to receive it before it threatened them with the penalties that failure to do so inevitably entailed. The 'No' of the Old Testament is fulfilled by the 'Yes' of the New, and if the element of surprise is still there, as it certainly is, its emphasis is the other way round. It lays its stress upon the indescribable blessedness which the future holds for those who take the appropriate action in the present rather than upon the inescapable doom which it holds for those who do not.

But it is not upon the contrast between Jesus and his prophetic predecessors that we should first lay stress. That contrast can only be understood against a background of fundamental agreement. He 'came not to destroy but to fulfil'[3] the eschatology of the prophets as well as the law of the Pentateuch. Therefore the first impression which we receive from the eschatology of the New Testament is that the day of the Lord is as sudden, unexpected, inescapable and imminent as it had ever been in the Old Testament. Whether we like this eschatological emphasis or not, whether we agree with it or not, no fair interpretation of the New Testament can possibly fail to see that it is central to its whole outlook upon the last things.

The earliest Christian documents we possess are perhaps St Paul's two letters to the Thessalonians and the epistle of St James, if that is really the work of the 'brother'[4] of our Lord. In St James the day of the Lord is imminent and indeed 'before the doors'[5] after the manner of the Old Testament expectation of the prophets. But there is a significant switch of emphasis, first of all on the person

[1] Matt. 4, 17; cf. 3, 2.
[2] Cf. R. Otto, *The Idea of the Holy*, E.T. (O.U.P., 1928), pp. 31 ff.
[3] Matt. 5, 17.
[4] Mark 6, 3. R. Heard (*An Introduction to the New Testament* (A. and C. Black, 1950)) supports this claim (pp. 164 ff.), as also that of Jude (pp. 215 ff.).
[5] Jas. 5, 7 ff.

whose arrival is imminent, and secondly upon his parousia (παρουσία) which is expected. The Septuagint never uses the latter term, which is distinctively Christian in its significance,[1] and the vividness of the description of the scene, 'Behold the judge standeth before the doors',[2] suggests a humanizing of the content of the day of Yahweh which is only explicable on the assumption that the personality of Jesus is at the heart of this primitive eschatological expectation, whether the use of the term ὁ κύριος, 'the Lord', with which the Septuagint translates Yahweh, is here deliberately intended to refer to Jesus or not.

When we turn from St James, with his evidence, whether early or late, of the way in which the future eschatological expectation of the Old Testament maintained its importance within the Christian church, to St Paul's earliest epistles, we find our first impressions confirmed. The day of the Lord finds its classical expression in 1 Thessalonians,[3] where God's activity is described as like that of a nocturnal housebreaker, and its content is given unmistakable Christian significance by the continual use of the expression, the parousia (ἡ παρουσία) of our Lord Jesus Christ, to expound its meaning.[4] And as if this was not enough, the evidence of St Paul about the middle of the first century A.D. is backed not only by his own assumption that his views have been thoroughly grasped by his converts,[5] but also by the witness of the three earliest sources for the Synoptic Gospels. It is the burden of the close of St Mark's 'little apocalypse',[6] it is the theme of the so-called Q apocalypse,[7] and it is in St Luke's special and primitive source, usually labelled L.[8] This is cumulative evidence as clear in its variety as in its unanimous convergent testimony to the primitive outlook of the early church about 50 A.D. No Old Testament prophet had ever depicted more vividly either the imminence of the day of the Lord or its inexorability. If we want a modern parable, Lawrence of Arabia will provide us with one in his description of Jeddah, the port of Mecca, as seen for the first time from a ship at sea. 'Then', he writes, 'the heat of Arabia came out like a drawn sword and struck us speechless. It was midday: and the noon sun in the East, like moonlight, put to sleep the colours. There were only lights and shadows, the white houses and the black gaps of streets.'[9] It is in just such vivid terms

---

[1] W. O. E. Oesterley, in *The Expositors Greek Testament* (Hodder and Stoughton, 1897), vol. iv, p. 471.
[2] Jas. 5, 9.   [3] 1 Thess. 5, 1 ff.
[4] 1 Thess. 2, 19; 3, 13; 4, 15; 5, 23; 2 Thess. 2, 1, 8.
[5] 1 Thess. 5, 1 ff.   [6] Mark 13, 32 ff.
[7] Luke 17, 22 ff.   [8] Luke 21, 34 ff.
[9] T. E. Lawrence, *Seven Pillars of Wisdom* (Jonathan Cape, 1935), p. 65.

that our Lord's parables add their *imprimatur* to the prophetic conception of the day of Yahweh.

The difference between the Old Testament and the New is therefore not to be conceived of as a blurring by love of the sharp outlines of the ancient eschatology of hate. On the contrary, if love could alter the old outlines it could only alter them by sharpening and not by blurring their decisive significance. Sentimentality never for one minute finds a place in biblical eschatology. But there is a difference in the content given to the day of Yahweh which does in fact completely transform its significance. And when we have done all we can to emphasize the identity of the new doctrine with the old we must go on to point out the difference. For eschatology is the last department of theology to be affected by any doctrinal reformation, and we must beware of so stressing the hang-over of pre-Christian eschatology that we miss the distinctive newness of the Christian hope.

Something of this newness can be glimpsed from the simple fact that whereas for the Old Testament the Lord's day meant an unknown future, for the New Testament its primary significance was the first day of every week. The eschatological day affected the Christian conception of Sunday, but far more important was the effect of Sunday upon the Christian conception of the eschatological day. The difference was at least as great as the difference between the Jewish sabbath and the Christian Sunday, though the gloom of the Jewish sabbath is often grossly exaggerated by Christians who know it only by analogy with the traditional idea of a Puritan Sunday. The note of resurrection joy suggests something unbelievably good rather than something unspeakably bad. Damnation is still a risk that can never be eliminated so long as the salvation of love is a possibility to be reckoned with.[1] But the accent has changed from the last day of the old week, the swan-song of the old order, to the first day of the new week, the in-breaking of the new order. It looks to the future rather than sums up the past. Far more important, the Lord who gives content to the meaning of the day is now Jesus, and Yahweh only as interpreted and revealed by Jesus. The glowing expectation of the new Israel is contrasted with the fearful foreboding of the old, and though the contrast may be overdrawn it may not be ignored.

Furthermore, the apocalyptic tendency was to transform the concrete time of the prophetic day, deriving its content solely from Yahweh who would then be operative as never before, into something much more like the abstract time of modern thinking, whereby it

[1] 1 Cor. 11, 29.

becomes a date in time, generally fixed but conceivably movable like Easter. This tendency was sharply corrected by the Christian insistence that 'the day' is only incidental to 'the Lord' who will come on it. The prospect of facing an unknown event is thus completely transformed into the certainty of meeting a known person.

This transformation should have meant the total elimination once and for all of all attempts to understand its significance or to estimate its imminence by any reckoning of 'times' or 'seasons'.[1] The fact that this has not yet been done only shows how hard it is even for the Christian church to abandon its securities in a datable temporal world in order to discover its only eschatological security in the undatable world of love. In such a world time is real, but it is time which 'flies' and is so transformed as to make 'times' and 'seasons' quite irrelevant. In this world of real but not of chronologically reckoned time there is no getting away from the inescapable element of surprise which is the hall-mark of all real meeting and intercourse in a relationship of love.

The Christian eschatological hope is built upon the coming of a person, and morbid introspection at the prospect gives way to the wonder of a faith which has no confidence in itself at all, but only in him who justifies 'the ungodly'.[2] Taken out of the context of a relationship of love this is a scandalously immoral and antinomian doctrine. Taken within that context, no other conceivable ground of eschatological confidence can be imagined. Election and predestination are lifted clean out of the grim context of iron necessity and given an entirely new meaning in the glorious context of romantic love. A new understanding, indeed a new dimension of time opens up, not in the abstract terms of a theological proposition or even in the concrete form of a Christological inference, but in the lived experience of how time does in fact 'fly' for those who are 'in love'. It is this speeded-up time which gives content to the theological distinctions between 'dynamic' and 'static' time, or between 'redeemed' and 'unredeemed' time. Without it the distinctions remain logically valid but experientially meaningless.

It is the transposition of chronological or clock time into lovers' time which is the key to the riddle of eschatological imminence, which is otherwise such a puzzle for those who wish to be loyal to the New Testament hope and yet cannot see how it can be valid in view of the time-lag of nearly two thousand years since it first gripped the minds of the early Christians. Given this transposition of time, there is no reason to discard the note of imminence, and we have no justification for making its presence in the New Testament

[1] 1 Thess. 5, 1.   [2] Rom. 4, 5.

record an excuse for discarding the whole of its eschatological outlook as an out-of-date mythology of merely academic and archæological interest to the twentieth century.

Undoubtedly liberal protestantism, until the effect of Schweitzer's work began to percolate through into Anglo-Saxon Christianity, thought that to all intents and purposes New Testament eschatology could be scrapped without injury to and indeed with positive gain for the essence of its message, which was held to be the ethical teaching of Jesus. The fact that the innate Pelagianism of the average Englishman, whether churchman or not, heartily endorsed this view and was only too ready to commit all eschatology to the limbo of an out-of-date mythology, merely shows how totally inadequate Pelagian morality is as a substitute for Augustinian love.[1] The ethical teaching of Jesus without his eschatology is as mutilated a fragment as is his teaching about love of our neighbour without its twin commandment about love of God.[2] 1 Corinthians 13 is inconceivable in the present except in the future context of 1 Corinthians 15, and 1 Corinthians 15 is just a display of intellectual fireworks about the future without its present basis in 1 Corinthians 13. What 'God hath joined together let no man put asunder'.[3]

If then we are prepared to take the eschatology of the New Testament seriously and face up to the problem caused by its delayed fulfilment, the first thing we realize is that this problem is no new problem. Even within the New Testament itself there is a re-interpretation of eschatology precisely because of the problem of its unaccountably delayed fulfilment. Almost the whole of the 'little apocalypse' of St Mark[4] is coloured by such a reinterpretative tendency. The original question of the apostles, 'Tell us, when shall these things be?'[5] may well have been answered by the final statement of certainty as to the fact and agnosticism as to the time, with which the long discourse concludes.[6] All in between, the 'little apocalypse' as it is called, may be authentic words of Jesus, but in their present setting and combination these words do not give a true impression of his meaning[7] by providing arguments for the non-appearance of the imminently expected parousia.

If this critical theory proves convincing, then the long Synoptic apocalypses[8] in their present form are a half-way house between

---

[1] Cf. J. Burnaby, *Amor Dei* (Hodder and Stoughton, 1938).
[2] Mark 12, 29 f.
[3] The Book of Common Prayer: The Form of Solemnization of Matrimony.
[4] Mark 13, 5 ff.   [5] Mark 13, 4.   [6] Mark 13, 32 ff.
[7] Cf. the increasing tendency to relate the little apocalypse to the Passion narrative, which is its immediate sequel (R. H. Lightfoot, *The Gospel Message of St Mark* (O.U.P., 1950), pp. 48 ff.).
[8] Mark 13, 1 ff.; Matt. 24, 1 ff.; Luke 21, 5 ff.

the original expectation of an imminent parousia, such as we have met with in the Thessalonian epistles, the terminus of Mark's 'little apocalypse', and the apocalypses of Q and L,[1] and the final term of New Testament eschatology which we meet with in St John's gospel.[2] That this is no arbitrary and unwarranted critical reconstruction of the textual evidence is clear from the way in which we know the prophecy of Mark 9, 1 was in fact reinterpreted.[3] So soon does the level of spiritual expectation fall from the mystical imminence of lovers' time to the calculated imminence of chronological time!

Our Lord certainly upset the eschatological time-table of Jewish expectations, and the future course of church history has upset what many Christians have regarded as his own eschatological time-table. There are two questions which this upset forces on our attention. First of all, have Christians rightly understood our Lord? Secondly, have they seriously faced the isolated disclaimer of knowledge which he is recorded to have made about precisely this point? The second is easier to clear up than the first. The conclusion of the Markan apocalypse says distinctly: 'Of that day and that hour knoweth no one, not even the angels in heaven, neither the Son, but the Father.' [4] To build an immense kenotic theory of our Lord's self-limitation of knowledge upon this completely isolated and unique piece of evidence is as unwarranted as to ignore such self-authenticating evidence on the precise point at which it is relevant. As far as the chronological date of the parousia is concerned, our Lord neither knew it nor (we may presume) was he interested in such a matter of idle curiosity. In any case, any dating is extremely dubious on the frontier of time and eternity.

On the first and more important question as to whether Christians have rightly understood our Lord's time-table at all, it would certainly appear that if there is anything in the Hebrew rejection of abstract time in favour of concrete time, deriving its meaning from its content, if there is anything in the distinction between the kairos (καίρος) of God and the chronos (χρόνος) of man, and if there is anything in the distinction between lovers' time and clock time (and if this last distinction makes sense in experiential analogy of the theological significance of the other two distinctions), then the Christian church has continually misinterpreted her Lord. He was talking of imminence in one time-scale: she has been thinking of imminence in another.

---

[1] 1 Thess. 5, 1 f.; Mark 13, 32 ff.; Luke 17, 22 ff.
[2] E.g. John 3, 17 ff.
[3] Cf. T. W. Manson, *The Teaching of Jesus* (C.U.P., 1931), pp. 277 ff.
[4] Mark 13, 32.

It is certain that the note of imminence is central to the authentic primitive Christian eschatological hope: it is certain that that note of imminence goes back to our Lord himself: it is certain that the early Christians soon found the apparent delay a problem: it is certain that they did their best to explain it. But though their arguments have been continually re-edited to meet the perplexity of every generation from the first century to the twentieth, they have never yet carried conviction except to the wishful thinking of a few pietists and fanatical enthusiasts.

How can the primitive Christian hope be retained in the face of such constant disillusionment? The most common answer to that question is to scrap the time factor altogether as being totally irrelevant to its real significance, viz. the stimulus to a moral urgency of decision which it provides. But in fact, though this may relieve intellectual tension, it does so at the cost of depriving the Christian gospel of a generator of genuine hope. It seems quite clear that the solution to the problem is not to scrap the time factor but to transpose it, not to the timeless world of abstract philosophy but to the world in which lovers live a life packed full with meaning every moment of time.

The nature of the day of the Lord, so imminently expected in both the Old Testament and the New, is determined by the indissoluble conjunction of the twin concepts of the parousia and the judgment. The millenarian sects often separate these, usually introducing the parousia as the prelude to the millennium, which will culminate in the judgment, rather than introducing the millennium as itself only the prelude to the parousia and the judgment. This bringing of the parousia forward to the beginning of the millennium proves in fact to be the generator of hope, which those who keep the parousia till the end of the millennium lack. It is incidental proof in contemporary religion of the permanent importance of the sense of imminence in all living eschatology.

Only the pre-millenarians appear to have a living, as opposed to a theoretical, hope at the centre of their eschatology. However fanatical or distorted their views may strike those who do not share their biblical fundamentalism, the significance of this basic fact should not be ignored. It not only supports the argument for the retention of the note of imminence: it also emphasizes in however extreme a manner the change-over effected by the certainty as to who the person is who will in the end appear. If this is the known Jesus, then he does not come in the end with the primary purpose of judgment. Judgment with him will be in the end what it has been all along, the inevitable corollary of his coming and not the deliberate purpose and intention of it. The surprise of the parousia is not its unlikeness from the presence, but its revelation of how little we realize the nature of him who is present.

The great church has lost the rapture of the early church: the pre-millenarian sects have recovered the rapture but without the balance of the early church.[1] The reason for the great church's apostasy is that she has fallen out of lovers' time and has retained a theoretical eschatology which is not integrated into her present experience. The result is that if Jesus is expected at all, it is only as the judge that he is expected, and in fact the judge who is expected is often no longer the authentic Jesus. The reason for the sectarian lack of balance is that so often the pre-millenarians as well as the great church have fallen out of lovers' time, and instead of basing their convictions of the imminence of the parousia upon the intuition of faith and love they have argued from reason and from calculations of 'times and seasons'.[2] Furthermore, by separating the parousia from the judgment they have ethically, if not hypostatically, divided the person of Jesus. If the great church has tended to view him in the end only as judge, the sects have tended to view him (so far as they themselves are concerned) not as judge at all.[3]

It is most important that the great church should not ignore the eschatological challenge of the sects, because their reasons for hope are often fantastic and their feverish excitement is far from the sober reality of the gospel. If their enthusiasm is forced, it is at least there. When it is so often completely absent elsewhere, this is something to which we all do well to pay heed, though we should pause before we allow ourselves to be carried away by an eschatology so suspiciously like the popular eschatology of the Old Testament, which the prophets so utterly disowned.

The prophetic tradition remains at the centre of the New Testament outlook. In the judgment there will be no pro-Israelite bias: its basis will be ethical and its scope universal. There will be no favourites and no under-privileged classes. 'It will be more tolerable for Tyre and Sidon in the judgment',[4] and even for Sodom and Gomorrah than for the chosen people themselves. Compared with the Queen of Sheba and even with Nineveh, 'the bloody city',[5] the Jews have thrown away their chances and stand irrevocably condemned.[6] In thus identifying himself with the heart of the prophetic

[1] Cf. K. E. Kirk, *The Vision of God* (Longmans, 1931), pp. 94 ff.
[2] 1 Thess. 5, 1.
[3] On fundamentalist eschatology in general and fundamentalist millenarianism in particular, cf. O. T. Allis, *Prophecy and the Church* (James Clarke, 1946); L. E. Froom, *The Prophetic Faith of our Fathers*, vols. i–iv (Review and Herald, 1950).
[4] Luke 10, 13–15 — Matt. 11, 21–23 (Q).
[5] Nahum 3, 1.   [6] Luke 11, 31 ff. = Matt. 12, 41 f. (Q).

9

protest against any reliance upon privileges or even any presumption upon God's promises, Jesus was carrying on the work of John the Baptist, who insisted that no mere reliance upon genealogy, pedigree or race would be of the slightest avail in the day of Yahweh, unless it was coupled with the ethical conduct which authenticated it.[1]

But there was in Jesus what we never read there was in John the Baptist, the anguish of heart of one who loved the people he condemned and who 'wept over'[2] Jerusalem when he approached it for the last time. Here is no Amos diagnosing evil from the outside with all the pitiless clarity of the spectator's view. Here is another and a greater Hosea implicated himself in the sin and sorrow and suffering of others, who was compelled to pass judgment upon his people and yet only did so by entering mysteriously into that judgment himself in the vicarious alchemy of the cross.

There is no getting away from this judgment: 'Many shall come from the east and the west and shall sit down with Abraham, and Isaac, and Jacob, in the kingdom of heaven: but the sons of the kingdom shall be cast forth into the outer darkness: there shall be the weeping and gnashing of teeth.'[3] Again and again Jesus in his teaching and especially in his parables[4] emphasized the same point. These parables lose their pungency if they are merely allegorized into general truths. They are first of all particular and pointed applications and interpretations of the message of our Lord's own life and ministry. As such they are the most significant support for the essential truth of realized eschatology.[5] But the fact that they reflect present realities, veiled in Jesus' presence during his lifetime, does not disprove the superficially transparently clear evidence that sometimes at least they refer to future realities, to be unveiled at his parousia. On the contrary, the clue to the future is found in the present. But a presence which does not point to a parousia is not a presence of love, nor is the judgment, which is its corollary, a judgment of love.

The verdict of judgment day, being the verdict of love, will be a surprise to all and a complete surprise to most. This is central to all strands of the earliest New Testament evidence. Everything will be, to our human understanding, completely topsy-turvy. It is impossible to exaggerate this New Testament underlining of Rosenzweig's warning to every member of the Christian church and

[1] Matt. 3, 8 ff.
[2] Luke 19, 41.
[3] Matt. 8, 11 f.
[4] Luke 14, 16 ff. (The Great Feast); Matt. 22, 1 ff.; cf. Matt. 21, 33 ff.; Mark 12, 1 ff.; Luke 20, 9 ff.
[5] Cf. C. H. Dodd, *The Parables of the Kingdom* (Nisbet, 1935).

especially to every eucharistic worshipper and communicant, 'Sir, remember the last things'.[1] There is no sound scriptural warrant for exempting the Christian church from the hazards which confronted the Jewish church. No Christian claim on the promises of Christ which is based on their unconditional form has any more validity than the Jewish claim on the promises of God, which from the time of Abraham onwards were none the less ethically conditioned for being apparently unconditional in form. God's purpose is always dependent upon faith for its fulfilment even when it takes the form of a fiat.

Judgment 'must begin at the house of God',[2] and this is as true to-day as it ever was. It is the ever-recurring apostasy of the Christian church to claim exemption from this inevitable accompaniment of all creaturely existence and by a one-sided emphasis on identity with Christ as his body to aspire to an apotheosis which must inevitably bring down the nemesis which awaits the *hybris* of any institution, however holy it may be.

To claim that the organic relationship between the church and Christ is a sufficient description of its place in the purposes of God and in his plans for society is to fly in the face of the strong Hebraic tradition of the difference at this very point between the relationship of Yahweh with his people and the relationship of the Baals with their people. It is also to fly in the face of the truth enshrined in Christian trinitarianism, for it is only at the risk of patent idolatry that the church as an extension of the incarnation can usurp the place of the Holy Spirit within the godhead. It is idle to deny the risk of this in fact happening when ecclesiology is treated simply as a part of Christology.

The surprise of the eschatological hope of the Christian church should be just the corrective which the church needs to prevent it falling into the peril of self-idolatry. It is not only in the conclusion of the Markan apocalypse and in the so-called apocalypses of Q and L [3] that the note of surprise is struck. It is in the pathetic cry, 'Lord, Lord, open to us'; [4] and if all the pathos has gone out of the passage in St Matthew,[5] that only serves to underline the stark reality, which is brought home inexorably in the Matthean eschatological parables [6] as well as in the Lukan corroboration of the Pauline imagery of the housebreaking activity of God on the day of the Lord.[7]

[1] M. Buber, *Mamre* (Melbourne U.P. and O.U.P., 1946), p. 30.
[2] 1 Pet. 4, 17.   [3] Mark 13, 32 ff.; Luke 17, 22 ff.; 21, 34 ff.
[4] Luke 13, 25.
[5] Matt. 7, 21; cf. Luke 6, 46.
[6] Matt. 25, 1 ff.; the Virgins, the Talents, the Sheep and the Goats.
[7] Luke 12, 39 f.

The pathos of Luke comes out again in the description of the irrevocability of judgment day implied in the parable of Dives and Lazarus.[1] Without turning this parable into an allegory by undue emphasis on the details of its picture, it can be seen that the conception of a 'great gulf fixed'[2] emphasizes in an almost Johannine way the present reality of a veiled judgment, which awaits the day of the Lord for its full disclosure. There is no escape from that final topsy-turvydom which is a present though hidden reality and which in the end will be made perfectly plain. This is a graphic way of presenting exactly the doctrine of the Fourth Gospel with its reiterated emphasis on the eschatological significance of the present moment.[3]

There is no warrant in the New Testament for complacent confidence that all will be well in the end for everybody and everything. Any dogmatic universalism[4] is likely to distort the clear evidence of the New Testament that love will not impose itself on anyone and that there is no limit to the evil to which in their freedom men may not choose to fall. 'In a universe of love' it may be true that there can be 'no hell for any which does not at the same time make it hell for God'. But it does not at all follow that 'God cannot endure that',[5] even though it certainly would be true that no one else can. The cross even suggests that perhaps that is just what God not only can but does endure. But be that as it may, no doctrine of love's final triumph can be true to the love whose triumph it asserts unless it leaves room for final surprise.[6] If love in the end is to be 'all and in all', that is not a dogma of logical proof, but a surprise of incredible grace.

No hope of God's final triumph is true to the New Testament which does not lay the most stringent emphasis upon the rigour of the moral and spiritual conditions, which bar the way to all easygoing reliance upon the mercy of God. The latter may indeed be free—that is the glorious gospel, which ecclesiastical timidity perpetually tends to modify and water down through fear of antinomian misinterpretation. But on the other hand it is never cheap, and the chances of self-exclusion from the kingdom of God in the last day remain for all a terrible reality. If the picture of nobody except the most resolute gate-crasher ever entering the kingdom of God may be slightly overdrawn,[7] nevertheless it remains true that the possibility of self-damnation is never removed and seldom relaxed either in the

---

[1] Luke 16, 19 ff.   [2] Luke 16, 26.   [3] E.g. John 3, 19.
[4] Cf., e.g., J. A. T. Robinson, *In the End, God*, pp. 108 ff.
[5] *Op. cit.*, p. 125   [6] *Op. cit.*, pp. 108 ff.
[7] For the picture, cf. Luke 13, 24; for the corrective, cf. Matt. 22, 11 ff. and John 10, 1.

ethical or in the eschatological teaching of our Lord. That we should not presume to judge others is the inevitable corollary which is so seldom drawn. Yet the one truth is as plain as the other, and never more clearly expressed than in the great eschatological trilogy of Matthew 25.

What is certainly true is that no one can speak about God's judgment in either the Old Testament or the New without recognizing its bias towards mercy.[1] 'The gift of a cup of cold water is just about the absolute minimum, but even the minimum counts if it is given from the right motive.'[2] There is, however, nothing in the New Testament to warrant the transference of this ground of confidence in God's free mercy for all into cheap assurance for any. To indulge in such presumption is likely to land us in a final surprise quite as unpleasant as that to which Dives eventually awoke, when he found that the Sheol he so complacently envisaged and ignored as a good Sadducee turned out to be a Gehenna no less agonizing because of the spiritual nature of the unselfish anguish involved on behalf of the rest of his family[3] than the crudest conception of penal retribution could conceive.

If, then, judgment is right in the centre of New Testament eschatology, there is in that fact no necessary advance upon Old Testament doctrine, except in so far as the New Testament emphasizes that total elimination both of vindictiveness and of sentimentality from its conception of the end, which it had been the aim of all the greatest Old Testament prophets to stress. The new element in New Testament eschatology is not bound up with the fact of judgment, however, but with the person of the judge. There is a reversal of emphasis and it is he who gives it. The judgment which his incarnation necessarily involved was the inevitable corollary of the grace and blessedness which he came to bestow. Those who refused the latter condemned themselves to the former. As it was in the incarnation so it is in the parousia, whether eucharistically or eschatologically interpreted.

The end will not reverse the entire process up to the end. It cannot, for the end has been already disclosed in Jesus Christ and no future manifestation can contradict that full disclosure. Nevertheless that disclosure will be misinterpreted either by the limited mental and spiritual understanding of the individual Christian exercising his right of private judgment upon it, or by the limited mental and spiritual understanding of the whole church, handing

---

[1] Cf. N. S. Snaith, *The Distinctive Ideas of the Old Testament* (Epworth Press, 1944), pp. 68 ff.

[2] T. W. Manson, *The Teaching of Jesus*, pp. 271 f.

[3] Luke 16, 27 f.

down its traditional interpretation of it, unless both individual and corporate understanding recognize the limits of their competence.

However right the individual judgment and however sacrosanct the corporate tradition, neither can presume to claim such full understanding of the self-disclosure of love (not even with the guidance of the Holy Spirit of love himself) as would preclude the possibility of any real surprise in the future as to the meaning of love. For to do that would neither be true to private judgment nor be loyal to corporate tradition, for it would deny to both any deep insight into the essential nature of the reality disclosed to them. If this reality is love, then full present understanding of it is only compatible with awareness of unlimited future revelations or discoveries of it. It is in fact no longer a thing which may be defined in propositional terms, but a person, who can only be indicated by apostolic witness. Confidence in the fullness of the revelation of God in Jesus Christ in his incarnation and atonement does not rule out the possibility of further revelation of his significance at Pentecost and the parousia. On the contrary it demands it, precisely because it is a revelation of love. Each individual and each generation is therefore judged by no arbitrary standard of reference, but by its response to the contemporary manifestation of God.[1] It is therefore of the utmost importance that the manner of his contemporary manifestation should be understood biblically as occurring in event and its interpretation, rather than in proposition and its acceptance. It is in the events of each day which we do not choose rather than in the speculative idea or the meditative object of our choosing or of our seeking that we are kept alive to the surprises of the self-disclosures of love and by our response to them decide our destiny.

But these events of each day are fraught with all the implications of the past and pregnant with all the possibilities of the future. They are in the present, but they are not confined to the present. It is through them that the impact of the past reaches us in all its contemporary significance. It is through them too that the possibilities of the future dawn upon us with all their load of fear or buoyancy of hope. It is through them, however mediated (as it generally is) or unmediated (as it occasionally may be), that the revelation of Jesus Christ comes home with saving significance to us or is rejected with damning implications by us.

The means of grace may be word, sacrament or silence, book, dogma or rite, an agelong tradition or an immediate illumination. But the Jesus of history is no self-disclosure of God to anyone unless he steps up out of the long ago and through the testimony of a heard

[1] Matt. 12, 41 f. = Luke 11, 31 f.

voice or a seen sight makes his claims upon us. How he does this does not matter: that he does it matters more than anything else in the world. To make rules as to how he has to do it is idolatry: to deny that he does it is apostasy. For love is the meaning of life, which we may glimpse in a momentary awareness or decision of consciousness, or in a prolonged process of which we are quite unconscious. It may come in a flash of intuition with a sense of undeniable givenness or in the gradual process of study and meditation, all too easily referred to our own effort and not to the prevenient grace of God, because his love does not advertise what it does or seek to get the credit for it.

To refuse to see the meaning of life in the events which confront us every day of life, or to refuse to respond to that meaning and to live by the implications of it, is the fatal possibility which is never far from the glorious prospect which responsible acceptance opens up. In this way is set before the community as well as before the individual the stark alternatives of 'life and death, the blessing and the curse'.[1] And thus the last day is but the final term of the present significance of every day, involving both the certainty and the surprise of every rendezvous with love.

For the whole New Testament church this last day had dawned in the coming of Jesus Christ. To confess that Jesus was the Christ meant precisely this. Whether he is thought of individually in the loneliness of his isolation as at least in his total dereliction on the cross the sole representative on earth of the true Israel of God, or whether he is conceived corporately as being himself involved in the conduct and behaviour of every member of his body, the church, does not matter. In either case he is the touchstone of judgment for all men, and often the most apparently individual conversion is effected through the most completely corporate means, as in the case of the corporate significance of the converting words which St Paul could never forget: 'Saul, Saul, why persecutest thou me?'[2] In either case 'the lot of the individual on the great day depends strictly on his attitude to Jesus in the intervening period'.[3] And there is nothing arbitrary about such a judgment, for it is no unknown and unattainable perfection with which we are confronted, but the known perfection of the 'man, Christ Jesus',[4] however he is manifested to us.

The closeness of the relationship of Christ with those who are his [5]

[1] Deut. 30, 19.   [2] Acts 9, 4.
[3] T. W. Manson, *op. cit.*, p. 263.   [4] 1 Tim. 2, 5.
[5] T. W. Manson, *op. cit.*, p. 269 n., where it is suggested that the 'son of man' in the gospels should be equated with 'the man from heaven', and so with Christ the first-fruits plus those that are Christ's, and so again with Christ the first-born plus many brethren, and so finally with Christ the head plus the members of his body.

brings the Synoptic doctrine into the closest possible relation with the Pauline, and the great cry which converted St Paul [1] provides the most vivid commentary both upon the ethical 'Inasmuch' [2] of Matthew 25 and also upon the eschatological understanding of the parousia as meaning the coming not of Christ alone, but of Christ with all the saints who have died before his coming again. [3]

If the heart of the eschatological gospel of the New Testament is that the end has come in Jesus Christ, so that our response to him is the criterion of our standing in the judgment, then it is important that the significance of the continuation of history after his coming should not be written down in the interests of realized eschatology, but should rather be written up in the interests of a true understanding of eschatology. In this connection the New Testament use not only of harvesting metaphors like 'firstfruits' [4] but also of commercial metaphors like 'earnest', [5] or first instalment, to express the secret of the eschatological truth of the gospel is most significant.

In so far as we have in Christ Jesus no mere anticipation of the end, but a first instalment of it, then that first instalment is no mere preliminary to a series of other equal instalments, as if the whole were like the price of something obtained on a hire purchase agreement, a thing which could be divided up and given piecemeal. It is a first instalment which is full and final and yet, because its nature is love, does not thereby rule out the possibility of further instalments, but on the contrary necessarily involves them. Understood in any other terms than those of love, the finality of the first coming of Jesus Christ and the fullness of his revelation of God must rule out the possibility of any further coming, whether at Pentecost or the parousia. But understood in terms of love, the exact reverse is true. The fullness and finality of love does not preclude further manifestations: on the contrary, because it is love it necessitates them.

It is because the first coming is interpreted in terms other than those of love that either it is regarded as final in the sense that no

---

[1] Acts 9, 4.   [2] Matt. 25, 40.

[3] 1 Thess. 4, 14, on which cf. W. Neil, *The Epistles of Paul to the Thessalonians* (Hodder and Stoughton, 1950): 'The Thessalonians were not principally in doubt about the resurrection of their dead, so much as about their share in the Parousia. Paul does not say, as we might expect, God will "raise up" (2 Cor. 4, 14). That is passed over, taken as a matter of course, and the word used, "will bring" (with Him), points to the Thessalonians' real problem. The resurrection of the dead is taken for granted as a prelude to the Second Advent' (p. 95).

[4] Rom. 8, 23; 1 Cor. 15, 20, 23.

[5] 2 Cor. 1, 22; 5, 5; Eph. 1, 14.

further coming can be expected [1] or else it is not thought of as final at all, in which case the essence of the once-for-all 'scandal of particularity',[2] which is at the heart of the Christian gospel, is lost. If, however, the category of love is allowed its full weight for the interpretation of Christian eschatology, then present presence by no means rules out future parousia: on the contrary it necessitates it. Judgment is now in veiled reality what it will be one day in unveiled reality, a present fact dependent for its issue upon no hypothetical future assize or trial but upon actual response in the present to the claims of Christ and of his church, however consciously or unconsciously mediated to us every day of our lives.

Our Lord constantly stressed this point, 'Whosoever shall be ashamed of me and of my words . . . the Son of man also shall be ashamed of him, when he cometh in the glory of his Father with the holy angels'; [3] and again, 'Whosoever shall give you a cup of water to drink because ye are Christ's, verily I say unto you, he shall in no wise lose his reward'.[4] This close identification of Jesus Christ as judge with his brethren, who are inseparable from him, leads to the daring promise that they will in the end share in that judgment, and the tragedy of the ecclesiastical misinterpretation of this fact should not blind us to its dominical guarantee: 'Verily, verily, I say unto you, that ye which have followed me, in the regeneration when the Son of man shall sit on the throne of his glory, ye also shall sit upon twelve thrones judging the twelve tribes of Israel.' [5] Something of the same meaning is implied by the Pauline conception of the parousia involving the manifestation not only of Jesus but also of the saints with him.[6] There can now be no revelation of the one without the others.

Where biblical eschatology has been taken seriously, the note of judgment has never been far from the centre of the panorama of the end. But its centrality in the Synoptic gospels takes on a very different look from the one-sided grimness with which much of the Old Testament in a bracing way and much of church history in either a morbid or a complacent manner have invested it. In the Synoptic gospels it is the reverse side of the thrilling joy and tingling hope with which the expectation of the end is again and again characterized

[1] Except, of course, out of loyalty to Christian tradition, the coming of the Holy Spirit, as if he was so distinct from Jesus Christ as not to be effectively related to him at all. He is in fact the *alter ego* of Jesus, never to be separated by us from Christ and yet never to be identified with him; cf. the definition of the Council of Chalcedon, A.D. 451, on the two natures of Christ (J. E. Fison, *op. cit.*, p. 137).

[2] G. K. A. Bell and A. Deissmann, ed., *Mysterium Christi* (Longmans, 1930), pp. 31 ff.

[3] Mark 8, 38; cf. Luke 12, 8 f. and Matt. 10, 32 f.   [4] Mark 9, 41.

[5] Matt. 19, 28; cf. Luke 22, 30.   [6] 1 Thess. 4, 14.

by our Lord. The second of the three great theological virtues, which alone abide [1] not only up to the very end but in the very end as well, is not fear (as some interpretations of Christianity seem to imagine) but hope. And hope everywhere,[2] and especially in the Synoptic gospels, has a future reference, which cannot possibly be brought within the compass of a present fully realized eschatology. We have already seen that what the Lord's Prayer expresses in the hope, 'Thy kingdom come',[3] the early church expresses in the ejaculation, 'Maran atha'.[4] It is not the neuter *eschaton* (ἔσχατον) or end, but the masculine eschatological man, *ho eschatos Adam* (ὁ ἔσχατος Ἀδάμ),[5] or better still, the personal coming one, *ho erchomenos* (ὁ ἐρχόμενος),[6] who is as much the focus of the expectation in the minds of the first Christians as he had been of the little group of pious folk who were looking forward to his coming before the incarnation.[7] Judgment is not viewed in the true New Testament perspective unless it is kept in its right place as the subordinate corollary to this.

We are apt to-day to recognize the practical identity of the coming of Jesus in the past with the coming of the kingdom of God, but we are strangely loath to commit ourselves to a similar identity in the future. Yet there is no getting away from the latter if we accept the former. In Jesus was the *autobasileia* (αὐτοβασιλεία), the ideal of *basileia* (βασιλεία) as Origen expressed it, or, as St John Chrysostom put it in still more authentically Christian terminology, Jesus was himself *autobasileus* (αὐτοβασιλεύς), a very king.[8] No other expression so adequately explains either the Synoptic facts or the conviction of the disciples that Jesus was the Messiah or the startling change in theological vocabulary between the Synoptic gospels and the Pauline epistles.

In the gospels the subject of the preaching is the kingdom of God; in the epistles it is 'Jesus Christ and him crucified',[9] and the Acts of the Apostles shows the transition from the one to the other. For the early church Jesus Christ himself was the clue to the significance of the kingdom of God. He preached what he practised and he practised what he preached. He was the revelation of the meaning of the kingdom of God. In using the term, the kingdom of God, he gave new content and new significance to words the meaning of which

---

[1] 1 Cor. 13, 13.
[2] Including the Epistle to the Hebrews; cf. W. Robinson, *The Eschatology of the Epistle to the Hebrews* (Overdale College, Selly Oak, Birmingham, 1950).
[3] Matt. 6, 10.   [4] 1 Cor. 16, 22.   [5] 1 Cor. 15, 45.
[6] Luke 7, 19.   [7] Luke 2, 38; 3, 15.
[8] Cf. H. G. Liddell and R. Scott, *A Greek-English Lexicon* (O.U.P.), s.v.
[9] 1 Cor. 2, 2.

everyone took for granted they knew until he came on the scene. No word sounded the same on his lips as it did on anyone elses's.[1]

The nearest the apostles could get to the meaning he conveyed by using the term, the kingdom of God, was to speak of him. He said everything depended on right relationship to the kingdom of God. They said it depended on right relationship to Jesus Christ. The change of vocabulary was essential to secure the identity of meaning. Verbal idolatry would have been fatal to the truth, as P. T. Forsyth clearly realized at a time when liberalism was seeking to drive a wedge between Jesus and the apostles in general and between Jesus and St Paul in particular.

> The gospel of Christ replaced the gospel of the Kingdom because by his death he became the Kingdom, because he became all that the Kingdom contained. . . . The Kingdom was great with Him. The gospel of the Kingdom was Christ in essence: Christ was the gospel of the Kingdom in power. The Kingdom was Christ in a mystery: Christ was the publication and the establishment of the Kingdom. . . . He was the truth of his own greatest gospel. It is wherever he is. To have him is to ensure it.[2]

But if this be so, if the kingdom of God has come in Jesus Christ and if, being love, that first coming is not only not incompatible with, but on the contrary bound up with future comings right up till the end at the parousia, then we can understand the dramatic change from timid fear to joyful hope which so markedly contrasts the main eschatological emphasis of the New Testament from the main prophetic emphasis of the Old. The prophets had to destroy the popular hope (which exempted the Jews from all the perils of doomsday), and ridiculed all such non-moral racial or national or ecclesiastical pretensions. And from the hope that they were able to offer they could not with all their present knowledge of God remove the fear of facing the unknown. But that is just what the New Testament does, for it presents us at the end not with the unknown, but with the known; not with the terrors of the infinite, but with the infinite and inescapable love of God manifested in Jesus Christ himself. In fact it is not afraid to transform doomsday into a wedding day.[3]

When every effort has been made to read out of the parables of Jesus any reference to his second coming in order to read into them a vivid relevance to his first coming, the fact remains that if they have

---

[1] Cf. C. A. A. Scott, *Living Issues in the New Testament* (C.U.P., 1933), p. 192; 'Jesus enhances every title that is given to him', quoting D. M. Macintyre.

[2] P. T. Forsyth, *The Person and Place of Jesus Christ* (Hodder and Stoughton, 1909), p. 122; not to be dismissed as 'fireworks in a fog' (Silvester Horne).

[3] Matt. 22, 1 ff.; Eph. 5, 27; Rev. 19, 7; 21, 2.

any such relevance at any time they will have a similar relevance at all times. Of course if the parousia is imagined as something entirely unrelated to the presence, then parables which have relevance to the presence have probably nothing to do with the parousia. But if presence and parousia are integrally connected, then the evidence in favour of applying the teaching of any parable to the situation arising out of the presence supports its application to the circumstances attending the parousia. To refer a parable merely to the parousia is almost certainly to allegorize it and make it into a trivial item of advance information calculated to whet the curiosity of the cranks. It is great gain that realized eschatology has redeemed many parables from this debased interpretation of their meaning. But it is an even greater loss when that same eschatology goes on to deny any future relevance because it is aware of present significance.[1]

It is both for the present and for the future that again and again the parables of our Lord create the atmosphere of tingling and expectant hope.[2] And even if this atmosphere has for its bracing corollary the peril of being caught unawares by the moment of decision, owing to the whole tenor of life up to that moment,[3] nevertheless it is the atmosphere of spring and not of autumn which pervades the whole New Testament from beginning to end, and which makes nonsense of the travesty of morbid and self-regarding introspection which has dogged the path of Christian holiness all down the history of the church. It is with tingling hope that the New Testament reflects the authentic primitive expectation of the church, and this hope finds its dominical sanction not in explicit definition of its ground and object but in the clearest possible inculcation of its spirit. The fact that the resurrection appearances of our Lord intensified the hope still more than any words of his could have done,[4] and the fact that Pentecost intensified it still more, is no disproof of its irrelevance at the very end. On the contrary, the vivid expectation with which at every eucharist at least the church transposed the focus of the words of the Lord's prayer, 'Thy Kingdom come',[5] into the expectation of the personal coming of the Lord himself, 'Maran atha',[6] is conclusive evidence of the attitude of the first Christians towards

---

[1] Cf. T. F. Glasson, *The Second Advent* (Epworth Press, 1945), pp. 89 ff.

[2] E.g. the Hid Treasure (Matt. 13, 44), the Good Pearl (Matt. 13, 45 f.), the Seed Growing Secretly (Mark 4, 26 ff.), the Leaven (Matt. 13, 33 = Luke 13, 20 f.), the Lost Sheep (Luke 15, 4 ff.), the Lost Coin (Luke 15, 8 ff.), as well as the more specific, the Servants Watching (Luke 12, 35 ff.), the Virgins (Matt. 25, 1 ff.), the Talents (Matt. 25, 14 ff.).

[3] E.g. the Wicked Husbandmen (Mark 12, 1·ff.; cf. Luke 20, 9 ff. and Matt. 21, 33 ff.), the Pounds (Luke 19, 12 ff.) and the Fig Tree (Mark 13, 28 f.; cf. Luke 21, 29 ff. and Matt. 24, 32 f.).

[4] Cf. 1 Pet. 1 ,3; 5, 4.   [5] Matt. 6, 10.   [6] 1 Cor. 16, 22.

the eschatological parousia, without which their present hopes were left entirely 'in the air'.

If in fact they went to the eucharist every Sunday in dread of the damnation of the presence, then the terrors of *Dies iræ, dies illa* might legitimately be given the centre of the stage at the parousia. But nothing could be imagined more untrue to the spirit of joyful eucharistic worship. In thankfulness for what they had been given the early Christians went to worship their Lord and to offer themselves to him in joyful expectation of what they would be given. And their hopes were fulfilled beyond all their expectations, so that the downright magic of the miracle of transubstantiation far more accurately describes the reality of Christian worship than any timid calculation of a *quid pro quo*.

In fact, what happens at the eucharist can no more be defined than what happens at the parousia. The reality is undeniable even if any definition is inconceivable. This is as it must be if that reality is love. To speak either of the presence or of the coming of love is to speak of something which it is impossible to prove, but to which it is vital to bear witness. As to its significance, whether St John the Divine was 'in the spirit'[1] on the first day of the week or on the first day of the new order ushered in by Christ's coming, whether in fact 'the Lord's day'[1] is to be interpreted primarily in terms of the eucharistic presence or of the eschatological parousia, can anyone for an instant imagine that that day was one of gloom and terror and not of joy and gladness? The hope of the day of the Lord is for Christians born of the hope of every Lord's day. To come to the table of the Lord with fear and trembling is one thing: to turn the day of the Lord into a day of gloom is quite another.

It is the joy, the assurance, the balanced rapture, the hope, the expectation and the confident 'boldness'[2] of the first Christians, without a trace of egotistical self-assertion, which is the hall-mark of the record of the Acts of the Apostles and of all the apostolic literature we possess. The apostles, who of all people are most aware of the wonders of the past,[3] are looking forward and their eyes are on the future. It is precisely this forward look that the Christian church has by comparison with them so conspicuously lost. This is not something born of some imagined reality at present unknown: it is born of an experienced reality at present known, however dimly. It is not born of the expectation of judgment day, though judgment is its inevitable corollary. It is not born of the prospect of an ultimate arrival at a state of bliss, whether in this world or the next, whether in some corporate utopia or some individual beatific

[1] Rev. 1, 10.   [2] Acts 4, 13.   [3] E.g. 1 John 1, 1 ff.

vision (if such an individual beatific vision is not in itself a contradiction in terms). It is born of the resurrection of Jesus Christ from the dead [1] and of the awareness of having been surprised by grace and overwhelmed by love beyond all possible expectations or desert.

It is out of the present wonder of such an awe-inspiring revelation of the depths of sacrificial love that the Christian soul and the Christian church as well look for the day when the immensity of the reality, which overwhelms them and of which the more they know the less they feel they know, will dawn upon the saints of God. Except in some such concept as the parousia, how can the future be regarded by those for whom the divine initiative, prevenient grace and the forgiveness of sins are a present reality?

To see the eschatological parousia in this way is no more to claim for it unmistakable and fool-proof dominical definition than for its corollary, the eucharistic presence. The New Testament evidence suggests that Jesus was as reticent of definition in the one case as he was in the other. It is the merit of Dr. T. F. Glasson's otherwise unsatisfactory treatment of New Testament eschatology [2] that he has raised in an acute way the problem as to how far our Lord actually prophesied his own second coming and was himself responsible for making it the eschatological focus of the hope of the Christian church. His argument is that the whole concept of a future parousia or second coming finds no place either in pre-Christian Jewish eschatology or in the Synoptic eschatology in its earliest form. He thinks it was later written into the Synoptic record out of the living expectation of the whole primitive church, which whether in Rome, Macedonia, Asia Minor or Palestine was by A.D. 50 quite obsessed with the idea. His suggestion is that the explanation of how this all came about is on the whole (apart from the part played by Caligula's attempt to set up his image in the Jerusalem Temple in A.D. 40) [3] to be found in the Christian adoption of the word used by the Septuagint to translate the Hebrew name of God, Yahweh, to describe Jesus himself. He is now *ho kurios* (ὁ κύριος), the Lord; and this meant that all the prophecies about 'the Lord' which he had not fulfilled in his first coming were transferred by the early church to his second coming, on the accepted principle that being in scripture they must be fulfilled.

In so far as objective definitions of the manner of the parousia are concerned, and in so far as the use of the actual Greek word, parousia (παρουσία), itself is concerned, there is no doubt that Dr. Glasson is right. These have no place in the earliest Synoptic

---

[1] 1 Pet. 1, 3.   [2] T. F. Glasson, *op. cit.*   [3] *Ibid.*, pp. 180 ff.

tradition of our Lord's teaching. But in so far as the reality of the eschatological hope of the early church is concerned, apart from the nature of its objective grounds, any attempt to eliminate from our Lord's own authentic parabolic teaching and from the conclusion of the apocalypses both of Mark, Q and L [1] the note of vivid, if un-defined, expectation is quite unwarranted, and any attempt to make its permanent validity for the church a matter of trivial significance is quite unjustified.

Unless some such vivid expectation of future hope in a person rather than in a thing, rooted in a present loving relationship with that person, is realized as central to the primitive gospel and grounded in the teaching of Jesus himself, the reverse side of the picture, a grim panorama of judgment, is bound to dominate the future horizon for sensitive consciences. It will be the more deadly in its numbing effects in proportion to the emphasis laid upon the relatively impersonal associations of its traditional setting in a law court or on a battlefield. There is still in the New Testament a strand of eschatology which speaks in such images. But the images, except perhaps in the Book of Revelation, are on the whole subordinated to the person of Jesus Christ himself and kept in their right place by reference to his actual historical life and teaching. And if the note of judgment is still there, as it undoubtedly is, it is only the reverse side of the Advent hope, which dominates the earliest Synoptic tradition.

The fact that Jesus himself did not define the grounds of this hope in so many words with the fool-proof clarity of later, even apostolic, writers is no disproof of the hope but a suggestive reminder that the secrets of love are neither in the present nor in the future to be found in objective or subjective definitions of what it is or how it works. They are only revealed or, as we say, 'given away' in that indefinable meeting ground between person and person which is the field of real human freedom and responsibility. To-day even if we venture on that 'holy ground' [2] we are blind to its full implications, privileges and responsibilities: but one day we shall no longer be blind. To-day its responsibilities, if we are aware of them at all, seem to us limited and we think we can dodge them: one day its unlimited responsibilities will be inescapable and we shall not be able to dodge them.

The dawning of that day will reveal the total range of the possi-bility of life lived in real I-Thou relationship not only between man and man, but also between man and God and between man and nature too. Then perhaps the whole hierarchic structure of the

[1] Mark 13, 32 ff. ; Luke 17, 22 ff. ; 21, 5 ff.   [2] Exod. 3, 5.

universe will open up an entirely new dimension of living, as in emancipation from the top-heavy mediæval universe and the bottom-heavy modern universe we realize something of the symmetry of love.[1] Certainly the new dimension of living of which we shall then have vision and to which we shall then have access will have both community significance and cosmic range and will by no means be limited to any individualistic rendezvous of the soul with its Beloved. On the other hand it may well be that it is the magic of that final lovers' meeting, more vividly visualized in terms of the future of the individual soul than of the community as a whole, which is the secret of the transformation of all else and the secret of the synthesis of the rival eschatologies of the soul beyond history and of the community in history. *Via* the parousia, presupposing the resurrection of the body, the summing up of all things in Christ becomes a Christian conceivability. Without the parousia and the resurrection it is Christianly inconceivable; and the trouble is that it is so often proclaimed as the climax of Christian eschatology without the two things which alone make it for a Christian a tenable doctrine.

That is the reason why the eschatology of the rest of the New Testament needs so badly to be interpreted and checked in the light of the Synoptic gospels. It is when the organic continuity of the unbroken purpose of God, leading via the Logos to the church as the body of Christ and so to the consummation of all things in him, is taken without reference to the Synoptic evidence that it becomes dangerously misleading and threatens to eliminate all genuine eschatology from its interpretation of the working out of the purpose of God in history. For, as with so many other aspects both of doctrine and of ethics, we do not have to go outside the New Testament itself to find ample evidence of a failure to grasp or at least to interpret the essential newness of the teaching of Christ and of the Christian gospel.

The consequence of such a failure is very serious, whether it results in an arrested development, which fails to push on towards a true understanding of Christ's message, or in an archaic reversion to a pre-Christian understanding of it. And at no point of doctrine is this failure more likely to be marked than in eschatology, which is always the last part of any theological system to be radically affected by any new revelation or reformation. Indeed the eschatological outlook of the Book of Revelation and of the non-Pauline epistles of the New Testament shows little advance upon pre-Christian conceptions of the end except for the all-important

[1] Cf. D. E. Harding, 'Are Angels Superfluous?' (*Theology*, S.P.C.K., March 1952), vol. lv, pp. 97 ff.

certainty of Jesus as the Messiah. But this conviction which should have recast the whole conception of the day of Yahweh is itself in danger of being submerged beneath the mass of Old Testament imagery which surrounds it in the Book of Revelation. Indeed Jesus himself is in danger of ceasing to bear any resemblance in the eschatological panorama to the only Jesus who ever actually lived on earth.

Outside the Pauline epistles the only New Testament letter to attempt any further drawing out of the eschatological significance of the Christian gospel is 1 Peter. However the harrowing of hell is interpreted, there is here [1] a definite attempt to replace an eschatology based on a mechanically rigid scheme whether of logic or chronology by an eschatology ethically conditioned by the necessity to provide room at some time or other in this life or the next for the preaching of the gospel to everyone.[2] This allows opportunity for ethical progress and is a possible, if not a necessary, interpretation of the Synoptic outlook.

Apart from 1 Peter, it is left to the Pauline epistles in gradual stages of progressively deepening understanding of the eschatological implications of the gospel and to the Johannine literature in one supreme and final corrective reinterpretation of the whole life and teaching of our Lord to give in regard to the doctrine of the future hope, as in regard to so many other things, the evidence of the power of the Holy Spirit to lead the thinkers about and the lovers of our Lord into a deeper understanding of his significance. It was the work of St Paul and St John to reform Jewish theology and make it Christian, and if it is an exaggeration to say that they achieved their object without quoting from anyone, it is an exaggeration which is pardonable, for though their creative work owes all its inspiration to the events of the Synoptic gospels and to their interpretation of them, it is achieved with a freedom and independence of the Synoptic tradition, which is as daring and courageous as anything in the history of the development of theological thought anywhere, whether inside the Christian religion or outside it.

The dynamic reformulation of theology which we owe to St Paul and St John is not an attempt to improve on the Synoptic doctrine any more than their ethical teaching is an attempt to improve upon the holiness of Jesus. It is an attempt to draw out the ultimate implications of that doctrine in the light of the tremendous events of the death, burial, resurrection and ascension of Jesus Christ and the coming of the Holy Spirit which were the sequel to it. It is these events which colour the Synoptic evidence as those who lived after them looked back through them at the life of Jesus and saw his

---

[1] 1 Pet. 3, 19 ff.; 4, 5 f.   [2] Cf. Matt. 24, 14.

10

teaching in the light of them. This is as true of his eschatological teaching as of his ethical.

It is a mistake to view the Pauline and the Johannine development of eschatology as a process involving the gradual replacement of a temporal future hope by a timeless present reality. That would be to deny any ultimate reality at all to time, which no one who believes that God the Son was manifested in time and lived in time can possibly do. The development is along other lines: it aims at correcting a futurism conceived solely in terms of calendar and chronological time by a mysticism which in the relative reality of time enters into the absolute reality of eternity. The true contrast is not between time and eternity, understood as contrasting opposites, but between time as it is ordinarily understood at least outside the Hebraic tradition and time as it is at least partially understood by those who are in love and as it opens up its new significance of 'eternal life' to those who are 'in Christ'. What St Paul is getting at in his mystical understanding of being 'in Christ', St John is getting at from another angle in his mystical understanding of 'eternal life'. Neither is speaking about a trance-like timelessness: each is trying to express a reality in which time is packed with the significance of eternity.

To see the Pauline and Johannine achievements in perspective it is important to reckon with the Book of Revelation. This may be an isolated exception to the general trend of New Testament eschatological development, as we now know it, but it is likely to be a significant illustration of a general attitude much more common in the primitive church than the daring reconstructions of St Paul and St John. To us, coming at the end of the New Testament and as the last book of the Bible, it may look like a throw-back to Judaism. In the church in which it originated it may have looked much more like a logical development of Judaism, introducing the name of Jesus indeed, but otherwise leaving its eschatological outlook largely untouched.

Perhaps it is true to say that if the Book of Revelation is taken as a book like other books, then it is a throw-back and a reversion to Judaism. But Revelation is not a book like other books: it is not even a book like other New Testament books. It is a book of symbols and images, taken from dreams and visions. They are not meant to be interpreted in logical sequence as if they referred to a series of different events, but they are intended to give by their very repetition an impressive weight of cumulative evidence about a few constant basic realities. Like Jung's archetypes,[1] the images of Revelation are likely therefore to be archaic. But even so, they

---

[1] J. Jacobi, *The Psychology of C. G. Jung*, E.T. (Kegan Paul, 1942), pp. 41 ff.

are evidence that at the deeper levels of unconscious thought the
new eschatology of Jesus himself with its fascinating symbol of the
little lamb [1] was battling against the old eschatology of the Jews
with its tremendous symbols of Har-Magedon [2] and Gog and Magog.[3]
The new eschatology had not yet worked through the superficial levels
of the mind to effect a complete penetration of the hinterland of
the subconscious and unconscious levels of the thinking of Christian
and even apostolic men.

It should not surprise us that it took longer than one generation
for Jesus' own deep reorientation of both the manner and the
matter of eschatology to sink into the depths of the souls of
his disciples. Even before that reorientation of eschatology was
effected there were two processes at work in the church, the one a
progressive and continuous reformulation of doctrine under the
guidance of the Holy Spirit, and the other a retrograde and reactionary reversal to pre-Christian Judaism, if not in matter at
least in manner. This latter process led to a spirit of controversy
in some of the patristic Christian writers which was often much more
akin to their Talmudic Jewish contemporaries than to their apostolic
Christian predecessors.[4] Such a spirit certainly finds expression in the
Book of Revelation, in which the present and invisible operations of
the parousia-judgment in the letters to the seven churches of Asia [5]
rapidly give place to an eschatological outlook which is in many
respects far more Jewish than it is Christian. All the reticence and
reserve of Jesus himself have completely disappeared. The coming
in the clouds [6] means reaping with the sickle [7] and treading the
winepress of wrath.[8] 'The great day of God, the Almighty',[9] will
involve the destruction of Antichrist at Megiddo [10] amid terrible
slaughter, ending with the consignment of all remaining opposition
to God to 'the lake of fire' for total destruction.[11] This great blood
and thunder panorama draws upon all the conventional apocalyptic
imagery to describe the details of the eschatological drama, war,
pestilence, famine and the break-up of society itself.[12] There is no
question of the grandeur and magnificence of the canvas which the

---

[1] arnion (ἀρνίον), twenty-eight times in Revelation and only once (John 21, 15)
elsewhere in the New Testament.

[2] Rev. 16, 16.   [3] Rev. 20, 8.

[4] A parallel which is not entirely to the discredit of the Fathers, for if 'the Jew was
able to maintain his identity in the course of the long centuries to come under conditions such as no other people has ever been able to surmount, it is to his Talmud,
above all, that the credit is due' (C. Roth, *A Short History of the Jewish People* (East
and West Library, 1943), pp. 131 f.). In any case the fair parallel is between the
Talmudists and the Fathers rather than between the Talmudists and the Apostles.

[5] Rev. 2, 5; 2, 16; 2, 22 f.; 3, 3, 20.   [6] Rev. 14, 14.
[7] Rev. 14, 14 ff.   [8] Rev. 14, 17 ff.; 19, 18.   [9] Rev. 16, 14.
[10] Rev. 16, 16.   [11] Rev. 19, 17 ff.   [12] Rev. 18, 14 ff.

author has painted, and its abiding appeal and significance is as
apparent in Michelangelo's 'Last Judgment' as in Julia Ward Howe's
' Battle Hymn of the Republic '.

Despite the marvellous depth and beauty of the image of the little
lamb and the at times almost lyrical acclamation of him,[1] there is
no doubt that the Book of Revelation by itself alone would have given
a distorted picture of the true development of Christian eschatology.
'The song of Moses' too often gets the better of 'the song of the
Lamb',[2] and even when the symbolism of the battlefield gives place
to the more rational picture of the great assize,[3] there is a twist from
the essential Christian outlook, as it was being developed by St Paul
and St John. The Gentiles are certainly allowed into the new order
that awaits the righteous on the yonder side of resurrection, parousia
and judgment, but it is a Jewish new order to which they are admitted.
It is the Old Testament day of the Lord, with all its paraphernalia of
books [4] and the second death and fire,[5] and with the Messiah, as
Jesus revealed him, relegated to a comparatively insignificant place
in the essential theodicy of God.[6]

As far as the development of Christian eschatology is concerned,
the one element in it which we owe particularly to the Book of
Revelation is the doctrine of the millennium.[7] This deserves to
be taken much more seriously as a symbol than it usually is, and
it ought not to be dismissed because of the ludicrous fantasies of
chiliastic literalists. It is completely misleading even as a symbol
unless it is closely related to the parousia and seen as its sequel and
not as its prelude. But as such it links up with other hints [8] of a two-
stage eschatology in which the purpose of God is achieved by means
of a preliminary kingdom of Christ, which is the prelude to the
ultimate kingdom of God. It is an attempt to safeguard the double
element of both *telos* ($\tau\acute{\epsilon}\lambda o\varsigma$) and *finis*, which is essential to any
truly Christian eschatology.[9] It reinforces the doctrine of the
parousia in its refusal to abandon hope for this world under the pre-
text of securing it in the next. Admittedly, apart from the parousia
the millennium enshrines a forced optimism about the future which
has no basis in the present, and as such it may well be a fanciful
psychological compensation for a real defeatism. But as the sequel, if
not as the prelude to the parousia, it can be integrated into a coherent
Christian eschatology, and is a valuable corrective to merely individualistic and otherworldly interpretations of the Christian hope.

[1] Rev. 5, 9; 14, 3; 15, 3.   [2] Rev. 15, 3.   [3] Rev. 20, 12.
[4] Rev. 20, 12.   [5] Rev. 20, 14; 21, 8.   [6] Rev. 6, 16 f.; 22, 12.
[7] Rev. 20, 2 ff.   [8] Matt. 13, 41, 43; 25, 34; 1 Cor. 15, 23 f.
[9] Cf. R. Niebuhr, *The Nature and Destiny of Man* (Nisbet, 1943), vol. ii, pp. 297 ff.

However it is not the millennium but the parousia which is the key to that hope, if we are to see it in its true New Testament perspective. An eschatology which concentrates hope upon another kind of existence in another kind of world is apt to leave this world without any final significance in the purpose of God and its history without any real *telos* at all. On the other hand, an eschatology which focuses hope upon a continuation of the same sort of existence in the same sort of world as we now know will in all probability provide no effective *finis* to the course of this world's history at all, and will make any doctrine of the resurrection of the body so crudely materialistic as to be quite untenable.

It is the parousia which links this world to the next, not by the emergence of this into that after the manner of a gradual evolutionary development, nor by the swallowing up of this in that after the pattern of the soul's mystical absorption in the divine.[1] It links it by the coming of that world to this, and out of the meeting of the two opens up on an infinitely wider scale the same sort of possibilities of newness of life which in ordinary human experience we know result so creatively from personal meetings, interviews, conversations and intercourse.

It offers a future beyond this life for the individual soul and a future beyond history, as we know it, for the corporate whole, which is by no means limited to humanity in its cosmic scope. This future is not attained by any magical transformation or transubstantiation of what is, but by such a meeting as will involve all that in this world is capable of entering in any way into the secrets of the next in such a meeting with Jesus Christ, who in himself sums up and embodies all those secrets, as will offer out of the meeting a new beginning beyond all present comprehension whatever.

As to what this means, perhaps the best we can say is that it is something analogous to, but infinitely transcending, the marvellous and the miraculous, but not the magical new dimension that from time to time opens up, whether of truth out of a genuine dialogue or conversation between two minds, or of beauty between an artist and something he sees, or of goodness between one soul and another or between a soul and God. It is the secret of natural physical birth; it is the secret of spiritual rebirth; [2] and it is the secret of final and eschatological rebirth.[3] The deepest secret of the way in which God is working his purpose out is not to be found in reconstruction or

---

[1] This is not the true doctrine of Christian mysticism, but it has infected much Christian mysticism; cf. J. Dalby, *Christian Mysticism and the Natural World* (James Clarke, n.d.), pp. 19 ff.

[2] John 3, 1 ff.   [3] Matt. 19, 28.

renovation, but it is to be found in regeneration. Reconstruction and renovation can be achieved without love: regeneration can never be.[1] The secret of the hope of regeneration is not to be thought of as being the final achievement of the effort of man, for however heroic that effort may be it can only be doomed to frustration and disappointment; if it could be conceived of as by itself bringing anything to birth, it would inevitably be something still-born. On the contrary the realization of the Christian hope, whether in individual experience or in corporate history or in an eschatological event which combines them both, is always to be regarded as the fulfilment of the purpose of God.

It is the way he goes about things, the way he always has and always will. It is of a piece with the covenant of the Old Testament which arose out of the meeting of God and man; and it is of a piece with the covenant of the New Testament which arose likewise out of a meeting between God and man. In the old covenant the meeting was lop-sided: Abraham and Moses stood on the oath and the promise of God. So at least the secret of their covenant meeting was interpreted from the earliest narrative of what happened at Sinai [2] to the latest biblical exposition of it in the Epistle to the Hebrews.[3] In the new covenant the meeting was no longer lop-sided but evenly balanced and fully reciprocal, Jesus in his own person being 'the mediator' [4] because in him there was the perfect meeting of God and man.

Each of these covenants pointed forward, the first to a better time ahead of which the coming of the Messiah was eventually proved to be the secret, and the second to a better time ahead of which the return of the Messiah is continually proved to be the secret, until in the end it fulfils the agelong purpose of God, only exhausting his truth and beauty and goodness so far as this world is concerned, and pointing still further on beyond itself to the truth and beauty and goodness God still has in store in 'the life of the world to come'. No end can be looked forward to which is the outcome of a present relationship of love and which is itself the fulfilment of that relationship unless that end itself is the beginning of something beyond itself, of which at present we have no inkling. This is the secret of the Christian eschatology of love, the fulfilment of which always looks forward beyond itself, as much when it is a future parousia as when it is a present presence. To seek for a finality without such looking forward is to desert the real and dangerous world of the relationship of love in order to secure the

---

[1] Cf. C. N. Cochrane, *Christianity and Classical Culture* (O.U.P., 1940), pp. 359 ff.
[2] Exod. 3, 14; 24, 1 ff.   [3] Heb. 3, 1 ff.; 6, 13 ff   [4] 1 Tim. 2, 5.

abstract and safe world the logic of the working of which excludes the reciprocal secret of love.

It is the merit of the developing eschatology of St Paul and St John to point to a future hope along such lines as these. The rest of the New Testament, apart from the Petrine references to a larger hope or at least to a wider extension of the possible range of hope,[1] adds little or nothing original to eschatology at all. 2 Peter and Jude make no advances upon the semi-Judaic outlook of Revelation, and they translate its poetry into prose and its symbols and images into propositions. As for the Epistle to the Hebrews, it remains in respect of its eschatology as much as its origin, authorship and destination a complete enigma, appearing in the midst of the New Testament rather like that Melchizedek himself for whom it has such a high regard.[2]

Does it try to convert the temporal realities of an Hebraic future into the timeless realities of a Platonic or a Philonic present? That is how it is often interpreted, but with no more justice than the Fourth Gospel. It looks forward,[3] as the Greeks never did and with their cyclical conception of time never could. But it adds little that is original to our understanding of the Christian hope. If the imminence and the surprise and the inexorability of the parousia-judgment do not appear as much as elsewhere in the New Testament, the actual and much maligned expression, the second (sic) coming, quite uniquely does.[4]

But for creative thought on this subject as on so much else we must turn to St Paul and St John. St Paul's doctrine shows an unmistakable trend away from a Synoptic towards a Johannine perspective. There is no need to press the differences of emphasis between his earlier and later epistles. The similarities far outweigh them: but they are there none the less, and no one who thinks for a minute can be surprised that they are. St Paul was a man whom even his worst enemies could never for one minute accuse either of standing still or (to change the metaphor) of resting on his oars. In his ardent pressing forward towards 'the prize of the high calling of God in Christ Jesus',[5] his mind was as active as his spirit and body. The parousia and judgment day are imminently expected in 1 and 2 Thessalonians, though 2 Thessalonians [6] begins that lengthening of perspective which we find also in 1 Corinthians.[7] But on the whole it remains true that 'the time is shortened',[8] and behaviour is

---

[1] 1 Pet. 3, 19 ff.; 4, 5 f.   [2] Heb. 6, 20 ff.
[3] Heb. 11, 1a; cf. W. Robinson, *The Eschatology of the Epistle to the Hebrews* (*ut supra*).   [4] Heb. 9, 28.   [5] Phil. 3, 14.
[6] 2 Thess. 2, 1 ff.   [7] 1 Cor. 7, 26.   [8] 1 Cor. 7, 29.

strictly rigorist and otherworldly in its emphasis in consequence. There is no expectation of any delay beyond the lifetime of the apostle,[1] and there is the clearest emphasis upon the hall-mark of judgment day being the appearance of Jesus himself and none other as judge.[2] Indeed throughout his epistles St Paul's eschatology is as Christocentric as is his mysticism, although he says in Romans that 'we shall all stand before the judgment seat of God',[3] rather than of Christ.

It is not at all true to say that he drops his early hope of an imminent parousia. Nothing could be more vivid, imminent and thoroughly in the spirit of Jesus' own parables than the terse staccato interjection, 'The Lord is at hand', *ho kurios eggus* (ὁ κύριος ἔγγυς), in the Epistle to the Philippians.[4] He may have altered his views as to the likelihood of his living to see the parousia. He never altered his views about its imminence. For him it was always imminent in terms of the only time that mattered, which was God's, and to imagine it very far off was to eliminate something of the very essence of the Christian hope.

What happened, however, was that he drew out the cosmic implications of his beliefs about the future, and so in the epistles to the Ephesians and Colossians followed up the indications in Romans 8 of an approach to the whole subject of eschatology which is much more akin to the Johannine outlook. For such an estimate of his later work much depends upon the authorship of the Epistle to the Ephesians.[5] If it is Pauline, then the perspective of an imminent parousia widens out on its further side to reveal the full extent of the wonder of the consummation of all things in Christ.[6] The common idea that the parousia can be left completely out of account in interpreting Ephesians seems entirely unwarranted. It might, for all St Paul says of it, be equally well left out of account in interpreting Galatians. Yet no one will use the *argumentum e silentio* in that case to deny that at the time he wrote Galatians the parousia was at the centre of St Paul's eschatological outlook.

And, of course, if Ephesians is not an authentic and original Pauline letter, then the centrality of the parousia in St Paul's outlook

---

[1] 1 Cor. 4, 5; 15, 51 ff.; 16, 22.
[2] 1 Cor. 1, 8; 3, 13; 4, 4 f.; 5, 5.
[3] Rom. 14, 10.
[4] Phil. 4, 5; cf. Col. 3, 4. Incidentally it is hard to resist the conclusion that the conscious or unconscious motive behind the effort to place Philippians earlier in St Paul's ministry and to date it perhaps from an Ephesian rather than a Roman imprisonment is the desire at all costs to rid the latest strata of St Paul's writings of the naive eschatological expectation of an imminent parousia.
[5] Seriously challenged, at least in its traditional form, by C. L. Mitton, *The Epistle to the Ephesians* (O.U.P. 1952). [6] Eph. 1, 10.

on the future stands so utterly unapproached in importance by any
other eschatological doctrine as to make it for all practical purposes
the one thing he looked forward to.   Nothing indeed could be more
natural if the secret of hope is the purging of memory.[1]   For the
memory of the Damascus road experience,[2] if not hugged for its
own enjoyment in retrospect, must have inevitably pointed forward
to something like the parousia as its true fulfilment in prospect.
If St Paul did not try to remember the most significant thing in his
past life, that is how it would inevitably come back to him.   Why
then, if his conversion experience is left as indisputably authentic
evidence of the secret of the beginning of his Christian life, should
his parousia hope be ridiculed and challenged as a naively crude
conception of its ending?[3]

With this strong caveat against the dismissal of the parousia from
the mature Pauline eschatological perspective it is possible to enter
without reserve into the wider vision of the universal and everlasting
purpose of God which his later epistles unfold before our wondering
eyes, more in Ephesians certainly[4] as a prayer and a meditation than
as an argument or a dogma.   His hope is that all that is not finally
impenitent (and the range of penitence is not limited to humanity
in its effect, though it may be in its practice) will eventually find its
place in the sum total included in the salvation of Christ.   Somehow
it will all get included in him.[5]

In the vision of his later captivity epistles St Paul has moved,
perhaps because of his physical confinement, right out of any
suspicion of that mood of restless expectation and feverish anticipation of a temporally imminent end of the world into a serene confidence in the present unfolding of the wonder of eternal life, which
links him at the end of his days so closely to St John, perhaps also
purged of his thunder and lightning[6] by imprisonment.[7]   He is
caught up, as nowhere else in all his writings, in amazement at the
transcendent wonder of the eternal purpose of God working from
beginning to end of creation and catching up everything in the sweep
of its vast comprehensive design of love, of which the inner secret
has been revealed in Christ and is now being manifested and worked
out through his body, the church.   Such is the grandeur and the

---

[1] Cf. St John of the Cross, *ut supra*.   [2] Acts 9, 1 ff.

[3] The most critical opponents of the naive parousia are only too glad to avail themselves of the most conservative support for the traditional authorship of Ephesians—
ostensibly to save St Paul's eschatological face, but perhaps unconsciously to save
theirs too!

[4] Eph. 1, 15 ff.; 3, 14 ff.

[5] Eph. 1, 10; Phil. 2, 10; Col. 1, 16 ff.   [6] Mark 3, 17.

[7] I do not regard a common Johannine authorship of the Fourth Gospel and
Revelation as completely disproved.

glory of St Paul's final contribution to the doctrine of the Christian hope. But if peace and serenity of vision befit old age, they do not befit youth. To attempt to by-pass the ethical rigour of the earlier Paul living under the pressure of his futurist eschatology in order to enjoy the mystical experience of the later Paul revelling in the contemplation of his realized eschatology is not to be loyal to the apostle either in his youth or in his old age. Complacent self-indulgence in the enjoyment of the end is as much apostasy from apostolic doctrine and behaviour as is any feverish attempt to quicken the *tempo* of the unfolding of the end.

If St Paul in the end leads on to St John, and if the Fourth Gospel is the climax of the whole New Testament doctrine, then the steps of the ladder which lead to the top must be climbed painfully one by one, and only so will the transmuted eschatology that we eventually reach be the real corrective of a crude futurism that it is meant to be and not some spurious substitute for it, claiming to stand in its own right as a complete and comprehensive account of the Christian hope. The Fourth Gospel is the final term of Hebrew doctrine and not an Hellenistic intrusion into it, and the doctrine of the Logos is esentially subordinate to the doctrine of the Christ, especially in his eschatological significance as the judge.[1] The Logos may legitimately correct current misinterpretations of the Messiah, but he may not be used as a substitute for the Messiah. It is in Christ that the end has come and therefore we are all now placed inescapably and unavoidably in his presence, whether we realize it or not. The present reality is often blurred and to some extent necessarily hidden: when it is finally revealed there will be a recognition of a judgment already consummated by God,[2] although not yet recognized by man. St John thus brings the future into inescapable relation to the present, and in doing so is merely drawing out the central message of genuine prophetic and New Testament eschatology, which interprets judgment on no abstract theory of the way a divine theodicy ought to work but on the basis of a concrete application of present convictions about God to every particular situation.

For St John the judgment is self-judgment and its criterion is man's attitude towards the light which has always been in the world,[3] but which has shone in all its fullness in Jesus Christ.[4] It is no part of the positive purpose of Christ to set himself up to be the judge of men.[5] Nevertheless judgment is the inevitable consequence of his coming: his presence inevitably involves it.[6] This means a carrying

---

[1] John 5, 22 ff.; 8, 18 f.; 9, 39; 12, 31.
[2] John 3, 18; 5, 24; contrasted with 5, 28 f.; 12, 48.   [3] John 1, 9.
[4] John 8, 12.   [5] John 3, 17 ff.; 5, 45; 12, 47.   [6] John 9, 39.

back in the Fourth Gospel of the traditional future judgment into the present actual life of Jesus Christ. This is a fearless reconstruction of doctrine which is always necessary, though seldom attempted, whenever eschatology pretends to be a preview of the shape of things to come and refuses to be content with the humbler rôle of showing the inevitable consequences of things as they are.

St John's eschatological corrective of the one-sided futurism prevalent in the church of his day is perhaps the clearest example of the way in which he puts into practice his doctrine of the Paraclete, whose self-effacing work is never to advertise himself but always to point to Christ and to draw out further implications of his original secret of love.[1] What he did appears at first sight to be a complete reorientation of the traditional expectation of a future and an imminently future end, but it is in fact only the necessary corrective of a one-sided emphasis which was in danger of so concentrating upon the future revelation of Christ as to forget the all-important central Christian conviction that the end had already come and that its nature had already been clearly revealed in Jesus Christ. Why on eschatology alone modern criticism should allow the Fourth Gospel to replace and supersede the Synoptists is inconceivable on any fair handling of the New Testament evidence. On the doctrines of the Logos and of the sacraments, the miracles and the messianic secret, and indeed on all other doctrines especially emphasized by St John, it is agreed that his work must be seen in the light of the Synoptic evidence and as a corrective of it but not as a substitute for it. This canon of interpretation should hold for his eschatological emphasis and his eschatological silence too.

For this is designed to bring out the fact that the eschatological significance of Jesus Christ is not to be interpreted as having reference to a merely historical and temporal event in time past. By the power of the Holy Spirit that past event is realized as present fact, and the presence of Christ is no mere memory of long ago but a present reality. Only those who know the secret of the presence can realize the secret of the parousia, and only those who look for the parousia can safely be entrusted with the secret of the presence. Failure to recognize this double-edged character of the revelation of love has fatal consequences, for it leads either to an apostasy from the presence in expectation of the parousia or to an idolatry of the presence with no hope in the parousia at all. The world of love with all the perils involved in its exploration is abandoned for the world of logic and of reason, which is impervious to the surprises of

[1] John 16, 18; cf. J. E. Fison, *The Blessing of the Holy Spirit* (Longmans, 1950), pp. 134 ff.

love. All is neat and tidy and secure and safe: surprise is eliminated: by formula or rite or gnosis God is caught within the grasp of man and by the apotheosis of the church or something else man thinks he can guarantee to himself God's final favour and benediction.

Nothing could possibly be a more disastrous travesty of the Christian gospel and nothing further from the purpose of St John. 'The peace of God which passeth all understanding',[1] which has been found in Christian experience to be the supreme legacy of St John to the church, is based upon an eschatological realization of the eternal presence, which is only arrived at on the yonder side of the almost intolerable tensions of history with which the Fourth Gospel abounds. The fact that for St John the eschatological event is a present reality does not mean that it has thereby ceased to be in any genuine sense eschatological at all. It is only because it is eschatological that it is present. That is the meaning of St John's transposition of the kingdom of God into eternal life. Time may now be taken up into eternity, though it may not be swallowed up by it; eternity may not be so pulled down within time as to be by nature as well as by grace within the grasp either of man alone or of the church as a whole. The peace of God is neither found in a timeless eternity nor achieved in a temporal certainty. It is realized only in the new dimension of time, revealed in the intercourse, conversation, exchange and reciprocity of love.

In such a relationship no awareness now of the presence with which we are confronted in the person of Christ can eliminate either the thrill or indeed the terror with which we await his parousia. This is at the heart of Pauline sacramentalism [2] and of Johannine eschatology. What St Paul says, 'Now we see through a glass darkly, but then face to face',[3] is exactly what St John endorses.[4] 'The main thing, after all, is that Jesus Christ himself is to appear: "we shall see him as he is". The writer has here put in the simplest possible words not indeed the whole content of Christian eschatology, but the controlling conviction which gives character to any eschatology which is to be distinctively Christian.' [5] And, significantly for Dr. C. H. Dodd, St John has expressed the heart of his eschatological hope in a tense which is not present, but future. St John knows quite clearly the limitations of any realized eschatology, however necessary it may be in his day and in ours as a corrective to a one-sided futurism. No one can ever know the presence of love without looking for the parousia.

[1] Phil. 4, 7.   [2] 1 Cor. 11, 27 ff.   [3] 1 Cor. 13, 12.   [4] 1 John 3, 2.
[5] C. H. Dodd, *The Johannine Epistles* (Hodder and Stoughton, 1946), p. xxxvi.

CHAPTER VI

THE PATTERN OF DEVELOPMENT *

IF there is a wholeness about revelation in general, and there must be if it is a revelation of the God who is one and who is love, then that wholeness will inevitably lead to parallels of development in the particular doctrines which serve to express and interpret it. If such parallels are forced into patterns which constrict the living truth they are meant to express, then the systematic theologian, who is guilty of imposing them as a strait-jacket upon the evidence which confronts him both inside the Bible and outside it too, will be 'a savour from death unto death'.[1] Nothing is more deadly to spiritual growth within either the soul or the community than such rigid impositions. But on the other hand nothing in an age of spiritual as well as mental and physical homelessness like our own can be more valuable than the use of such patterns and parallels as sign-posts and pointers to the wholeness of the revelation of him in whom 'we live and move and have our being'.[2] This is the apostolic secret, 'a savour from life unto life',[3] and just the corrective needed to save men from relapsing into departmentalism in their despair of ever seeing the significance of the whole at all.

In looking for such biblical patterns it is possible to sum up the New Testament evidence by saying that it contains within its pages three different eschatologies, not capable of rigid distinction, but lending themselves to a difference of emphasis, which is undeniable. First of all there is the pattern of realized eschatology, set out by Professor C. H. Dodd,[4] which certainly includes the last judgment as one element in the primitive preaching or *kerugma* both in the Acts of the Apostles[5] and in St Paul.[6] So integral is this to the original Christian message that it is taken for granted not as something to be argued for but as something to be argued from, a datum of apostolic faith[7] rather than a probandum of

---

* The biblical evidence for the development of the doctrine of the Holy Spirit is set out fully in my book, *The Blessing of the Holy Spirit* (Longmans, 1950), pp. 36–147, and is not repeated here.

[1] 2 Cor. 2, 16.   [2] Acts 17, 28.   [3] 2 Cor. 2, 16.

[4] C. H. Dodd, *The Apostolic Preaching and its Developments* (Hodder and Stoughton, 1936).

[5] Acts 10, 42; cf. 3, 21.

[6] Rom. 2, 16; 14, 10; 1 Cor. 4, 5; 2 Cor. 5, 10.   [7] Cf. Heb. 6, 1 f.

apologetic argument. Judgment is a function of the lordship of the Messiah,[1] on which the early church was so insistent, and which it did not conceive as beginning in some distant future but as having already begun in the life, death and resurrection of Jesus Christ.

For St Paul the judgment was visible in the cross of Jesus Christ [2] and the new order began with the resurrection.[3] That was why he placed so much emphasis upon the doctrine of justification by faith. If present judgment was a fact and not a fiction, so was present justification. But no moral sense can be made of this, unless it is interpreted in the context of that realized eschatology of the early church, for which the reiterated refrain in the gospels, 'that it might be fulfilled', is the clearest possible evidence. For such an outlook the temptation is great to reinterpret our Lord's confession before Caiaphas [4] back into the terms of its Danielic original and so see in the whole sequence of our Lord's life and death one coming, and that a coming *to* the Father finding its fulfilment through one unbroken progress of triumph, eliminating the need or indeed the possibility of any second coming at all.

Over against this first pattern of realized eschatology is set another pattern of futurist eschatology. This was an attempt by the early church to retain the central Christian conviction that in the coming of Jesus the end had in some real sense arrived, and yet at the same time to make intelligible and meaningful the continued going on of history since his coming. It is urged on behalf of this futurist eschatology that it is an attempt to get out of the self-contradiction, involved in the belief that the end had come and the stubborn fact that the end of history had self-evidently not come, by a reinterpretation of the original concept of a single coming of Christ along the lines of a twofold coming.

The first coming of Christ in humility and eventual humiliation was to be balanced by a second coming in triumph and glory, and the eschatology of the primitive gospel was worked over and reinterpreted in this sense to justify the time-lag between the two advents. This is why we have the long Synoptic apocalypses in their present form,[5] and why the direction of Daniel's vision is reversed in Jesus' confession before Caiaphas, as we now have it recorded.[6] A similar motive lies behind St Paul's warning to the Thessalonians against being deceived by those who proclaimed a single advent.[7] And the

---

[1] Ps. 110, 1 is the proof text which the New Testament quotes again and again, e.g. Mark 12, 36; Acts 2, 34 f.; 1 Cor. 15, 25; Heb. 1, 13.
[2] Rom. 8, 3; Col. 2, 15.   [3] 1 Cor. 15, 20; Col. 1, 18.
[4] Mark 14, 62.   [5] Mark 13, 1-37; Matt. 24, 1-51; Luke 21, 5-36.
[6] Mark 14, 62; Dan. 7, 13 f.   [7] 2 Thess. 2, 3-10.

whole weight of the Book of Revelation is laid on the side of the same futurist reinterpretation of eschatology.

As for its reasons, it is quite clear that once the eschatological significance of the once-for-all act of God in Jesus Christ was lost, and once that act began to be looked back to as one among many other events of past history, then a futurist eschatology of compensation was inevitable if faith was to survive. Also the inevitable corollary of the loss of the eschatological understanding of the Christian gospel was the increasing tendency to substitute good advice for good news, *didache* for *kerugma*, teaching for preaching. This meant in effect the substitution of lists of spiritual vitamins for the offer of spiritual food, and it was to try to combat its disastrous effects that St Matthew's gospel, which lays so much stress upon the teaching of Jesus, tries to compensate for this one-sidedness by its heightened emphasis upon a futurist eschatology. But the unity of the original primitive gospel had to be broken up in order to do this, and in consequence its saving significance was gravely impaired.

Finally, on top of realized and futurist eschatology, the New Testament offers a third pattern of the shape of things to come, in which there is such a sublimation or transformation of the futurist conception that it is hardly an exaggeration to say that the Fourth Gospel has replaced eschatology by mysticism. The last judgment is a present fact and eternal life a present reality. The whole eschatological programme is completed in the triumphant 'It is finished' [1] of the crucified Jesus himself. This is no humiliation to be reversed by future glory. It is the present glorification of Christ for those who have eyes to see it, the climax of no hidden or secret messiahship but of a life and ministry of which every act and word in time was a 'sign',[2] a transparency, revealing the eternal world to men. For this transmuted eschatology the coming of the Paraclete fulfilled all the hopes placed by the futurists in the parousia, and that coming was not even delayed till Pentecost. It occurred on the evening of Easter day itself.[3]

In the light of this outlook it is no surprise to find in the Fourth Gospel the most tremendous claims made for what might almost be described as the present 'divinization' of man. It is easy to read the evidence of the Fourth Gospel for the necessity of the new birth and for the possibilities of the new and eternal life without being aware of the ethical conditions of all fully personal relationships on which the Synoptic gospels lay such emphasis. But it is only on the yonder side of their moral tensions that there is any possibility of

[1] John 19, 30. [2] Cf. John 2, 11. [3] John 20, 19 ff.

entering the mystical peace of St John, and any attempt at a short-cut into his eternal world is spiritually suicidal.

If only protestantism would press on into the mystical world which the Fourth Gospel reveals, and if only catholicism would face resolutely the ethical conditions of all access to that world which the Synoptic gospels lay down, then a reunited church might again experience both the present salvation and the present judgment of a realized and transmuted eschatology. Then indeed we should be 'born anew'[1] into the wonder and curiosity of the little child's outlook upon life and the poet's words would be true:

> For the end of the world was long ago—
> And all we dwell to-day
> As children of some second birth,
> Like a strange people left on earth
> After a judgment day.[2]

To look at the New Testament in this way, to see the threefold pattern of realized, futurist and transmuted eschatology and so to get an intelligible grip upon its outlook upon the shape of things to come, is much better than to see the whole as an amorphous mass of contradictory evidence, impossible to integrate into any coherent scheme at all. But it has a fatal defect, for even though faith is saved by being made intelligible, hope is so easily lost because the secret of love has been missed.

This threefold pattern so easily becomes a scheme of temporal logic rather than a signpost to eternal love. What was realized in the coming of Jesus Christ was the fullness of the love of God. When that realization began to grow dim, a future compensation for what was lacking in the present was emphasized. St John saw that this was futile and led nowhere, and so he reasserted the present reality as the only key to the future possibility, for the realization of present love does not rule out the possibility of future love. On the contrary it demands it, not as a contradiction of the present but as a corollary to it; not to compensate for what is not but to balance what is.

The prospect of fulfilment is imminent in terms of lovers' time, and for such imminence delay in terms of calendar time is no problem and apologetic arguments no support. The trouble with the three-fold pattern of the realized, futurist and transmuted eschatologies is that it can be so easily interpreted as implying no knowledge of

[1] John 3, 3.
[2] G. K. Chesterton, *Ballad of the White Horse* (quoted by C. H. Dodd, *op. cit.*, p. 218).

any time save calendar time or of any mysticism save timeless mysticism. This involves such a contrast between time and eternity that the essential Christian conviction of the relative validity of time within eternity is abandoned. The result is to make havoc of biblical eschatology, however neat and tidy the pattern by which it appears to safeguard its intelligibility. Whatever the biblical pattern is, it is certainly not the pattern of a ruthlessly consistent realized eschatology, for the Synoptic evidence just will not fit into such a pattern. In it there is future hope as well as present faith, and the kingdom of God has not been so realized on earth that there is no real need to pray, 'Thy kingdom come'.[1]

It is true that as Christians we are dead already,[2] with an actual end to our old life and a real beginning of a new one. That is the heart of the secret of Christian initiation, and the early church is full of the implications of this vivid awareness of the meaning of holy baptism. The first Christians knew what it was to be risen already with Christ and to enjoy a new beginning of life. They knew what it meant to be born all over again.[3] But this does not mean that death, which is still future, is for them a trivial incident. There is no such cheapness in St Paul's awareness of 'the last enemy'[4] or in the way Jesus himself faced the cross.

Christian eschatology dare not make the future trivial if it would remain true to the New Testament evidence, and it is bound to make it trivial unless it takes time with all seriousness and refuses the short-cut out of its problems by denying its significance since the crucifixion, even if it admits it beforehand. There is no biblical escape from time into a timeless mysticism. It is not true to say that in the New Testament gospel, as it was originally understood, there is only one coming of Christ, and that a coming not to earth, but to the Father. Such an outlook reverses the whole direction of the New Testament movement, the emphasis of which is always upon the coming of God to man, whether in incarnation, atonement, Pentecost or parousia. This is not just a relic of Synoptic naïveté. It is Johannine doctrine too, for the triumph of Jesus in the Fourth Gospel is the climax of his coming not to his session in heaven but to his cross on earth.

It is not true that because of the reiterated Synoptic refrain, 'that it might be fulfilled', therefore the New Testament church felt that the end had so come that there was really nothing more to look forward to in the future. On the contrary, precisely because of the fullness of the past revelation, it knew that there was everything to look forward to in the future, for that revelation was a revelation of

[1] Matt. 6, 10.   [2] Rom. 6, 2.   [3] John 3, 1 ff.   [4] 1 Cor. 15, 26.

11

love, whose fullness is of such a nature that the more there is of it the more there is to be.

As for the problem of the delayed parousia, that, it must be repeated, is a New Testament problem, but only for those who have not grasped the nature of the imminence implied in the original expectation. Once this is realized to be imminence in terms of lovers' rather than of calendar time, the problem disappears and the attempted solutions of it are seen to be irrelevant. So far from an eschatological expectation of a second advent being a perversion of the original gospel, it was inherent in any true understanding of its nature as love. The traditional Christian interpretation of Jesus' confession before Caiaphas [1] is right, and St Paul's warning to the Thessalonians should not be disregarded as if it were merely due to a futurist misunderstanding of the gospel: on the contrary it should be faced up to for what it is, a downright apostolic condemnation of all strictly realized eschatology.[2]

It is true that the primitive eschatological understanding of the gospel was soon lost, but that does not mean that the futurist attempt to safeguard it was wrong. On the contrary, if the eschatological revelation of Jesus Christ was a revelation of love, then a future parousia is a necessary corollary to a present presence. As for the heightened objectivity of the grounds of future hope, that indeed may legitimately be characterized as a falling away from the primitive understanding of eschatology and as in part due to an attempt to correct present moralism with future supernaturalism. But such heightened objectivity is no necessary part of New Testament futurist eschatology whatever, unless the images and symbols carried forward from the Old Testament and from the apocryphal and pseudepigraphical literature of the inter-testamental period are allowed to dominate the reinterpretation of them given by the New Testament.

As for the claim that St John has transmuted eschatology into mysticism, that is a tenable interpretation of the facts if two conditions are granted. In the first place it is to be understood in the same way as so much of the Fourth Gospel is to be understood, not as a full-orbed presentation of Christian doctrine, but as a one-sided corrective of the doctrinal outlook prevalent in the writer's day. Secondly, too, it must be realized that the mysticism into which the eschatology of the Synoptic gospels is said to be transmuted is not the timeless mysticism of the Platonic and neo-Platonic tradition, finding its secret in escape from the material world, but the embodied mysticism of a time packed with the meaning

---

[1] Mark 14, 62.   [2] 2 Thess. 2, 1 ff.

of love, which is the true climax of the whole Hebrew understanding of time.

It is time seen in a new light with lovers' eyes which the Johannine mystic enters. And his time 'flies' not in a disembodied trance-world outside space and time, but in the embodied world of space and time. Its secret is found not by those who seek to escape from reality, but by those who face it; not by those who choose the heroic cross, but by those who do not dodge the humdrum one; not by those who get away from life's material conditions, but by those who let love transform them; not by those who escape from evil, but by those who 'overcome evil with good'.[1]

There is a mystical corrective in St John's Gospel, but it is a corrective and must not be taken for anything more than it is. It is a corrective relevant to the merely temporal futurism as con-spicuously present in the Christian church at the end of the first century A.D. as it is absent from the great church in the middle of the twentieth century A.D. As a corrective to the millenarian sects it is just the emphasis required to-day, but it can no more speak to the condition of the great church as a whole than can the Pauline injunction, 'let all things be done decently and in order',[2] which was originally addressed to the licentious, disorderly and enthusiastic church in Corinth, be applied as gospel truth to a typical middle-class Anglican congregation in England.

Further, the mysticism of St John is Hebraic in essence and not Hellenic: its basis is not the Word, but the Word who 'became flesh'.[3] Any attempt to interpret it in terms of disembodied time-lessness is treachery to the intention of the gospel. It sounds attractive to much modern thinking to be allowed to escape from the problems of history into the answers of eternity by the mystical short-cut. But such an escape is neither true to the real meaning of eschatology nor consistent with a true understanding of Christian mysticism.

The popular tripartite division of New Testament eschatology into realized, futurist and mystical patterns stands therefore in need of correction, and a comparison between the development of eschatology and pneumatology suggests the right approach. There is a parallel between the development of the doctrine of the last things in both the Old Testament and the New on the one hand and the development of the doctrine of the Holy Spirit on the

---

[1] Rom. 12, 21. Whatever may be thought of Luther's protest against the monastery in favour of the family as 'the school for character', this is the point at issue. Cf. R. H. Bainton, *Here I Stand* (Hodder and Stoughton, 1951), pp. 286 ff.
[2] 1 Cor. 14, 40.   [3] John 1, 14.

other, which is worth working out in some detail in order that the pattern may become clear.

In the Old Testament the actual use of the term, holy spirit, is confined to two or, at the most, three references all told.[1] But each term, holy and spirit, is used separately throughout the Old Testament and there is a striking parallel between the development of their usage. To begin with, there is nothing particularly ethical about holiness, because there is nothing particularly ethical about the Holy One, from whom the idea of the holy derives its content. Then the great prophets, without breaking the line of the tradition of faith by introducing a new deity, proceed to give to the concept of the holy that ethical connotation which is the inevitable corollary of their deepened ethical understanding of the Holy One himself.

Holiness throughout the Bible has to do with God, and the God it has to do with is the real God of the Old Testament, always Yahweh and never a Baal, not even when the Baal masquerades under the name of Yahweh. Yahweh can be met as a person. He cannot be mastered like a proposition. That is the difference between Yahweh and Baal. The Baals can be owned or possessed or manipulated and used by the people who acknowledge their lordship. Not so Yahweh—the propositions that can be used to describe him can only be rightly used if their limitations are kept clearly in mind. The mystical *via negativa* is a necessary corrective to all theological trespassing on this holy ground.

Propositions about Yahweh are dealing with someone of whom the classic and original formula of definition, 'I am that I am',[2] is, as we have seen, much more like an exclamation 'He!' than an interpretation lending itself to metaphysical explanation. The mystery of the identity of this 'He!' is probed again and again throughout the progressive understanding of his nature and character which the Old Testament unfolds.[3] But to the very end he remains a mystery, not because he tries to make a mystery of himself after the manner of a magician, but because he is in his inner being that holy love which can only be disclosed in actual meeting and can never be comprehended by any objective speculative analysis, however acute its vision or skilled its technique. The light which shines in such a meeting cannot help serving to reveal the darkness which surrounds it.[4]

As long as Hebrew religion lived and grew, progressive interpretations of the Holy One could be offered as clues to reality without

---

[1] Cf. J. E. Fison, *The Blessing of the Holy Spirit* (Longmans, 1950), pp. 42 ff.
[2] Exod. 3, 14.
[3] Cf. M. Buber, *Moses* (East and West Library, 1946), pp. 39 ff.　　　[4] Ps. 97, 2.

danger of their becoming safe abstractions from the danger of that reality. But in the end the living faith of the people of God ceased to support and vitalize its theological interpretations. This was the eventual tragedy of post-exilic Judaism. In the end the reality of the Holy One was safeguarded by his removal to a distant sphere safely under ecclesiastical control and far removed from any actual danger of his interference in daily life. At the same time the holy name, Yahweh, no longer known as a living power in real life, was safeguarded as a dead talisman; it was never spoken, and the result was that even its pronunciation came by continual disuse to be completely forgotten.

Such a religion is a far cry from that vital relationship with the living and the holy God, who (whether symbolized by a burning bush [1] or by holy bread [2]) could never be approached with impunity or treated as some innocuous and ineffective reality, which could be equally well taken for granted or ignored. From being an active and dynamic force, the idea of the holy degenerated into being a passive and a static and an entirely negative conception.[3] The Jews insulated the Holy One from his own world in order to keep him safe! None of the advance in philosophical understanding of his relation to the world, which we owe to the wisdom literature, should blind us to the disastrous apostasy involved in any loss of the prophetic understanding of his meeting with the world.

As with the holy, so with the spirit—there is a development in the Old Testament doctrine and the pattern is even clearer. To begin with, the spirit is introduced as an explanation of the abnormal and ecstatic behaviour of individuals and groups, such as we meet with in the books of Judges and 1 Samuel.[4] But if at first the spirit accounts for the strange way in which prophets speak and act and behave, there follows in the Old Testament the striking silence about the spirit of the great writing prophets before the exile. These prophets are not proud of their association, at least by name, with much of the contemporary phenomena of prophecy. They much prefer to attribute their inspiration to the word rather than to the spirit of God.[5]

Only when their lives and their words have demonstrated this new and deeper understanding of what the prophet and the spirit really mean can the actual words, prophet and spirit, be safely reintroduced explicitly and made once again current coin in the prophetic vocabulary. The debased verbal coinage has to be redeemed before it can be brought into circulation again. But when it has thus been redeemed, then it bursts into full prominence, first

---

[1] Exod. 3, 1 ff.   [2] 1 Sam. 21, 1 ff.   [3] Hag. 2, 10 ff.
[4] Cf. J. E. Fison, *op. cit.*, pp. 61 ff.   [5] *Ibid.*, pp. 78 ff.

as the explanation of Ezekiel's strange psychological behaviour, and then as at least one of the factors in that mystical communion with God, which marks out Deutero-Isaiah so distinctly from every other prophet in the Old Testament. Finally the word, spirit, is used as the hall-mark of that eschatological future prospect, on which through thick and thin, either nationally in this life or, later, individually in the next, the profoundest prophetic and apocalyptic minds increasingly based their hopes. If in the silence of the pre-exilic writing prophets the meaning of spirit became first and foremost ethical, though it never ceased for a moment to be supernatural, then in the speech of the exilic prophets the emphasis changed again from the ethical and the intellectual to the mystical and the eschatological.

A similar pattern of development may be discerned in the New Testament, provided due recognition is taken of the fact that the primitive church of Jerusalem after Pentecost, though of course the sequel in time to the revelation of Jesus Christ himself, was nevertheless its prelude and predecessor in the stage of spiritual life which it represents and in its consequent understanding of theological terms. Spiritually and intellectually the primitive Jerusalem church lies behind Jesus and is much nearer to Simeon and Anna.[1] There was necessarily a time-lag between the revelation of Jesus Christ and the church's understanding of it. St Peter and St Paul and St John all had to 'grow in the grace and knowledge of our Lord and Saviour Jesus Christ',[2] and even at the end of their lives no one of them could do more than point to him. There can never be any going beyond his holiness or improving upon his fullness of the Spirit.

If this is granted, then the Synoptic gospels do not portray a lower level of spirituality than the epistles to the Romans or the Ephesians or the Hebrews, however much these epistles may be valued for their insights into the deeper meaning of the gospel revelation. The order of progress, which in the Old Testament runs in straight historical sequence from Judges and 1 Samuel on to the pre-exilic and so to the exilic prophets, in the New Testament begins with the Pentecostal Jerusalem church with its links with the birth stories of Jesus and John the Baptist; it then goes back in time to the life and teaching and death and resurrection of our Lord, as recorded in the Synoptic gospels; and so proceeds via St Paul to its climax in St John.

In this line of progress, the first stage of the doctrine of the words, holy and spirit, is marked by the same slightly negative and ecclesiastical conception of holiness to which post-exilic Judaism reverted

---

[1] Luke 2, 25 ff.   [2] 2 Pet. 3, 18.

from the deepest positive levels of prophetic understanding. All the good characters of the primitive Jerusalem scene are in this sense holy. And as for spirit, it is the otherwise abnormal and inexplicable which, whether in the case of the birth of our Lord or in the case of the birthday of the church, is explained in pneumatological terms by reference to the working of the Holy Spirit.

But there is one most important difference between the first stage of the New Testament development and the first stage of the Old, for whereas in the latter there is no eschatological significance in references to the spirit to begin with, in the former that significance is from the first unmistakable and very definite. The strange behaviour of the day of Pentecost was connected with believers in Jesus as the Messiah and with them alone. Therefore since the Messiah was expected in the end of history and not just at any time within history, the concept of the spirit had an eschatological reference to begin with. It was the combination of strange and unaccountable behaviour and the occurrence of such behaviour only among those who believed either that the end had arrived or was on the eve of arriving, which justified St Peter's claim that this was the fulfilment of the prophecy of Joel and the outpouring of the Holy Spirit.[1] Thus the earliest Christian understanding of the meaning of the words, holy and spirit, was entirely Jewish and pre-Christian in its significance, except for the vital difference that eschatology took on an entirely new appearance for those who believed that Jesus was the Messiah.

For the understanding of the ultimate Christian significance of the words, it is vital to discover how Jesus himself handled the current ethical and pneumatological vocabulary of his day, and on this subject the Synoptic gospels leave us in no sort of doubt. There is a striking absence of the words on the lips of Jesus himself, and an even more striking absence of them in the records of the evangelists, who on any hypothesis of Synoptic authorship must have been writing in the midst of and for the instruction and edification of churches, which were abounding in evidences of the working of the Holy Spirit in the lives of the holy people.[2]

This remarkable Synoptic silence is made more remarkable still by a critical study of the gospel evidence, for that study eliminates almost every reference to the Spirit from the most primitive Synoptic tradition.[3] The only possible adequate explanation for this silence

---

[1] Acts 2, 15 ff.

[2] The early Christians were 'the saints', *hoi hagioi* (οἱ ἅγιοι) = 'the holy people'.

[3] C. K. Barrett, *The Holy Spirit and the Gospel Tradition* (S.P.C.K., 1947), pp. 122 ff.; and also J. E. Fison, *op. cit.*, pp. 103 ff.

is that Jesus himself, like the great pre-exilic writing prophets of the Old Testament, was reinterpreting in his life the meaning of the current pneumatological vocabulary. So impressive was his silence that even the evangelists, writing in the midst of communities constantly speaking of the Holy Spirit and witnessing his work in their midst, maintained the same reticence even in their interpretation of the gospel story.

The life of Jesus Christ made it impossible afterwards for any true Christian insight to find in the ecstatic or the abnormal the hall-mark of the spirit, or to find in the negative and the ecclesiastical the hall-mark of the holy. His life made the conjunction of the two words, holy and spirit, for the first time inevitable. They could never afterwards be separated in Christian tradition, and the meaning to which they pointed was not only something eschatological, but also something intellectual, ethical and mystical; something, furthermore, essentially dynamic and positive rather than basically static and negative. Just as Jesus had to reinterpret the meaning of the word, Messiah, by his life before he could safely speak of it with his lips, so he also had to reinterpret the words, holy and spirit. Otherwise holiness would have remained at best Pharisaical and at worst the key to pneumatology might have been found in abnormalities, attributed to good spirits in precisely the same way as others were attributed to evil spirits. This would have meant the debasing of the idea of being 'filled with the Spirit'[1] to the level of demon possession.

It was St Paul's achievement to show in his own spiritual pilgrimage how the abnormal gave way to the ethical as the key to the understanding of the Holy Spirit and how the ethical in the end was transformed in the mystical. Always for him the Spirit was closely connected with the end,[2] but his thought developed, and there is not the same emphasis upon the *charismata* in his later as there is in his earlier letters. By his refusal to allow the Holy Spirit to run away with or run away from the actual lived life on earth of Jesus himself, St Paul was putting the most effective barrier in the way of all attempts to improve on the holiness of Jesus himself, while at the same time leaving room for infinite originality in the interpretation and understanding of that holiness in the lives of the saints all down the history of the Christian church. In St Paul's own personal life, it was this referring of the work of the Holy Spirit back to Jesus himself and the continued check that this reference supplied which caused the apostle, while never denying his own spiritual ecstasies,

---

[1] Eph. 5, 18.
[2] Cf. G. Vos, in *Biblical and Theological Studies* (Charles Scribner, New York, 1912), pp. 209 ff.

to value far higher that ethical fruit and mystical root of the Spirit, which lie at the very heart of his pneumatology. In him a vivid eschatology, a realistic ethic and a transparent mysticism are vitally related. This is the work of the Holy Spirit, whose gifts and fruit and witness are indissolubly connected.

Thus the trend of the development of St Paul's thought leads straight on to the Johannine climax of the whole New Testament doctrine. This is found in the doctrine of the Paraclete, the only real *alter ego* of our Lord Jesus Christ. It is the Holy Spirit, not of the ostentatious display of Pentecost but of the self-effacing sequel to the Last Supper, who is the climax of New Testament pneumatology. And it is his deposition from the godhead which is the besetting sin of all ecclesiastical, biblical or experiential idolaters.

Here is the secret both of ethical conduct in individual lives and of corporate fellowship in a vital and growing organism. Here is the key to the continued vitality of the body of Christ and the ever renewed confidence of the people of the new covenant. Here is the way towards a Christo-centric mysticism, which is neither a relapse to a religion of works of supererogation in time nor a decline into the passive inertia of a timeless *kismet*. Here is the truth of a final fellowship with God which shall be such a true state of 'being in love' that it will be marked by an inexpressibly intimate union and yet never result in absorption. Here is the life which by its very mystery of love transcends all propositional attempts either to explain it or to explain it away. Here is in fact the Holy Spirit, so fully personal that he can neither be separated from nor identified with the means of grace he uses to indwell the individual or the community. He is neither to be identified with the spirit of man nor with the body of Christ, and yet he cannot be separated from either of them by any fool-proof yardstick or criterion of human reckoning.

If the evidence for the development of the word, holy, is not so extensive as that for the word, spirit, it is because the whole emphasis of the New Testament lies upon the dynamic rather than upon the static, upon the concrete rather than the abstract, and within such a context of love it is the good news of the spirit which corrects in the New Testament the undue emphasis upon holiness with which post-exilic Judaism became eventually so lopsidedly obsessed. Though for this reason the word, holy, is far less prominent in the New Testament than we should naturally have expected it to be, nevertheless what comparatively little evidence there is supports the pattern of development outlined above for the word, spirit. Jesus' own reinterpretative silence is followed by the apostolic reintroduction of the word as the technical term used to describe the Christians of any particular locality. And it is to be noted that 'the saints' in New Testament usage are not the saints of any ecclesiastical calendar; they are all the members of the Christian church and not any specially selected minority, qualified by particularly eminent virtues.

Thus, before passing on to consider in the light of the pneumatological evidence the striking eschatological parallel which it suggests, we can summarize our conclusions so far as follows. First, in both Testaments, the spirit is the explanation of the abnormal and the ecstatic; and the holy is the abnormal, if not the ecstatic. Secondly, in both Testaments, there is the striking silence—not only of the pre-exilic prophets but also of our Lord himself. The word, spirit, and the word, holy, are put out of commission for a time while a new meaning is given to them. This meaning becomes intellectual and above all ethical; it remains supernatural, but is not essentially abnormal.

Finally, in both Testaments, the word, spirit, and to a lesser degree the word, holy, and to a pre-eminent degree in the New Testament the combined phrase, holy spirit, come back into current usage as the hall-mark of the ethical and the mystical and the eschatological life both of the individual and of the community. It is this life which the biblical revelation offers not as speculative good advice for a few, but as practical good news for all.

In view of the close connection between pneumatology and eschatology it is not surprising that the pattern of development of the biblical doctrine of the end is unfolded upon lines very similar to that of the doctrine of the spirit. In the Old Testament there is no clear evidence of any positive spiritual and moral eschatology before the time of the writing prophets. Individual survival in Sheol was looked forward to as a bleak prospect indeed.[1] As far as any corporate purpose in history was concerned, when we first meet it in the Book of Amos, it is so obviously a prospect encouraging the worst excesses of jingoistic nationalism that the prophet roundly denounces it,[2] and it is very uncertain how far he, or indeed any of the pre-exilic prophets (except Isaiah), offered any solidly based ethical hope in its place.

On any view their relative silence about a future hope for the nation in this life is as marked as their absolute silence about a future hope for the individual after this life, and both are coupled with the most categorical denunciation of the false hopes engendered

[1] Job 10, 21 f.; Ps. 39, 12 f.; 88, 9 ff.; 115, 17 f.; Isa. 38, 18 f.
[2] Amos 5, 18.

by the popular eschatology of their time. They were as much by their silence as by their speech reinterpreting eschatology in the same way as they reinterpreted pneumatology.

And the sequel is strikingly similar. Ezekiel brings back a positive pneumatology and a positive eschatology and links them both together.[1] He introduces the spirit to explain his abnormal psychological experiences, and he introduces a prospect of an ecclesiastical heaven upon earth to give reality to his future hopes.[2] In both cases he is the link with the pre-prophetic ideas of the spirit as the explanation of the abnormal and of the end as the good time coming for the Jews after the destruction of their enemies.[3] But in both cases he introduces a new moral and spiritual element into the originally psychological and racial hope of the pre-prophetic outlook. The future holds the certainty of renewal and regeneration, but the realization of the eschatological prospect depends upon its pneumatological secret.[4]

Deutero-Isaiah succeeds Ezekiel, and with him a positive spiritual and moral eschatology for the nation begins to open out in all its universal implications for good for other people as well as the Jews, and indeed for the whole of creation, not merely for humanity itself.[5] The fact that these hopes were not realized in the immediate historical sequel either by Haggai and Zechariah or by Ezra and Nehemiah should not blind us to the fact that in the prophet's mind there was no incongruity whatever between their thoroughly ethical and spiritual character and their concrete and material this-worldly fulfilment. The realism of the prophetic faith leads to the materialism of the incarnation and lends no support to a supposedly higher spirituality in another and a non-material world.

In this respect the hopes of the greatest prophets have more in common with the expectations of the pre-prophetic jingoists than

[1] Ezek. 37, 1 ff.
[2] Ezek. 40, 1 ff. For a summary of the present attitude to the critical questions connected with the Book of Ezekiel, cf. H. H. Rowley, ed., *The Old Testament and Modern Study* (O.U.P., 1951), pp. 153 ff. A relatively conservative attitude towards the book appears increasingly justifiable. What is needed is not a dissection of Ezekiel into prophet and priest, ecclesiastic and ecstatic, but a new appreciation derived from the Book of Ezekiel as a whole of the richness and comprehensiveness of the spiritual stature and vision of the true prophet.
[3] Ezek. 38, 1 ff.
[4] Ezek. 37, 1 ff. Ezekiel is dependent upon the new covenant of Jeremiah 31, 31 ff. For his views, cf. W. F. Lofthouse, *The Prophet of Reconstruction* (James Clarke, n.d.), pp. 162 ff.
[5] Deutero-Isaiah's eschatological vision links directly with Isaiah 11, 1–9, whether the conclusion of that passage refers to the peace of peoples or to the peace of animals, and its universal scope is the natural sequel to Isaiah 19, 23 ff. M. Buber (*The Prophetic Faith* (Macmillan, 1949)) regards both these passages as 'inimitably Isaianic' (p. 150).

with any philosophical idealists. It is the popular hope for Israel here on earth, shattered by one catastrophe after another from the fall of Samaria in 721 B.C. to the fall of Jerusalem itself in 586 B.C., which is revived by the greatest prophets in the form of a hope for all men here on earth. The extent and the scope of the hope has widened, but not its sphere. It is on earth and not in heaven. Conditions of enjoyment may now be ethical and spiritual rather than racial and national, but only the eschatological generation is offered a chance of sharing the eschatological heaven on earth.

Clearly the hope thus conceived had only to be expressed to be realized to be inadequate to represent the future corollary of the deepest present awareness of God, as the prophets knew him. It might satisfy those who knew no god other than the nation: it might indeed satisfy a Baal worshipper, and there were always in Israel many who worshipped Yahweh as a Baal. But it could not satisfy any real worshipper of Yahweh himself. Just as in the beginning Yahweh's relationship to his people was not an organic and natural relationship of indissoluble unity, but a relationship of covenant choice and grace, which itself created a unity rather than expressed it, so also in the end Yahweh's relationship was not so bound up with any one people racially as to offer satisfaction to a last generation of them alone. On the contrary it was bound to them, and through them to all men, morally and spiritually, and therefore offered satisfaction either to all generations of them or to none at all.

Temporary relief from the acuteness of this problem might be reached by trying to believe that in the end, in the very end of this life just before death, the righteous would be rewarded with the happiness their virtue deserved and the wicked with the misery their sin merited; but this was a desperate expedient which was bound to come to grief sooner or later upon the apparently shattering injustices of this life not only right up to the very end but in the very end of death itself. It was with the individual as with the nation. A last moment's reward or a last generation's reward, even if based on moral and spiritual grounds, could not possibly satisfy the spirit of those who drew from life the portrait of Job or of the heroes of the Book of Daniel.

An adequate eschatology is bound in the end to offer a double hope, in time and on earth for the nation and beyond time and space as we know them for the individual. Thus the conclusion of the prophetic eschatology is realized in the apocalyptic vision, which matched the millennium of the nation with the resurrection of the individual. As long as this apocalyptic future hope was rooted in the present moral awareness of the prophetic understanding of God, it provided the essential link between the corporate hope of the community in this life and the individual hope of every member of it in the next. But all too easily it lost its prophetic roots and then future phantasy ran away from present reality.

Thus the pattern of the development of eschatology confirms in its main outline the pattern of the development of pneumatology. First there is the popular notion, not necessarily originally wrong, but certainly always limited. Then there is its refutation or, at least, its correction either by the eloquence of prophetic speech or by the still greater eloquence of prophetic silence. Finally both the doctrine of the spirit and the doctrine of the end come back into the centre of the scene in all the glowing colours of prophetic and apocalyptic vision.

The nation has a future once more, but it will enjoy it on other than racial or national grounds. The individual has a future once more (the prophets are simply not interested in Sheol; their silence about it is as marked as their speech about the popular idea of the day of Yahweh), but he will share it on other than psychological grounds. If the progress of the doctrine of the spirit is from the abnormal *via* the ethical to the mystical, the progress of the doctrine of the end is from the racial or psychological *via* the moral to the mystical. It is the present conviction of relationship with God and the present awareness of his presence which provide the ground of future confidence and hope as much in the climax of the eschatology of the Old Testament as in the core of the eschatology of the New.

When we turn to the New Testament we see that its radical intellectual problem was how to express at one and the same time the Christian eschatological conviction both that in Christ the end had already arrived and also that it was in some equally vivid way to be imminently expected in the future. But what is intellectually obscure and incomprehensible for logical reasoning becomes mystically clear and unmistakable in the relationship of love, for whereas in logic, as we have seen, if you now possess something it is unreasonable to go on hoping for it, in love that is exactly what you must do. The extent of your present possession is the measure of your future expectation.

To begin with, the primitive church of Pentecost looked for the coming of the Lord very much on the old lines of racial and national expectation.[1] It was not the unknown Yahweh but the known Jesus for whom the early Christians were looking. But apart from that vital difference, it was the old Jewish hope which still dominated the Christian outlook. Neither in pneumatology nor in eschatology

[1] Acts 1, 6.

was the Jerusalem church far in advance of Judaism. It was indeed the known Jesus for whom they looked, but it seems as if to begin with they thought that the unknown future must be so controlled by the known present that all possibility of real surprise could be eliminated. The coming of the Lord must conform to the literal terms of a geographically conditioned appearance.[1]

It is the clinging of memory to the past which so allows the locality as well as the certainty of the Lord's return to be determined in advance. This is no real purging of memory into hope, but rather the attempt of logic to keep love within its grasp. It is the pretension of what can easily become a false idolatry rather than the expectation of a true theology. As with the spirit, so with the end; the church at Pentecost had hardly begun to catch up with the thinking of her Lord. We are back in the great expectations of the beginning of the gospel story.[2] They had to be purged into something better if they were not to result in the bleak house of disappointment and disillusionment, and it was the work of our Lord to do precisely this very thing and so redeem eschatology as well as every other branch of theology from its debased to its true meaning.

For him future speculation was controlled by present reality, but it was not so bound to it as to eliminate that note of surprise, without which it ceases to speak of the living hope of the real world of love at all. No future hope is valid unless it is related to present experience, but no future hope is efficacious if it is limited by present experience. Jesus' own life was orientated not towards an unknown future, but towards his Father, known in the present here and now. It was the Father who guaranteed the future, and it was faith in him here and now which generated hope in him hereafter. Jesus' own attitude combined reticence about the details of the end with vivid expectation of the end. But for him the end was never some static impersonal thing. If he did not precisely define its nature, he clearly indicated his own attitude towards it and thereby gave us the best clues we have from which to infer its nature.

For Jesus hope is a tingling expectation, a permanent and natural and quite unforced 'alert' not only of the mind but of the whole personality. He is always on the *qui vive*, never bored with doing nothing and never feverish with doing everything. If his teaching seldom in so many words says, 'I am coming again', it inculcates a vivid hope among his disciples which could hardly be better phrased than in those words. It is a hope which is both certain and also certain to be a surprise. And that is precisely the nature of the only kind of hope which is based on love as its objective

[1] Acts 1, 11.   [2] Luke 3, 15.

ground and born of love as its subjective principle. It is a hope which by being neither unsure nor cocksure proves its secret to be the work of the Holy Spirit of love himself. It opens up a future which is a tonic to the timorous rather than a terror to the tormented.

As far as any further definition of the object of hope is concerned, the way of Jesus was the mystic way, by which memory is purged into hope. Within forms and expressions which in many respects conformed to the contemporary Jewish eschatological pattern, he managed to convey an entirely new meaning by his use of the expression, 'the kingdom of God', to which he gave all the richness of his own experience, suggested to us by the wonderful variety of his parabolic illustrations of its significance.

For us the meaning of 'the kingdom of God' is seen far and away more clearly in the person of Jesus himself than in any definition he gave of it. He gave its secret away by the sort of things he did and the sort of words he spoke, by the way he prayed and the way he preached and the way he healed, above all by the way he suffered and the way he died and the way he rose again. That is our clue to his meaning, but of course it was a clue not available to him. If our memories are or should be full of him, his memory was certainly and could only be full of his Father and his Father's house and his Father's kingdom and his Father's will and his Father's love. What this meant to him he could only convey by indirect suggestion to others, and that is exactly what he tried to do by the use of the expression, the kingdom of God, and by hinting at its meaning in parables rather than imposing it by definition. The secret of love can be got across in no other way: it can never be transmitted direct.

If then the kingdom of God was the expression he used to express his hopes for the future, should we be content with expressing our hopes in the same terms? On the whole the great church has always thought it should, though it rather likes to transpose the terms into ecclesiastical language and to pin its faith and its hope on its own promised indestructibility and eventual triumph.[1] The early church, however, manifestly thought otherwise, and expressed its hope once and for all in the unforgettable simplicity of the original 'Maran atha'.[2] And there can be no shadow of doubt that this verbal change of formula is as much the secret of retaining identity of meaning in eschatology as it is in soteriology. The way the apostles preached what Jesus meant by the kingdom of God was to preach 'Jesus Christ and him crucified'.[3] To fall back upon verbal repetition to secure identity of meaning would have been to them as

[1] Matt. 16, 18.   [2] 1 Cor. 16, 22.   [3] 1 Cor. 2, 2.

much a betrayal of the gospel as outright denial of the words of the Lord himself. Love is utterly ruthless against any attempt at securing, whether by verbal formula or by any other method, that which may only be grasped at [1] by lust.

Jesus' reinterpretation of current eschatology involved the rejection not only of the nationalist hopes of the Zealots but also of the detailed information about the future, with which apocalyptic visionaries were filling in the Pharisaic outlook. As for the conservative Sadducean ecclesiastics they are given short shrift in the gospels,[2] and it would appear from Jesus' comments upon them that they had lost all contact with the living God. With such people there was not even a possible basis for eschatological argument, for Jesus' attitude to all problems of the future was to make plain that the only real basis on which they could be discussed lay in the present.[3] Ignorance of the present kingdom of God ruled out all possibility of discussion about the future kingdom of God. It is the present reality of love which guarantees the future, for love is inexhaustible and its presence necessitates its parousia. Any understanding of its presence which rules out or leaves no room for its parousia shows a total failure to grasp the very nature of love itself. It is not an object to be possessed or an idea to be entertained; it is a relationship to be entered. Man cannot grasp it: it enfolds man, and it is man's blessedness to realize that it does.

It is impossible even to begin to understand Jesus' reinterpretation of eschatology unless its setting in the context of the real world of love and of relationship and of meeting is fully appreciated. Only those born again into this world of love like little children [4] can begin to see what he is driving at. It took at least as much time for the early church to grasp the significance of his eschatology as it did to understand his pneumatology. To begin with, the vivid but largely undefined Synoptic expectation is replaced by the clearly defined object of hope, which went along with the primitive nationalistic outlook still current after the crucifixion in the Jerusalem church.[5] The epistles to the Thessalonians dropped the nationalism, but remained full of the traditional Jewish accompaniments of the Sinai theophany, the optical and acoustical pomp and circumstance of the parousia being quite as ostentatious as the display of power by the Holy Spirit at Pentecost.

But the framework and the setting of this primitive doctrine both of the spirit and of the end must not blind us to the fact that by relating both spirit and end so closely to Jesus himself, the early

---

[1] Cf. Phil. 2, 6; R.V. margin.   [2] Mark 12, 18 ff.   [3] Mark 12, 26.
[4] John 3, 1 ff.; Mark 10, 13 ff.; Matt. 18, 1 ff.   [5] Acts 1, 6, 11.

church had in fact made it possible for the setting to be abandoned and for the secret enshrined within it to be retained. Pentecost *via* our Lord's silence can lead to the Paraclete, and just in the same way the ostentatious parousia *via* his silence can lead to the real parousia. At the heart of the primitive Pauline outlook lay that meeting with the Lord which is the heart of the eschatological hope and the secret source of all its cosmic implications.

The continued delay of the parousia, however, presented the early church with a problem, which was found insoluble until Jesus' own distinction between lovers' time and eternal life on the one hand and chronological time and temporal existence on the other was to point the way to the discovery of a simultaneity which did not destroy time and so emancipate Christians from bondage to a successiveness which was delimited by time. Before this secret of Jesus' own relationship with the Father percolated through into the deep consciousness of the Christian church, there was only one way in which the problem of the delayed parousia could be tackled, and the fact that it has so often been tackled in this way from the days of the apostles to our own time shows how continually the church is in need of that rebirth into eternal life and lovers' time which is the secret of the eschatological gospel of the New Testament.

In the absence of such an understanding of the gospel or out of accommodation to the evangelistic needs of the time, the early church, as we have seen, tried out the line of apologetic argument which we find in such striking similarity in 2 Thessalonians [1] and in all the Synoptic apocalypses as they now stand.[2] Certain things must happen which have not yet happened: some of these are good, like the preaching of the gospel to all the world;[3] others are bad, like the great tribulation [4] and the great apostasy [5] and the appearance of antichrist or the man of sin.[6] Until these things have happened there can be no parousia.

All this apologetic argument alleviates the acute problem which is bound to face those Christians, not only in the primitive church but also all down church history and not least in our own day, who desire to remain loyal to the New Testament hope and yet know only the categories of chronological and calendar time within which to interpret it. But it does not fully meet the case even at the level at which it aims at doing so, within the categories of chronological and calendar time. Nero came—he might be antichrist: Jerusalem fell—that might be the great tribulation: Vesuvius erupted and

---

[1] 2 Thess. 2, 1 ff.   [2] Mark 13, 1 ff.; Matt. 24, 1 ff.; Luke 21, 5 ff.
[3] Matt. 24, 14.   [4] Matt. 24, 9.
[5] Matt. 24, 4 ff.; 2 Thess. 2, 3.   [6] 2 Thess. 2, 3.

12

destroyed Pompeii—what further signs were needed? Surely the
end must be imminent—and yet it still delayed. It was clear that
the apologetic argument was not enough and so it was necessary
to buttress it by the evidential. The object of the Christian hope
needed clearer definition, not in regard to the necessary preconditions
of its fulfilment but in regard to its own nature and the manner of its
manifestation. Otherwise the church was in grave danger either of
spiritualizing it away out of disappointment or of being led astray
by false claims to its fulfilment. It was to meet this need that St
Matthew's gospel touched up the Synoptic eschatological picture
and introduced the actual word, parousia, into the Synoptic record.[1]

This was the end of the New Testament attempt to buttress the
fading hope of the parousia in so far as that was conceived in terms
of chronological imminence. The fact that it was still alive and
dominant in the church many centuries later is proof that its real
inner vitality sprang not from the logic of reasoning in terms of
chronological time, but from the expectation of surprisingly imminent
fulfilment in terms of lovers' time. St Paul as a mystic as well as
a theologian had realized this from the first. The difference in his
eschatological outlook is not that at the beginning of his extant
epistles he expected an imminent parousia whereas at the end he
looked for something quite different and much more like Tennyson's

> . . . one far-off divine event,
> To which the whole creation moves.[2]

The difference is not to be understood in this way (even if Ephesians
is authentically and originally Pauline), but rather to be accounted
for by the growth of his theology, as he grew older, into an integrated
whole.

In that whole other aspects besides the parousia legitimately
found their place in his future perspective, just as other things
besides his conversion experience began to fill his present horizon.
Not only the resurrection of the body, which was a doctrine he held
before his conversion as much as after it, but also the consummation
of all things in Christ through his body, the church, came into his
vision of the working out of the eschatological drama, on which the
parousia would lift the curtain. As the different elements in his
eschatology began to fall into their place in a coherent and integrated
whole, St Paul let fall hints and suggestions of a time interval
between the parousia and the very end, between a particular and a
general resurrection, between the kingdom of Christ and the kingdom

[1] Matt. 24, 3, 27, 37, 39.
[2] Alfred, Lord Tennyson, *In Memoriam*, Conclusion, st. xxxvi.

of God. Only in such a way could he symbolize or express the fullness of his eschatological hope within which he looked both for the vindication and triumph of Christ in this world and also through that triumph in some mysterious way for the dawning of the inconceivable divine possibilities of another world beyond this.

But with all this widening of his horizon, the apostle never lost sight of the coming of the Lord and the meeting with him and with his saints as the secret of the future revelation of the love of God which was the inevitable corollary of his present awareness of it. This was always the core of the apostolic hope and conditioned all the rest of it. But the increasingly objective manner in which the fulfilment of that hope was portrayed and the increasingly rational and temporal terms in which the reason for its delay was explained away, and perhaps the increasingly neat schematic pattern into which the church tended to fit the different aspects of its eschatology—all tended to undermine and overthrow its essential nature.

It meant the transformation of what was originally the climax of hope into a refuge of despair. What was originally conceived in the context of a meeting in lovers' time became a fixed date and place in chronological time and geographical space. The secret of a memory purged became the compensation for a memory blighted, and the immediate corollary of a life of faith and love became the final term of a calculation of reason and logic. It was to deal with this exceedingly dangerous perversion of the eschatological gospel that St John wrote his corrective, which he couched in the form of a gospel.

To realize the situation with which he was confronted, we must take into account not only the increasing definiteness of the apologetic and evidential proofs of the object of the Christian hope, of which we find such clear evidence in St Matthew's Gospel, but also the increasing influence of apocalyptic ideas such as we find in the Book of Revelation. The temptation was almost irresistible to take the great dream symbols of this literature with their repetitive emphasis upon a few basic truths and transform them into rational concepts, each with a different meaning, and all bound to be fulfilled literally and separately one after another.[1] The result was certain to be utterly disastrous: nothing is easier than to transfer the meaning of rite or symbol into the interpretation of logic and reason, but to do so and to imagine that we have thereby grasped and secured their significance is to lose the whole secret of the world of love, which can only be pointed to or suggested indirectly and can never be proved by any rational process whatever. Not to try to interpret

[1] Rev. 22, 18 f.

the symbol is intellectually suicidal, but to imagine that the interpretation exhausts the symbol or is in any sense an adequate substitute for it is a spiritual calamity, the disastrous consequences of which cannot possibly be exaggerated.

St John's corrective of the current eschatology of his day was on a par with his corrective of the current pneumatology and sacramentalism. He did not deny the element of truth in the current outlook, but he set alongside it another element of truth which was in danger of being overlooked. He was out to correct the fatal one-sidedness which inevitably besets all attempts to rationalize the revelation of love, which never allows itself to be caught within the logic of any theological system whatever.

As far as eschatology is concerned, St John was faced by the current problem of the delayed parousia. It is conceivable that he wrote his gospel because his own approaching death raised that problem in its most acute form.[1] Certainly at the very end of the apostolic era there was no further point in trying to defend the imminence of the parousia in terms of temporal immediacy or defined objectivity. It was indeed hopeless to go on stressing the future reality of the kingdom of God at all unless present experience was allowed to give the clue as to its meaning. That was why St John chose to speak of it in terms of eternal life and so sought to insist that any future 'come back' of Jesus must be strictly related to his original coming, not as if that were merely an isolated event in past history but as it provided the clue to his permanent attitude and activity, which it was the work of the Paraclete to make a present reality to every Christian soul and to the Christian community as a whole.

The manifestation of what was hidden of the glory of God in this world is the purpose of the incarnation and the whole life and death of Jesus Christ. Every miracle is a transparency or epiphany revealing the eternal world of love at work within the confines of space and time. It is this present reality which points forward to that final blazing manifestation of love, which could be conceived almost impersonally as the final term of the revelation of the Logos, were it not that in his doctrine of the Logos, as in all other doctrines peculiar to the Fourth Gospel, St John is not attempting to set out the whole truth, but to correct a partial misunderstanding of it. The Logos within the world before Bethlehem, the Holy Spirit given on Easter day before Pentecost, the coming as the final manifestation of the light within rather than the final intervention of the light

---

[1] John 21, 23. The question of precisely who wrote the Fourth Gospel is not important for the argument. If it was written at the end of the first century A.D., the argument holds whether the author was John the apostle or John the elder.

without—all these are glorious correctives, pointing to the world of love. They are fatally misunderstood if they are regarded as comprehensive statements of the whole truth about that world.

In regard to eschatology, St John's problem was the difficult one inevitable for anyone aware of the true nature of love. He had to correct an over-defined and over-objectified hope without falling into the error of a completely indefinable subjectivism, just as he had to correct the current sacramentalism of his day in a precisely similar manner. To deal with the eschatological problem he replaced the Synoptic last apocalyptic discourse of our Lord with his own last discourses leading up to our Lord's high priestly prayer of consecration, just as to deal with the sacramental problem he replaced the Synoptic account of the institution of the eucharist with his own account of the feet-washing and his emphasis upon the 'new commandment'.[1] Eschatologically the result of his corrective was to focus attention upon the coming of the Holy Spirit, understood in the sense of the self-effacing Paraclete, rather than upon the parousia, understood in an ostentatious manner analogous to the coming of the Holy Spirit at Pentecost.

But the deepest issue confronting St John in his attempt to interpret the revelation and operation of love both in the present and the future was not between an explanation in either objective or subjective terms. It was between a way of revelation and of operation which was really personal and a self-disclosure of love on the one hand, and a way of working which was really impersonal and certainly in no true sense a self-disclosure of love on the other hand. To many it always seems as if belief in the personal Holy Spirit must involve acceptance of objectively verifiable phenomena, such as those of Pentecost, as the invariable hall-mark of his work. To others in reaction from this view it seems impossible to believe in any holy spirit at all other than as a constituent element in man's psychological make-up and as merely a subjective influence within his soul. Similarly with the parousia, to many it seems as if belief in the personal coming again of Jesus Christ necessarily involves expectation of objectively verifiable ostentatious phenomena. And in reaction from this view there is bound to grow up a tendency to disbelieve in any future coming at all, with the result that all that is left of the original eschatological parousia is a merely mystical presence.

St John saw a possible *via media* between these two extremes, neither discarding eschatology in favour of mysticism nor mysticism in favour of eschatology. He reinterpreted the ostentatious Pentecostal Holy Spirit by the self-effacing Paraclete. This did not mean

[1] John 13, 34.

that he denied the work of the Holy Spirit on the day of Pentecost, but that he saw it in its right perspective, not as the highest but as the lowest evidence of the way in which love expresses itself. Similarly he reinterpreted the ostentatious idea of the kingdom of God and of the parousia of Jesus Christ by emphasizing the secret of eternal life and the self-effacing parousia. In doing this, he was entirely and absolutely true to the central reinterpretative conviction of Jesus himself; 'the kingdom of God cometh not with observation'[1] of any sort, whether in the present or in the future, for it is the manifestation of the real presence of love, and that at its clearest and simplest can never be in the least ostentatious, however much it may be surrounded by ostentation.

To mistake the setting of the eschatological secret for the secret itself inevitably means the loss of the eschatological secret altogether; and all well-meaning attempts to safeguard it are suicidal. That is the meaning of the life and the death of Jesus himself, for he preferred to risk the existence of love in order to safeguard its meaning rather than to safeguard its existence in order to secure its meaning. It took more than a generation for the church to catch up with his meaning, and in the meantime much of what he had said had been twisted back and given a pre-Christian connotation.

St John realized that the essence of a personal parousia as much as of a personal presence (and in love as much as in etymology the two terms are inseparable) can never be ostentatious. For the meaning of personality is most clearly shown in love, and love is always self-effacing. This does not in the least mean that the presence or the parousia of love is subjective rather than objective. It means that persons are most truly revealed as persons not when they stand in definable objectivity over against each other, nor certainly when they lose their identity and merge it in some indefinable and perhaps disembodied assimilation of each other, but on the contrary when they meet each other in love and in the meeting disclose to each other the secret of their personalities. That is the secret of revelation, for that is the secret of love, which cannot disclose itself in any other way. It is the secret of the embodied sacramental presence as much as of the embodied eschatological parousia. It is in such reciprocal intercourse of love that the meaning of the new dimension of eternal life is disclosed.

The final term of the development of New Testament eschatology thus makes inescapably clear that love is the essential nature of the eschatological manifestation of God. And we are now in a position to see that the pattern of the development of New Testament doctrine,

[1] Luke 17, 20.

as it moves to its Johannine corrective and climax, is not quite as simple as the triple pattern of realized, futurist and mystical or transmuted eschatology might lead us to suppose.

The parallel development of pneumatology suggests that the first stage of the Christian New Testament eschatology was that of the primitive Jerusalem church at Pentecost, which was living in the same state of great expectations as the pre-Christian community into whose midst both Jesus and John the Baptist were born. The difference between the two little groups of ardent believers was simply that the Jews were looking for a messiah they did not know, whereas the Christians were looking for a messiah they now knew. Apart from this, the attitude of the Christians had hardly begun to be affected by Jesus' own eschatological teaching and outlook.

It is his outlook which marks the second stage of New Testament eschatology. He was reserved and reticent and sometimes completely silent about the future. At the same time he both inculcated the most vivid expectation and also refused every attempt to define precisely the object of that expectation. For him the future was so unmistakably based upon the present and so inextricably bound up with it, that his teaching about the kingdom of God has caused endless dispute as to whether he thought of it as present or as future or as in some mysterious way a mixture of both. He gave no encouragement to speculation as to the details of the eschatological programme, though on the reality of the eschatological prospect he manifestly sided with the Pharisees rather than the Sadducees.

His silence about the parousia was as marked as his silence about the Paraclete. He completely reinterpreted the significance of eschatological doctrine by his life before he made any attempt at its reformulation with his lips. Indeed, he inevitably left the working out of that reformulation to his church, which could only see its true significance in the light of his resurrection.

St Paul took up the theological legacy of our Lord in a way no other apostle attempted. He shared and expressed the primitive expectation of an imminent parousia, his own conversion experience probably being the key to his vivid apocalypticism. What was central in his memory remained central for his hope, which was always focused upon the person of Jesus Christ himself rather than upon any theological concept like the kingdom of God, however hallowed its dominical sanction.

If after the resurrection appearances of the great forty days the primitive Christian expectation of the future parousia tended to become increasingly unrelated to present experience, it was St Paul's task to bring back that interrelatedness of the present and the future which was such an essential feature of our Lord's own eschatological outlook. By his doctrine of the work of the Holy Spirit in the present experience of the church he was able to supply the link between the past resurrection of our Lord and his future parousia.

If his own conversion had seemed to him as a bolt from the blue at the moment of experience, he came to see it as part of a wider prospect and of the whole unchanging purpose of God, as he reflected upon it in retrospect. Similarly, as he pondered on the future in the light of his growing and deepening understanding of God's working in the past and in the present, he came to see the parousia in its relation to the whole body of integrated eschatological doctrine. The parousia remained central in his conviction, but each new element of future expectation, as it gripped his mind, enabled him to see it in a clearer and grander perspective.

Meanwhile the Christian church as a whole found the apparent delay of the parousia an increasingly difficult problem. Those who did not share St Paul's mystical understanding of the meaning of life 'in Christ', and who had never experienced anything comparable to his conversion, tended to think of the future in terms of compensation hereafter for something lacking here and now. Knowing little or nothing of the secret of lovers' time, they imagined eternity as an infinitely long-drawn-out extension of chronological time. Consequently, they attempted to buttress the fading hope of the parousia by an increasingly defined objectivity of manifestation in order to silence all doubt, and by an increasingly elaborated preparatory programme in order to explain away all delay.

It was to correct this tendency, which was bound to lead nowhere in the end, that St John crowned the development of New Testament eschatology by so relating its future prospect to present reality in the gospel record itself that he lifted the chronological successiveness of a series of temporal events on to the level of the simultaneity of eternal life. This final corrective of a one-sided futurism is no philosophical substitute for the eschatological gospel. If this is Platonizing, it is no disembodied timeless Platonizing of the gospel of the day of the Lord, but a thoroughgoing application of that eschatological gospel to every moment of every day. Its basis is not the word as a Platonic idea, but the Word made flesh as an eschatological fact.

Normally we all live in the shadows of Plato's cave,[1] unaware of life's realities because we have never seen them, and therefore certain that the shadows are the realities because they are all that we have

---

[1] Plato, *Republic*, Bk. VII, 514 A ff. Cf. J. Adam, *The Republic of Plato* (C.U.P., 1902), vol. ii, pp. 156 ff.

ever seen. We take the shadow for the substance. What we need is a new awareness, a new mode of consciousness, emancipated from the limitations of the 'cave man's' consciousness. And only love can give us what we need. However they have sought to attain it, this has been the conviction of all the saints. To get to this has been the intention behind all the spiritual exercises of the mystics. Disagreement about the method should not obscure wholehearted agreement about the goal. But disagreement about the method may be due to serious divergence of opinion as to how to reach the goal.

This is where the eschatological emphasis upon the parousia is so important. For it corrects, as no other eschatological emphasis succeeds in doing, every method of discipline to reach a distant goal which obscures the central conviction of the Christian gospel that it is not so much our going to God as his coming to us which opens up the possibility of the new consciousness and the new awareness of love into which we cave-men so badly need to be reborn. The outlook of the gospel reverses the direction both of Plato's philosopher stumbling out of the cave up to the light and of so many seekers after God, both inside and outside the Christian church. This gospel reversal of emphasis needs continually to be remembered, for we are more likely to miss the *rendezvous* of love's appointed trysting-place with us by concentration upon attaining the *rendezvous* of our own choosing than in any other way.

We can so easily miss it by the heroic adventure down the long one-way traffic street of giving, if that makes us blind to the much more humdrum opportunities of the two-way street of giving and taking. The goal of the former is very far off: the goal of the latter is 'very nigh'.[1] The former may lead to crucifixion, but only the latter offers the opportunity of being 'crucified with Christ'.[2] To attain to the former in this life or in any other is incredibly hard: to realize the latter is unbelievably simple. The logic of the former may be impeccable: but it is the love of the latter which is irresistible. St John knew this, and therefore he laid alongside the hope of a futurist eschatology the hope of a realized mysticism. But the mysticism of love which is the secret of the latter is no timeless and disembodied reality for him. It is no hope in some thing beyond space and time, introduced to correct a hope limited to some thing in space and time. Rather, it is a new way of looking at all things in space and time so that in and through them we may fall not out of life but into love. Almost all St John's correctives of theological tendencies current in his day are designed to open his readers' eyes to the secret of this mystical and eschatological world of love. He

---

[1] Deut. 30, 14.   [2] Gal. 2, 20.

knew far deeper than Marcus Aurelius that 'just to look at things from another angle than that from which we have seen them hitherto, may actually mean the beginning of a new life'.[1]

A present mysticism to correct a crude futurist eschatology is as vital as is a future eschatology to correct a vague sentimental mysticism.   Only where mysticism and eschatology combine do we do justice to the secret of the New Testament hope, and they can never combine on the level of logic in terms of temporal and chrono-logical existence.   They can only come together on the level of love and in terms of that reciprocal relationship of eternal life which is offered to us not at the end of our present time-scale of existence, but in the midst of it as it is transmuted from clock time into lovers' time here and now.

'Journeys end in lovers meeting'[2] is as much the secret of the Johannine as of the Synoptic perspective.   Eschatology like pneumatology finds the final term of its development not in a sub-Christian mysticism which escapes from time, but in the true Christo-centric mysticism which transmutes clock time into lovers' time and temporal existence into eternal life.   It is the tragedy of Christendom that mysticism so easily runs away from eschatology and eschatology so seldom has any use for mysticism.   Mysticism by itself may give hope to the individual soul and eschatology by itself may give hope to the corporate whole, but only in their combination do they do justice to the range and scope of the New Testament hope.

If mysticism and eschatology are to come together in the New Testament way so that the secret of neither is sacrificed to the other, but the secret of each is enriched by the other, then a futurist escha-tology with no reference to present experience except by way of compensation is as much ruled out as is a timeless mysticism with no reference to future history except by way of condescension.   The eschatological corrective of a timeless mysticism asserts in the doctrine of the parousia the surpassing wonder of what will be, no matter how great the reality of what now is.   The mystical corrective of an unrelated futurist eschatology asserts in the doctrine of the presence the abiding reality of what now is, no matter how surpassing the wonder of what one day will be.

New Testament reticence about explicit reference to the presence is as marked as it is about explicit reference to the parousia.   For neither the one nor the other can be grasped in the logic of words or in the action of rites.   Word and rite point beyond themselves to

---

[1] Quoted by F. W. Dillistone, *The Structure of the Divine Society* (Lutterworth Press, 1951), p. 246.

[2] W. Shakespeare, *Twelfth Night*, II, iii.

love, and love can only possess us as we cease to claim to possess it. We may bear witness both to the presence and to the parousia of love. We cannot prove either the one or the other. The apologist dare not trespass here upon the apostles' ground, and one purpose of the closing of the canon of the New Testament was to prevent his attempts to do so.

NOTE

VON HÜGEL'S 'LUMINOUS' TEXTS

It is the central conviction of this book that the parousia is the key to New Testament eschatology. But it is not the conviction of this book that the parousia as such is the key to our Lord's own explicit teaching about the future. It is therefore important to examine von Hügel's claim that the 'Second Coming is an entirely original conception of Jesus himself', and the five 'texts of immense weight and luminous clearness, which stand above all suspicion of a secondary origin',[1] which he produces to show what Jesus himself meant by it. All these texts [2] are in fact from St Matthew's Gospel, and a close examination of them amply confirms Dr. T. F. Glasson's verdict that 'Matthew did not hesitate to alter Mark, no doubt from a pious motive!' [3] The pious motive was an eschatological one. St Matthew wanted to arrest the falling away from the vivid expectation of an imminent parousia, which he saw all around him in the Christian church of his day and perhaps most of all in the non-Greek portion of it.[4]

As one after another the last of the original apostolic band began to die out, the problem of the delayed parousia became increasingly acute for all who reckoned its imminence in terms of clock or calendar time. St Matthew's is perhaps the last 'apostolic' attempt to buttress the fading hope by emphasizing the objectivity of the parousia and by rationalizing the whole conception of the triumph of God which it represents by importing a logical series of necessary preliminaries before its fulfilment.

[1] F. von Hügel, *Essays and Addresses on the Philosophy of Religion* (Dent, 1921), p. 123.
[2] Matt. 16, 28; 19, 28; 24, 29 f.; 26, 29, 64.
[3] T. F. Glasson, *The Second Advent* (Epworth Press, 1945), p. 72.
[4] For the Syrian or possibly Phœnician origin of the First Gospel, cf. G. D. Kilpatrick, *The Origins of the Gospel according to St Matthew* (O.U.P., 1946), pp. 124 ff.

The first of von Hügel's texts of 'luminous clearness'[1] is Matthew 16, 28, 'Verily I say unto you, there be some of them that stand here, which shall in no wise taste death, till they see the Son of man coming in his kingdom'. This text shows St Matthew's procedure. In St Mark the prophecy is of a coming of the kingdom of God in power in the lifetime of some of the bystanders.[2] St Luke interprets this in a spiritual and non-apocalyptic way: it is the kingdom of God that will still be seen by some of the bystanders, but nothing is said about the manner of its working or manifestation.[3] St Matthew on the other hand interprets it apocalyptically: he knows exactly what it will mean. It is 'the Son of man coming in his kingdom' who will be seen.

This prophecy is a *crux interpretum*,[4] and attempts to explain it or explain it away have been many and varied. The basic issue must be that either the prophecy was falsified or else its fulfilment at least began during the lifetime of some of the bystanders, who heard Jesus' own actual words. The idea that it refers to or is in any way exhaustively fulfilled by a concrete historical event like the fall of Jerusalem in A.D. 70 falls down completely on the fact that judgment, though an inevitable corollary of the New Testament eschatological hope, is never the primary purpose of the parousia. There was nothing thrilling for anybody except perhaps Titus and the Roman soldiers in the prospect of Jerusalem's fall.

The idea that the prophecy may be partly fulfilled by Pentecost is tenable, but certainly not the notion that Pentecost exhausts its meaning. Pentecost, in so far as it at all adequately reveals the nature of the operations of the self-effacing and unostentatious Paraclete, not only does not exhaust its meaning, but in fact itself points to some such reality as the parousia for its fulfilment. The last word of the Holy Spirit on any subject is not about himself, but about Jesus. Thus neither the fall of Jerusalem nor the coming of the Holy Spirit on the day of Pentecost adequately fulfils the prophecy, and the temptation is great to take the way out of the dilemma offered by the Lukan omission of any reference to any coming of any sort. But while this omission is understandable as a correction of such an emphasis upon the coming as would seem for all practical purposes to exclude the presence, it does not invalidate the eschatological significance and relevance of the coming. St Matthew's interpretation may err in the opposite direction to St Luke's, but at least it makes this fact plain.

The eschatological coming is the future fulfilment of the present

---

[1] F. von Hügel, *loc. cit.*   [2] Mark 9, 1.   [3] Luke 9, 27.
[4] Cf. T. W. Manson, *The Teaching of Jesus* (C.U.P., 1931), pp. 278 ff.

secret of the Christian gospel, for it is not the going of man to God, but the coming of God to man which is the heart and soul of that gospel. And the symbolism of the spatial imagery, suggested by a coming, is as necessary to keep future eschatology in its true Christian perspective as it is to safeguard the real significance of the past incarnation or of the present working of the Holy Spirit. If Christology and pneumatology are allowed fulfilment in eschatology, then the doctrine of the parousia must be at the centre of it.

There is no doubt about the truth of the Markan prediction. The coming of the kingdom of God was a reality before Calvary: it was even more of a reality after Pentecost. Thus it was a reality in the experience of the contemporaries of Jesus himself, but it was a reality which the generation of his contemporaries did not exhaust by possessing its secret, but rather one which by its very nature of love pointed anyone, who possessed its secret, on towards a further future fulfilment of it.

Luke took the notion of coming out of the text and by implication left his readers satisfied with presence. This is a valuable corrective, but a dangerous precedent if taken out of its context in the universal apocalyptic expectation of the church for which and in the midst of which his gospel was written, and if applied indiscriminately to church situations and attitudes far different from those prevailing in the first century A.D. St Luke as much as St John can only be rightly interpreted in the light of the church situation for which he composed his gospel.

St Matthew, unlike St Luke, left the original Markan coming in his text, but tried to define its nature more concretely than St Mark did. The object of hope is made more concrete, more objective, more visible, as if St Matthew were concerned to stress the coming of one who was absent rather than to point to the coming of one who was present. In logic it may be that he is right, and that the possibility of coming depends upon the fact of absence, but on the level of love he is wrong, for in love there can be no coming unless there is presence.

The conclusion is that if we want to know what our Lord actually said, we must look not at St Matthew's 'luminous' text nor at St Luke's alternative interpretation, but at St Mark's original statement. If, however, we want to know what our Lord meant by his enigmatical statement, then we can see St Matthew and St Luke each pointing, like the two sides of a cloud-capped mountain, to a hidden reality of love, which is as much future and apocalyptic as St Matthew asserts and as much present and mystical as St Luke realizes.

The second of von Hügel's 'luminous' texts is Matthew 19, 28, 'Verily I say unto you, that ye which have followed me, in the regeneration when the Son of man shall sit on the throne of his glory, ye also shall sit on thrones, judging the twelve tribes of Israel'. This passage and the characteristic Lukan parallel to it [1] are important eschatological texts, and the apostolic privilege in sharing in the eschatological judgment is a natural corollary of the Pauline idea that the parousia involves a revelation not only of the Lord Jesus Christ himself but also of the saints whom God will 'bring with him'.[2] But von Hügel's text hardly bears one way or the other upon the question of the parousia itself or upon the problem as to how far our Lord himself actually looked forward to his own coming again.

The third text is in the apocalypse found in Matthew 24, 'immediately, after the tribulation of those days . . . the stars shall fall from heaven . . . and then shall appear the sign of the Son of man in heaven . . . and they shall see the Son of man coming on the clouds of heaven in power and great glory'.[3] This passage in its whole context shows the way in which St Matthew heightened, objectified and to some extent rationalized the focus of the primitive expectation of the church. But it adds nothing essential to the final confession of Jesus before Caiaphas,[4] and its significance for the doctrine of the parousia depends upon the weight and interpretation given to that final confession.

Before dealing with that, von Hügel introduces his fourth Matthæan text, 'I say unto you, I will not drink henceforth of this fruit of the vine, until that day when I drink it new with you in my Father's kingdom'.[5] This text is verbally almost identical with Mark 14, 25, except for (a) the addition of 'henceforth', ap' arti (ἀπ' ἄρτι), (b) the addition of 'this', (c) the addition of 'with you', and (d) the substitution of 'my Father's kingdom' for the Markan 'kingdom of God'. The first three alterations all stress the present crisis of the Last Supper and its immediate sequel as marking the transition from the old order to the new. 'Henceforth' is exactly the same little phrase that St Matthew introduces into our Lord's final confession before Caiaphas. It is 'from this very moment' that the break comes, just as it is 'from this very moment' that the coming or the parousia begins. The guests at the last supper outside the kingdom are identical with the guests at the first meal inside it. It is no distant prospect which Jesus has in view, but something beginning almost at once. This is the heart of the parousia expectation, even though this text has no specific reference to the second coming.

---

[1] Luke 22, 28 ff. [2] 1 Thess. 4, 14. [3] Matt. 24, 29 f.
[4] Matt. 26, 64. [5] Matt. 26, 29.

Finally, the last of von Hügel's five texts is Jesus' confession before Caiaphas, 'I say unto you, Henceforth ye shall see the Son of man sitting at the right hand of power, and coming in the clouds of heaven'.[1] On the strictest view of messianic secrecy, here is Jesus' self-disclosure of his messiahship. He had done everything in his power to reinterpret in his life the meaning of the term. Now he could do no more. Even if he did not use the term himself to describe his life and work, he could not deny its applicability to himself, when challenged by the high priest. The confession at Cæsarea Philippi[2] which is demanded of St Peter and the rest of the apostles is here confirmed by Jesus himself in Jerusalem before the Sanhedrin.

But for our purpose the confession before Caiaphas is not important for the fact that it affirmed Jesus' messiahship, but for the significance which it attached to that messiahship. In St Mark and St Matthew this significance is drawn out of two Old Testament texts,[3] of which St Luke significantly omits one.[4] By quoting from Daniel, Jesus sanctions at least a limited apocalyptic understanding of his final triumph. But it needs to be remembered that the audience in which Jesus made his confession was largely composed of Sadducees, who were not only passively unapocalyptic but decidedly active in opposing the apocalyptic future hopes both of pietists and Pharisees. It was precisely in terms of that element in Judaism, of which in experience they were totally ignorant and to which in doctrine they were practically hostile, that Jesus interpreted his messiahship. His word was in such a context more corrective than constructive: it did not sanction all the apocalyptic hope, but it did sanction some of it.[5]

Daniel's prophecy of the triumph of 'one like unto a son of man' is described in terms of his going to 'the ancient of days' to share his reign. The setting of the enthronement is full of nebulous celestial imagery, but the fact remains, no matter what the setting. The sense of Daniel is quite clear: the mysterious figure 'like unto a son of man' is either coming or going to 'the ancient of days' or, as we should say, to heaven or to God. In popular Christian exegesis of Jesus' quotation of Daniel the direction of this coming or going has been reversed: it is no longer from earth to heaven, but from heaven to earth. The all-important question is whether this redirection of the royal progress is true to Jesus' own intention or a distortion of it. In other words, did Jesus use Daniel's words in Daniel's sense or did he give them a new sense of his own?

---

[1] Matt. 26, 64.
[2] Mark 8, 27 ff.
[3] Ps. 110, 1; Dan. 7, 13; Mark 14, 62; Matt. 26, 64.
[4] Luke 22, 69.
[5] Cf. Mark 12, 18 ff.

In attempting to answer this question, the first point to notice is the significant additions made both by St Matthew and St Luke to St Mark's account of Jesus' confession. The triumph in St Matthew is 'henceforth', *ap' arti* (ἀπ' ἄρτι), and in St Luke it is 'from henceforth', *apo tou nun* (ἀπὸ τοῦ νῦν). The meaning is clear: the triumph begins from this very moment. But the wording is different, and this difference suggests a double and independent evidence as to the primitive tradition, which may very possibly therefore be original and authentic. If it is, then the movement of royal triumph which Jesus said Caiaphas himself would witness must be regarded as beginning from the moment of the trial before the Sanhedrin. This is the Johannine perspective, which sees the crucifixion as itself a triumph and not a tragedy, turned into a triumph by the resurrection. If this interpretation of our Lord's confession before Caiaphas is correct, then the apocalyptic imagery is clearly framework rather than fact, for there was certainly no triumph 'in the clouds' on Good Friday.

So much may be granted, and yet the main question as to the direction of the royal progress is not thereby answered. Only St Mark and St Matthew interpret the messiahship in terms of Daniel's prophecy. But all three Synoptic gospels interpret it in terms of Psalm 110, 1, and in St Mark and St Matthew the quotation from the Psalms precedes the quotation from Daniel. This means that the session 'at the right hand of power' begins on the cross at the right hand of a thief and precedes the movement, whether that be interpreted as a coming or a going. And there is surely not the slightest doubt that, whatever Jesus himself meant by the words he used, the two Synoptic evangelists meant by them and understood him to mean by them a return to earth and a coming to man rather than a going away to heaven and to God. If they understood the words in this sense, then there would need to be abundant evidence, of which there is in fact hardly a shred, that Jesus himself meant something quite different.

If the royal triumph was going to be visible from that very moment onwards to Caiaphas, if only he had eyes to see it, then the setting of that triumph would be on earth and not in heaven. It is only as a royal progress of coming to men and not of departing from men that it can be described as a triumph visible to men. In other words the kingdom of heaven would come upon earth. If Jesus or the evangelists had wanted to retain the direction of Daniel's progress instead of clearly reversing it, they could have made this plain by putting the quotation from the Psalms after that from Daniel. The fact that they did what they did and placed the session before the coming suggests that in this, as in so many other things, Jesus retained the language of the old pre-Christian tradition but entirely transformed its meaning. The meaning of Daniel is not to be imposed upon Jesus, even if the language of Daniel is chosen by him. He used old thought forms, but gave them new meaning. The direction of Daniel's royal progress is completely reversed. Jesus fulfilled the apocalyptic expectations but not in the way the apocalyptists expected.

The movement of love's triumph is not thought of by him as a going but as a coming, and this coming is not some far-off distant event, designed to reverse the direction of his present exodus (ἔξοδος) or going.[1] It is meant to be, as St Matthew and St Luke by their additions to St Mark make perfectly plain, a coming in the immediate future to be seen by anyone who had eyes to see it on Good Friday and on Easter day as well as on the day of Pentecost and right onwards till the parousia. The future coming is only rightly understood as the final term of a whole series of comings. But without the final term the whole series is in jeopardy. And if the clue to the future is found in the present and if the significance of the present is seen, as Christians believe it is, in the incarnation and atonement of Jesus Christ himself, then the whole gospel is of one piece, a coming throughout of God in his prevenient grace to man. It is to safeguard this vital secret of the divine initiative that the parousia must remain at the centre of the eschatological gospel.

If it was only in his confession before Caiaphas at the very end of his earthly life that Jesus in so many words pointed to the secret of the eschatological gospel, that need not surprise us. It is exactly what he did in the case of the secret of the pneumatological gospel as well. The evidence for the Paraclete, if we look for explicit or indubitably authentic dominical sanction in so many words, is as scanty as it is for the parousia. If the former is not mentioned till the very end of his life, nor is the latter. The Paraclete and the parousia go together. The one sanctions the other and the one without the other is inconceivable. The final coming is not so completely *sui generis* as not to be of a piece with all the comings which are the manifestation of God's love and power and glory from Calvary onwards. At Calvary, if not before, the Lord's prayer began to be answered. It has been answered ever since and it is still being answered to-day. But no member of the early church ever imagined for one moment that because it was being answered it did not still need to be prayed. In fact it was the consciousness that it was being answered which provided the stimulus for its being prayed.

[1] Luke 9, 31.

13

It was the awareness of the presence which had come which emboldened prayer for the parousia which was to come.

Von Hügel's 'luminous' texts have been reduced to one. But the one is enough, for the hope of the Christian church does not depend upon the definition of its future ground, but upon the awareness of its present realization. The presence alone guarantees the parousia. But the presence without the parousia is as much idolatry as the parousia without the presence is phantasy. The one without the other is a contradiction of that love which the Christian gospel reveals as the very nature of God himself.

There is one other 'luminous' text, though von Hügel does not mention it as such, and that is the famous Schweitzerian crux, 'Verily I say unto you, ye shall not have gone through the cities of Israel till the Son of man be come'.[1] If these are the words of Jesus and not, as many modern scholars think,[2] the ideas of the primitive Palestinian church read back into the mouth of Jesus, then they can be interpreted along the same lines as those suggested for the right understanding of Jesus' confession before Caiaphas. In that case the coming is from now onwards and its starting-point is put back before the crucifixion.

Bishop Barry is quite right in saying that Jesus 'spoke of his coming as immediate. There is nothing in the authentic tradition about a defined and distant parousia'.[3] The question is whether he is right in saying that it is this 'deferred and distant parousia' which we mean when we speak about the second coming. If it is, then our perspective is false to the authentic and original Christian gospel, in which eschatology is not an appendage to an otherwise self-contained theological system, but an integral part of that system. In that gospel the imminence of the parousia is not just a way of stressing the urgency of its ethical implications, though of course it does help to do that. It is an expression of the truth as it is seen from within lovers' time. It is not true because it is fulfilled at Pentecost, as Bishop Barry suggests: it is true because what is true always will be found and proved true at the end. The final parousia at the end of time is of a piece with the manner of the presence throughout time, and of this the coming of the Paraclete is the clue. But the coming of the Paraclete does not exhaust the meaning of the hope of the coming of the Lord. On the contrary, on the Johannine view the former presupposes the latter.[4] It will be Jesus who

---

[1] Matt. 10, 23.

[2] T. W. Manson, *The Teaching of Jesus*, p. 221.   A. M. Hunter, *The Work and Words of Jesus* (S.C.M., 1950), p. 108.

[3] F. R. Barry, *The Relevance of Christianity*, p. 96 (quoted by A. M. Hunter, *op. cit.*, p. 110).   [4] John 14, 16 ff. ; 15, 26

comes and who will be seen in the end when the last veil that hides him from our eyes is taken away.

But his coming even in the end does not so much wind up as inaugurate the eschatological fulfilment of history. It is *via* his parousia that all the other secrets of eschatology will be made manifest. And if this seems to postpone the very end indefinitely, the Christian answer can only be that if there is to be hope as well as faith and love in the very end, then there can be no end which for the Christian is not also a new beginning. In this way the parousia fulfils the feeling of many sensitive souls that a further and greater manifestation of God's love and power is needed before the end, whether that feeling focuses on Christian reunion, 'that the world may know'[1] the truth of the incarnation, or upon world evangelization, that the world may have a chance of believing.[2]

In this way the parousia itself looks forward, and Lagrange's comment on Jesus' confession before Caiaphas is seen to be only a half-truth. It is true that 'cette venue n'est pas celle de la consummation mais de l'inauguration',[3] but it is not true therefore that the parousia, as part of the eschatological drama of the end, is not referred to. For the parousia is itself the inauguration of the consummation. The trouble with the church's attitude to it has been that it has all too often, as in the Apostles' Creed, tended to regard the parousia not as inaugurating the untold blessedness of the end but as confirming the judgment at the very end. But in fact the parousia itself points forward, not backward, and only so can it fulfil the covenant expectation of the church. It is the covenant which explains and justifies the parousia as the secret and the clue to the whole Christian hope and the key to the whole eschatological drama.

---

[1] John 17, 23.   [2] Matt. 24, 14.
[3] Quoted by T. F. Glasson, *The Second Advent*, p. 68.

CHAPTER VII

THE SECRET OF MYSTICISM

THE primitive church was sure that in Jesus the end had come and that was why it called him Christ. But because it was therefore sure that the nature of that end was love, it was also sure that the end was still to come. Furthermore, because it lived in lovers' time it reckoned in terms of lovers' time, and so by lovers' time the end, which was still to come, was very near—a fact which the subsequent passage of two thousand years of clock or chronological time has done nothing either to prove or to disprove.

As soon as the level of Christian eschatological thinking descended from that of love to that of logic, as soon as the nature of the love revealed in Jesus Christ descended from the person who may be met to the proposition which can be grasped, the church started to argue imminence in terms of chronological time. And from that day within the New Testament church to this day within the contemporary church there have been calculations to prove imminence and arguments to explain away delay.

Once, however, the imminence is grasped as imminence in terms of lovers' and not of clock time, the reckoning whether of the expanded Synoptic apocalypses [1] or of the rabbinizing apostle [2] or of the great apocalyptist himself,[3] if he is misinterpreted as expressing in propositions of conscious logic what he is in fact embodying in images of unconscious love, is seen to be of a piece with the reasoning of the so-called modern 'students of prophecy'. Such arguments may have value to steady faith on the lower level of logic; they are powerless to lift it to the higher level of love: and they are paralysing if their apologetic *tours de force* are allowed to usurp the place of the apostolic preaching of the eschatological gospel.

This latter, if it remains true to its original title-deeds, remains always a standing witness to love 'not in persuasive words of wisdom, but in demonstration of the Spirit and of power',[4] and never presumes to make the Satanic trespass of attempting proof of it. At the mystical level of love the end can be both expected imminently at any minute and also experienced or realized immanently as having

---

[1] Mark 13, 5 ff., and parallels.   [2] 2 Thess. 2, 1 ff.
[3] The author of the Book of Revelation, whoever he was.   [4] 1 Cor. 2, 4.

already occurred. The parousia can be the presence too: indeed it must be, or else the future reality is merely phantasy.

Within such a context, what of the details of the New Testament eschatological prospect? The outlook of the early church is not dominated by the hope of immortality or by the glimpse of the millennium. It faces the judgment more as the inevitable and immediate conclusion of every individual's life than as a final verdict administered in a universal court. In neither case, however, is judgment so central as to dominate the perspective or to distort a future prospect which for the first Christians is as full of hope as the present scene is full of faith and both are full of love.

In the New Testament the Christian future prospect focuses on the coming of the Lord, with the resurrection of the body as the necessary corollary of that final embodied meeting in which all mankind and nature too will share and by which all will be transformed. What for the Old Testament was the day of the Lord, so easily imagined by the apocalyptists as a date fixed in some time-scale of calendar or astronomical time, becomes for the New Testament once again the prophetic day which derives all its meaning from him whose activity alone gives it content and significance. And now it is no longer Yahweh but Jesus who gives it its content. He is the Lord, moving in love towards those he loves. It is no longer some one largely unknown, but some one intimately known who is expected, and hope is focused on a person and not on any abstract [1] absolute whatever.

If Christians move towards a date it is a lovers' date, and if they move towards a place it is a lovers' trysting-place. And if they move towards a lovers' date and a lovers' trysting-place, they move on no fixed point either in calendar and chronological time or in geographical and astronomical space. They move towards a meeting which may open up surprisingly at any point in historical time or geographical space. It may open up at any minute, and if it does, there are no limits to the transformation of all space and time which in its turn it opens up.

That is the eschatological truth gripped by the New Testament church and tragically distorted if it is either denied all reality altogether here and now or given a non-eschatological reality here and now. The break-up of the New Testament outlook may take one of two forms. Either the real Jesus himself is no longer expected, however much in theory his name is used of the central figure in the eschatological prospect. This is in essence the mediæval heresy,

[1] Cf. the scathing criticism of the curse of abstraction in modern western civilization in E. Brunner, *The Scandal of Christianity* (S.C.M., 1951), p. 91.

where the focus of hope in the parousia of Jesus Christ is replaced by the focus of fear in the last judgment of the *pantokrator* (παντοκράτωρ). In this way all real eschatological significance in the present here and now is denied.

Or alternatively eschatology in any real sense is abandoned and there is no future parousia or judgment at all. This is in essence the modern heresy in which the pagan believes in no future at all and the Christian enjoys a spurious security, which is grounded upon a non-eschatological understanding of the basis of his faith. The result of both heresies is a loss of the essential New Testament doctrine of assurance, and means the abandonment of the world of the I-Thou relationship of love, in which alone that assurance can be found.

On the mediæval view there is either no assurance because the last judgment of *Dies irae, dies illa* is administered by one who, if he retains the name of Christ, bears no relation in his unknown and terrible splendour to the authentic Jesus; or else, alternatively, there is a false assurance, based upon the claims of the church to provide by some temporal infallibility an insurance policy valid against any eschatological eventuality.

As far as the modern outlook is concerned, the inevitable reaction from the mediæval distortion of the New Testament prospect and from the post-Reformation distortion which followed it has led to a general abandonment of the whole concept of the last judgment and of hell. Where these doctrines have been retained, post-Reformation protestantism has been as full of fictional ideas of justification as mediæval catholicism was of ecclesiastical dodges for escaping the wrath to come.

The tragedy of so much protestant biblicism and catholic ecclesiasticism is that the assurance they profess to offer is quite unable to stand the test of the essence of New Testament eschatology. It is the parousia of Jesus Christ himself which reveals the standard of judgment by which we are all judged. And his parousia is bound to be a surprise to everyone, for if no human lovers, however deep their mutual sympathy and understanding, can ever meet without surprise, how inconceivable is the elimination of surprise from the final meeting between our Lord Jesus Christ and those who love him and those who do not!

To offer assurance on any other basis than the mercy of the Lord is to betray a total ignorance of Christian eschatology. It is both false to the essence of any relationship of love and also entirely unworthy of such knowledge as we possess of the character of Jesus Christ himself. It is also quite useless in view of the inevitable surprise of our final meeting with him.

From failure to come to grips with the essence of New Testament eschatology, which is unintelligible as soon as its inner secret of love is lost, the church is in constant danger of division and schism on this very issue of assurance. It is so easy to replace the New Testament confidence in God alone either by no confidence whatever or by a false confidence which is not really based on God at all.

When we look at the mediæval eschatological scheme in detail its outline is not difficult to grasp. 'Universal immortality is assumed; for those who are beyond pardon there is Hell; for those who are pardonable, Purgatory; for those whose pardon is accomplished, Paradise. And alongside of these, for the unawakened soul there is Limbo.' [1] In this scheme, apart from its entirely individualistic reference and apparent ignoring of the significance of the onward sweep of history as a whole, there are, as Archbishop Temple suggests, 'certain administrative difficulties.' [2] 'How can there be Paradise for any while there is Hell, conceived as unending torment, for some? Each supposedly damned soul was born into the world as a mother's child, and Paradise cannot be a Paradise for her if her child is in such a Hell.' [3]

At the Reformation the difficulties of the mediæval scheme, so far from being eliminated, were in fact accentuated. The abuses connected with the doctrine of purgatory were plain for all to see. The Reformers searched the scriptures for evidence of such a doctrine and they found little or none at all. They therefore [4] eliminated purgatory from their eschatological scheme and left the stark alternatives of heaven or hell confronting all except the unawakened immediately after death.

This meant that judgment, which rather than the parousia still held the centre of the eschatological stage, became ultimately purely vindictive. There could no longer be any deterrent or reformative purpose in it. In fact, if not in theory, Jesus Christ is no longer the judge of all. His vindication is theoretically assumed, but at the cost of sacrificing everything he set out to vindicate. The real Jesus 'sacrificed His existence to the integrity of His Ultimate Meaning on the Cross'.[5] The ecclesiastical Jesus of traditional eschatology

[1] W. Temple, *Nature, Man and God* (Macmillan, 1934), p. 454.
[2] *Ibid.*   [3] *Ibid.*
[4] The lack of scriptural evidence for the mediæval doctrine of purgatory—'grounded upon no warranty of Scripture, but rather repugnant to the Word of God' (Article 22) —may have been the ostensible reason for its elimination at the Reformation. Perhaps deeper was the subconscious realization of the need of integrating eschatology into the rest of Christian doctrine, and of the difficulty of doing so as long as its main emphasis was upon the soul's long pilgrimage to God rather than of God's prior and prevenient pilgrimage to the soul.
[5] A D. Galloway, *The Cosmic Christ* (Nisbet, 1951), p. 258.

may almost be said to have vindicated his existence at the cost of sacrificing his meaning.

Thus for all practical purposes it looks as if the most significant move in the eschatological thinking of the Christian church has occurred not at the Reformation but in our own day, when both biblical and liturgical scholarship are rediscovering the unity and integrated wholeness of the New Testament doctrine of the last things.[1] This significant move is the response of the Christian church to the final breakdown of both the traditional mediæval and also the modern reformed eschatological programme.

For what has happened is clearly this: modern man has eliminated hell from the reformed scheme just as the Reformers eliminated purgatory from the mediæval scheme. Conceived as a clear-cut vindication of a vindictiveness ultimately sovereign in the universe, hell is an offence both to the natural conscience of man and also to his understanding of the work and character of Jesus Christ.

The Reformers eliminated purgatory, but they kept the mediævally distorted and vindictive judgment. Modern man has scrapped both purgatory and also hell and judgment too, although the two latter have certainly the 'warranty of Scripture'.[2] And for this scrapping of the whole traditional eschatological set-up modern man must not be too harshly blamed. For only if the church can rediscover for herself the essence of the unity of the New Testament outlook on the end, and only if she can demonstrate anew the secret of the New Testament hope, can she rightly claim the allegiance of the world to her eschatological doctrine.

If she still insists on the fact of life after death, as she must, and if this means that all who die go automatically either at once or after an interval to paradise or heaven, as seemed to be the implication of so many Armisticetide sermons between the two Great Wars, then the result is clear. There can be no gain-saying the truth of the communist charge in all the venom of its contemporary significance: 'religion is the opium of the people'. For God on this view is regarded as so genially tolerant that he becomes morally indifferent, and belief in life after death becomes a moral narcotic instead of a moral stimulant.

It is idle to deny that this is in fact the grave disservice that so much distorted and emasculated Christian eschatology has rendered to the modern world. The reaction from a vindictive to a senti-mental notion of 'our Father which art in heaven' has inevitably

[1] Only waiting, in my judgment, for the fearless realization that the parousia is the key to that wholeness.
[2] Article 22.

produced the lamentably similar swing of the pendulum in all earthly approximations to that fatherhood, of which St Paul tells us the pattern and prototype is in heaven.[1] The result is plain to see in the homes, the schools, the law courts, and the whole social and political structure of twentieth-century democracy.

So we are confronted with an inescapable dilemma. Either we must rediscover the eschatological secret of the New Testament, or we must resign ourselves to a rôle of complete futility in the face of the ideological issues of to-day. We cannot possibly do without any eschatology at all, for eschatology is but the final term of faith in God. Without an eschatology such faith is at best wishful thinking and at worst sheer humbug. Time is short: just as in physical and material things, so also in spiritual and moral, the western world, which is the inheritor of a Christian civilization, has been living upon the inherited capital of the past. The imminence of judgment upon this sort of thing is no less clear spiritually than it manifestly is politically and socially.

Either we must rediscover the New Testament faith, or we must give up all hope of ever practising the New Testament ethic. It is sheer nonsense to pretend that we can go on producing the fruit when we have lost all touch with the root. And it is the great merit of the best contemporary scholarship, both biblical and liturgical, to have proved how indissoluble are the ethics and the eschatology of Jesus himself.

Two conclusions may be drawn from the distinctive Christian eschatology, the first of which gives the lie to any vindictiveness at the end, and the second to any sentimentalism. It is the real Jesus with whom we shall be confronted at the end.[2] When we 'see him as he is',[3] it will not be another Christ, but the same, for Jesus Christ is 'the same yesterday, to-day and forever'.[4] This means that in the end the last judgment will not be of finitude, but of sin; the criterion on which the verdict of judgment is now being based, whether we realize it or not, and will then finally be seen by all to be based is one and the same. It is not the unknown and eternal character of God that will judge historical and temporal man, but rather the ideal possibility of his own historical and finite existence. All distinctively Christian eschatology must stand squarely and unequivocally for the parousia of Jesus Christ himself as being the clue to the meaning of judgment and so give the lie to all vindictive eschatologies, whether ecclesiastical or political.

[1] Eph. 3, 14 ff.
[2] Cf. R. Niebuhr, *The Nature and Destiny of Man* (Nisbet, 1943), vol. ii, pp. 302 ff.; St Augustine, *De Civitate Dei*, xix, 27.
[3] 1 John 3, 2.
[4] Heb. 13, 8.

Secondly, against all sentimentalism the distinctive message of any truly Christian eschatology is that history has a meaning even if in history that meaning is ambiguous. The parable of the tares [1] is sufficient warning against any attempt to draw lines of absolute distinction to separate good from evil in history. But it is equally sufficient warning against drawing from this the typical modern conclusion that all such historical distinctions are meaningless and will ultimately be swallowed up in a distinctionless eternity. We cannot read 'the wrath' [2] and the 'severity of God' [3] out of the eschatology of the New Testament, [4] or pretend that they do not find a place very near the centre of the eschatological teaching of Jesus himself.

The righteous, in so far as their confidence is in any righteousness of their own, are bound to have an uneasy conscience at the last day, [5] and this only shows that before God, as Jesus reveals him, 'shall no man living be justified' [6] by any merits of his own. As the parable of the Pharisee and the publican makes unmistakably clear, our eschatological confidence can only be in the mercy of God. [7] This can easily be misunderstood, but for those who have the slightest inkling of the true significance of the New Testament doctrine of the atonement nothing could be more blasphemous than to interpret the fact that salvation is free as if it meant that it was cheap. It is at the cross that we are at the heart of the eschatology of the New Testament. It is tempting to go beyond the fact of Calvary and to spin out the fancies of an undreamt-of futurist eschatology, unrelated to past or present historical fact and experience. [8] But we do so at our peril, for if the resultant picture means the displacement of Jesus Christ crucified from the centre of the final panorama, then we have lost all sure ground of hope and confidence, however entrancing and enticing to fanaticism or wishful thinking may be the prospect opened up.

Not the field of Megiddo but the tree of Golgotha is our ground of confidence and hope. It may seem an inadequate substitute for the wilder apocalypses that continually dazzle the eyes of would-be

---

[1] Matt. 13, 24 ff.   [2] E.g. John 3, 36.   [3] Rom. 11, 22.

[4] Cf. E. Brunner, *The Scandal of Christianity*, pp. 76 ff. It is much better to explain the wrath of God on the analogy of human relationship, however imperfect that analogy may be, than to explain it away in terms of some impersonal necessity or fate. 'The man who cannot become angry cannot truly love' (E. Brunner, *op. cit.*, p. 78). That is not the whole explanation of the wrath of God, but it is sufficient warning against all attempts to explain it away. God does not share William Temple's most conspicuous failing. He can say 'No' and he can 'tick you off properly' (cf. F. A. Iremonger, *William Temple* (O.U.P., 1948), p. 498).

[5] Matt. 25, 31 ff.   [6] Ps. 143, 2.   [7] Luke 18, 9 ff.

[8] Cf. L. E. Froom, *The Prophetic Faith of our Fathers* (Review and Herald, 1950), vols. i–iv.

political and spiritual reformers, but it is the only basis of assurance that the Christian has to offer, if he is loyal to the gospel of the New Testament. It was at Calvary, not in opposition to Bethlehem but as the climax and clue to all that Bethlehem meant and stood for, that the eternal order was fully manifested in time in that 'scandal of particularity' [1] which is as much an offence to all idealists as to all cynics.

We cannot go back to Calvary or force our way forward to the millennium, but we can allow the significance of Calvary to confront us here and now with all its stark realism and all its gracious and glorious divine reality. By thus allowing God to meet us day by day we can enter into the secret of that meeting in which all real life now consists and in which one day it will be seen by all to consist. There is no possible short-cut to utopia, not even if we volunteer for the most exacting tasks and shoulder the heaviest crosses of our own choosing. It is only by crucifixion with Christ, which means not dodging the cross of God's appointment, that we can hasten his coming and find sure ground of solid confidence and hope.

In the light of the tremendous affirmations [2] which emerge as the inevitable conclusion of sharing the faith of the primitive church that the apparent defeat of the cross of Jesus Christ was in fact his final victory, we are in a position to realize the grandeur of the Christian outlook on the future. History is no puppet-show put on by a stage manager and manipulated by mechanical and determined forces behind the scenes. On the other hand it is no uncharted ocean with perhaps inescapable rocks and reefs barring all possible channels to the haven where we would be. We are left with no propositional certainty as to how the future will unfold, but we have complete and securely grounded personal confidence that its final issue will be a glory beyond our wildest dreams.

When Jesus Christ came into the world, he upset the propositional eschatology of the Jews: and any attempt to revert from confidence in the truth, as personally revealed in him, to the truth, as propositionally expressed about him, is eschatologically suicidal. We may neither find confidence in an idealism which escapes from the

---

[1] Cf. G. K. A. Bell and A. Deissmann, *Mysterium Christi* (Longmans, 1930), pp. 31 ff.; E. Brunner, *The Scandal of Christianity*, pp. 9 ff.

[2] I should summarize them as:

    (1) This is a law-abiding universe.
    (2) This is a freedom-loving universe.
    (3) This is a reciprocally related universe.

The penal, 'classic' and sacrificial doctrines of the atonement attempt to express these three truths (cf. J. E. Fison, *The Blessing of the Holy Spirit* (Longmans, 1950), ch. 10, pp. 178 ff.).

material half of life, nor in a realism which is blind to the tragic distortion of the pattern of the whole universe as we know it. Only in the conviction that in Jesus Christ the end has come, and in the realization that to share in his triumph we do not have to force ourselves back in memory two thousand years or force ourselves forward in some fevered imagination of a millennium round the corner, can we enter into the secret of the Christian eschatological gospel.

If we do enter into that secret, we discover that all we have to do is to allow the eternal truth revealed on the cross in time in all its full reality to step up to us and address us in the humdrum contemporaneity of our daily life. If we do not dodge its invitation and its challenge to take up our cross daily, we shall realize the continual initiative of the love of God towards us, and by responding to it find the secret of the real life of meeting and of holy communion, which is the birthplace of the radiant and indestructible Christian hope.

But to venture here means to take great risks. False grounds of hope must go before the true hope can take their place. So it must be in any relationship of love. 'We shall all stand before the judgment seat of Christ' [1]—there in a word is the inescapable and ultimate fact. And what good is a confidence now that is then of no avail? Then the issues, which are now blurred, will be crystal clear. There is something about the cruel brilliance of the light above the atmosphere, unspoiled by the pollutions it contains, in the apocalyptic vision of the 'great white throne',[2] and we are not surprised at the terrible picture of the expanding universe which accompanies it.

Take away the cruelty of an imported vindictiveness foreign certainly to Jesus Christ himself, and perhaps to the great apocalyptist too, and here is the inevitable effect of that stripping of the mask from the hypocrite and the humbug which confrontation with Jesus Christ always involves. The hypocrites of the New Testament, like the hypocrites of to-day, were largely unconscious and unaware of their hypocrisy. Until the prodigal son 'came to himself' it was impossible for him to 'arise and go' to his father.[3] Here and now, whether we know it or not, we are all constantly cushioning ourselves against the full impact of the ultimate reality of God revealed in Jesus Christ. One day we shall be in his presence stripped and naked. Not one of our protective measures, however holy its appearance, will then be of the slightest use. We shall have to make the response to him then which we so constantly avoid now.

[1] Rom. 14, 10.   [2] Rev. 20, 11.   [3] Luke 15, 17 f.

How shall we fare? That is the urgent eschatological question, and to it the whole New Testament gives us back one unanimous answer, 'Not as you expect'. Then how can we face the ultimate issues, to which now we are unconsciously or wilfully blind, but which we cannot always dodge? On what security can we build our hope in face of the last judgment?

There can be only one answer to this question. If we want to speak of the end as a judgment we must use the vocabulary appropriate to a judgment, and that is the vocabulary of the law court. And if we do, we are at once confronted with the glorious secret of the gospel of justification by faith. It cannot too often be insisted that this is no Pauline innovation. It was our Lord himself who countered the typical wrong-headedness of the lawyer, 'desiring to justify himself',[1] with the parable of the good Samaritan, and who passed his verdict of acquittal not upon the Pharisee, but upon the publican, who 'went down to his house justified rather than the other'.[2] When we come to grips with the meaning of a term like justification by faith, which at a certain moment in history can seem to contain within itself the whole content of the Christian gospel,[3] we can only find its secret if we realize the eschatological setting within which it was originally understood by the early church.

Confronted with the end, revealed in Jesus Christ, there is no ground of confidence for the Christian or for anyone else except in the mercy of God. 'God, be merciful to me the sinner'[4] is the only plea that can be sure of acceptance because no surprise can upset it. But how can anyone be sure of God's mercy? Only because Jesus Christ himself is the final revelation of God, and through his life and death manifested the fundamental and indeed eschatological mercy of God.

If he is not the judge on judgment day, there can be no confidence. But if he is the judge (and if with whatever regal or legal trappings we invest him in our imagination, we still let him dominate his setting and refuse the temptation to improve upon his actual revelation in time of God's eternal order), then there is confidence, but there will be no presumption. We cannot compel him to confront us in the way we want: we can only face him as he confronts us in the way he wants. Face to face with the ultimately inevitable surprise of his revelation there can be no ground of confidence or hope except in him.

[1] Luke 10, 29.   [2] Luke 18, 14.
[3] Cf. E. C. Hoskyns and F. N. Davey, *The Fourth Gospel*, 2nd ed. (Faber and Faber, 1947), p. 5.   [4] Luke 18, 13, R.V. margin.

To venture here is to move right out of the safe world of objects, whether they be persons or things, and to move right into the perilous world of relationship: it is to move out of the delimited and manageable abstract world of logic into the undefined and limitless reality of the world of love. In this world we may have the ark to point to our security, but we may not possess the golden calf as our security. This Old Testament analogy goes for all the Christian symbols, rites, dogmas and codes of ethical behaviour. They may all be means of grace: none of them may be an end or it will insulate us from grace.

To abandon confidence in these holy things (and holy book and holy sacrament and all our holiest experiences are here equally involved) seems to many to be sheer apostasy. But it is in fact the only gateway to dynamic as opposed to static faith. It seems like the loss of all assurance and hope: it is in fact the gateway to all true assurance and firmly grounded hope. It is in such apparent dereliction that we find the secret of justification by faith, to which baptism (as opposed to all other passports to the Christian life) so significantly points.

Justification is, as Article 11 says, a 'most wholesome doctrine and very full of comfort', but it is a snare and a delusion, however interpreted, unless it is set in its true eschatological context. In that context our confidence may perhaps be more safely formulated in guarded theological terminology, but it certainly can never be more vividly expressed than in John Wesley's graphic couplet—

> I give up every plea beside—
> Lord, I am damn'd; but Thou hast died.[1]

It would take much longer to expound the full implications of the doctrine of justification by faith.[2] But this *punctum stantis aut cadentis ecclesiæ* has become such a touchstone of religious controversy that it is difficult to find common ground between catholics and protestants on its fundamental significance. Only in an eschatological setting and only at a mystical level of understanding can we move towards a solution of our differences. That is why the doctrine of the parousia is so vitally important, for only if it is at the centre of our future hope can we look for that coming together of eschatology and mysticism which is the secret of the New Testament gospel.

[1] J. Wesley, *Sermons on Several Occasions*, First Series (Wesleyan Conference Office, 1878), p. 142.
[2] For a tentative beginning, cf. J. E. Fison, in *The Gospel of Grace* (Lutterworth Press, 1936), pp. 48 ff.

It must be cleared of that uniqueness which so often marks it off in complete and splendid isolation from all other elements of the Christian faith. In such isolation it may provide a refuge of compensation or a mirage of hope, but it cannot give us the grounded confidence and optimism of which we are in such sore need. That confidence, it is clear, can only be obtained in a person known in the present and not merely surmised in the future. No impersonal concept of a universal restoration of all things can take the place of the centrality of Jesus Christ himself in our understanding of the end.

If all things are to be summed up in him,[1] that is a very different thing from the all too common expectation of the reverse movement, whereby he is included in the summing up of a final totality, of which he is only a part. The church as a whole has often been guilty of this depersonalizing of the entire eschatological scheme, which in fact only holds together in the person of Jesus Christ and only opens out in its totality as a result of his parousia. She has gone back upon the apostolic reinterpretation of the vocabulary of the Lord, and sought by slavish and literal adherence to his own vocabulary to secure the identity of her gospel with his. Nothing in fact leads more certainly to apostasy from him than the perennial attempt to improve upon the apostolic preaching of Jesus Christ by reversion to an imitation of Jesus' own preaching of the kingdom of God.

If we recover the secret of the person as the ground of our confidence, then he must be at the centre of our eschatological outlook, and so we have to come to grips with the meaning of his parousia. This Greek word, by its double meaning of presence and coming, is singularly apt as an indication of the abiding significance of what the Old Testament had glimpsed in the doctrine of the *shekinah*. But as a technical term, used in this sense, it is very rare in the New Testament, for the significant reason that the presence or coming of which it speaks is the presence or coming of that which cannot exist by itself as an object *in vacuo* at all.

It is the presence or coming of love. As such it is the presence which guarantees the coming and saves it from phantasy, and it is the coming, or parousia, which is the corollary of the presence and saves it from idolatry. The presence of love meant for the early church a vivid expectation of its parousia. But, as we have seen, as soon as the indefinable presence of love began to be replaced and not merely interpreted by the definitions of propositions and dogmas about it, then it was inevitable that the originally indissoluble but unidentifiable presence/parousia should split into two.

[1] Eph. 1, 10.

In logic what is here cannot come here, and so the presence and the parousia became separated, and the first coming and the presence of Christ was de-eschatologized in order to safeguard the eschatological character of his second coming and his parousia.

The result of this was ultimately disastrous both for the understanding of the biblical gospel and also for the full realization of the liturgical worship of the church. The expectation of the experienced present revelation of the eternal in time was lost in the attempt either to recollect the past revelation of the eternal in time or to force the speeding up of the future revelation of the eternal in time. Elaborate biblical and ecclesiastical devices seeking to perpetuate and continually renew the expectation of the parousia were self-evidently unable to provide by rite or text, formula or gnosis, for that meeting of man and God in which real life consists. Instead of realizing the personal possibility of meeting in a genuine I-Thou relationship, the temptation was almost overwhelming to fall back upon an object of communion or contemplation which could never arise above the I-It world where propositional infallibility so easily replaces personal confidence.

Whether in Bible, sacrament or second coming attention became increasingly focused upon the manner of the parousia, and attempts were made by doctrines of infallibility and transubstantiation to guarantee that which, if truly understood as the eschatological parousia of personal love, could never be so guaranteed. The resulting idolatry and bigoted fanaticism is plain to see all down the history of the Christian church. But whereas it has been generally agreed that the eucharistic and biblical dogmas need redeeming rather than scrapping, it has not been so with the doctrine of the eschatological parousia itself. Yet without its redemption though we may have faith from the Bible and love from the sacrament we miss the note of radiant hope which sounds so clearly from the parousia in the theological harmony of the early church.

This hope is centred upon the personal manifestation of God in Christ. It looks for the personal triumph of love rather than for the propositional triumph of logic or for the impersonal triumph of goodness, truth and beauty, whether by evolutionary process or by catastrophic crisis. But so often the object of this hope is degraded in the cruder doctrines of the second coming, for it is so easy to forget that, if 'God is love',[1] then there must always be a proportion between a revelation received and the mental and spiritual state of the receiver. Even the much quoted Ascension text, 'This Jesus, which was received up into heaven, shall so come in like manner as

[1] 1 John 4, 8.

ye beheld him going into heaven',[1] is no evidence for the conventional picture of the second coming any more than it is for the conventional picture of the Ascension. Surely the ascending Christ was as invisible to the unbeliever as was the risen Lord.

If we accept the eschatological significance of the life, death and resurrection of Jesus Christ upon the testimony of the apostles, which we are convinced was not based upon an illusion, then we cannot introduce a completely alien and fool-proof objectivity into any future completion of the eschatological programme, which was altogether absent from that part of it, to which we already have reliable testimony. In the face of the loss of all living faith when the supernatural is abandoned, the good intentions of believers have turned continually to attempts to safeguard that supernatural world, to the reality of which the whole eschatology of the Bible is the clearest possible witness. But these attempts, however well intentioned, are misguided and ultimately idolatrous, because they deny the essence of the supernatural order, which is that it is an order of love.[2]

It is love which will be revealed at the parousia, and it is love which will be revealed in the last judgment. The two cannot be separated, though it matters a great deal whether we are looking with hope for the appearance of a saviour we love or expecting with despair the arrival of a judge we fear. Christ is the judge and he is the saviour, and 'we shall see him even as he is',[3] but the sight will not be of another Christ than him, whom we now know by faith. He will not then be safeguarded from all possibility of subjective misinterpretation by a fool-proof objectivity. No such conflict between a present life of faith and a future beatific vision is possible if the object of the former and the latter is love.

Arguments as to whether the beatific vision is a possibility in any sense in this life or whether it may only be enjoyed hereafter, lose all their point when once the conception of the philosophical God, over against us as an objective abstraction, is abandoned in favour of the biblical God meeting us in an inextricably intertwined objective-subjective relationship. We may have the philosophical God, and often the theological God too, within our mental and spiritual grasp. We can conjure him by holy rite or word, though of course we shall claim his sanction for the conjuring.[4]

[1] Acts 1, 11.
[2] Part of the purpose of the Fourth Gospel is, as we have seen, to check the danger of idolatry both in a present sacramentalism and a future eschatology.
[3] 1 John 3, 2.
[4] Cf. M. Buber, *Moses* (East and West Library, 1946), pp. 52 f.

14

But the biblical and eschatological God revealed in Jesus Christ is the one with whom we have to deal. He is no Baal, tied in irrevocable organic unity to his people, regardless of their moral and spiritual behaviour: he is Yahweh, the living and the covenantal God, and he meets us in his covenanted trysting-places and in all the uncovenanted and surprising *rendezvous* of love. We may never have him within our grasp and, though he longs to have us within his own, he will never use compulsion to secure his ends. In all sorts of ways and through all sorts of means he steps up to us and confronts us with his living presence.

It is the living God who has revealed himself in Jesus Christ with a finality and a fullness, to which the parousia can add nothing, but of which it will disclose depths of meaning at present hidden from our blurred and distorted vision. That meaning will not be of another order than the love, of which we already have partial understanding, though the element of surprise inevitably associated with all genuine eschatological expectation means that the revelation of the whole always appears to be more than the sum of its parts.

'God having of old time spoken unto the fathers in the prophets by divers portions and in divers manners, hath at the end of these days spoken unto us in his Son.' [1] There is no fuller revelation. But there is the full implication of this revelation. That is what we long for: that is the thrilling and the terrible Christian hope. That is the parousia and the last judgment and the end of this world, at least as we now know it.

Exactly what this means and how it will come about, human language is quite unable to express and human thought can supply only the barest analogy and human experience offer only the slightest clue. But perhaps the clue is there, if we look for it in the right place. The climax of the biblical revelation of God is the un-equivocal Johannine assertion that he is love.[2] In the language and the experience of love there is a clue. Just as Dante's shape of things to come dawned on him in the first instance *via* that fateful passing glimpse of Beatrice, so for each of us it may well be that romantic love [3] provides the least inadequate approach to any true understanding of the eschatological secrets of the gospel.

The parable of the ten virgins [4] suggests some such approach, and the situation described in the Thessalonian epistles almost demands it. For in human terms that situation seems like that in which

---

[1] Heb. 1, 1 f.   [2] John 3, 16; 1 John 4, 8.
[3] Cf. C. Williams, *Religion and Love in Dante* (Dacre Press, n.d.), *passim.*
[4] Matt. 25, 1 ff.; cf. I. A. Muirhead, *Scottish Journal of Theology* (Oliver and Boyd, 1952), vol. v, no. 2, pp. 175 ff.

every young man and woman find themselves, not after marriage, but when they first fall in love. Each lives for the next meeting with the other and, if the love is genuine, then the in-between times pass 'in the twinkling of an eye',[1] as Jacob found when he 'served seven years for Rachel; and they seemed unto him but a few days, for the love he had to her'.[2] If on the other hand the love is not genuine, then the fevered frustration of the interminable in-between time drags out its futile repetition of one thing after another, and there is all the forced fanaticism and lust to possess which mark the cruder Adventist hopes.

St Paul corrects the fever but confirms the hope: and in the language of romantic love the object of that hope is the marriage which is still future. That is the hope which sustains and braces the New Testament church. It is at least as true in the New Testament that the church is waiting for the marriage as that she is already married. Even the Epistle to the Ephesians brings out this future reference quite unmistakably.[3] The trouble has been that over against the fevered future expectation of the sects the church has tended either to ignore the marriage similes and metaphors altogether (and so has reduced Christian discipleship to a distant following of a great example), or else to claim in the present such a union 'betwixt Christ and his church'[4] as is a very one-sided interpretation of the whole New Testament evidence. It cuts the nerve of genuine eschatology and leaves nothing to look forward to in the future which is in any way vitally related to what is experienced in the present.

In the New Testament the church looks forward with romantic love and thrilling expectation towards a future consummation, and the measure of present love is shown by the foreshortened future time-scale. For the church and the Christian really in love with the Lord the end is always very near. It is only when love grows cold that the time-scale lengthens out and what is really one day becomes a thousand years. It is a measure of our lack of love that we forget this, and believe that the reality is the thousand years and the one day mere illusion.

If we are truly born again into the lovers' time-scale of the kingdom of God, if we truly and continually 'turn, and become as little children',[5] then we repent and change our whole conception of the meaning and the duration of time and find in the imminence of the

---

[1] 1 Cor. 15, 52.   [2] Gen. 29, 20.
[3] Eph. 5, 27; cf. 2 Cor. 11, 2; Rev. 19, 7; 21, 2; 22, 7.
[4] The Book of Common Prayer, 'The Form of Solemnization of Matrimony'.
[5] Matt. 18, 3. It is characteristic of a little child to foreshorten the future and to think of death, e.g., in a matter-of-fact way as something immediate.

parousia no stumbling-block to be explained away, but the very secret of that life, of which Henry Drummond used to say the perfect tense was love. The fact that the language of love can so easily be debased is no excuse from scrapping it from our theological vocabulary but every reason for seeking to redeem it to its true and divine significance.

Marriage thus conceived of as the climax to all the meetings that precede it involves of course a double movement. Any attempt to force the love of God into a one-way traffic movement does grave disservice to a charity which is always in danger of being debased into a patronizing one-way traffic condescension and constantly needs to be redeemed into its true significance of a mutual two-way traffic reciprocity of exchange. 'Love on the dole' is not meant to be the Christian experience in the present and is certainly not the Christian hope in the future.

In our advent and eschatological hope there is therefore no denial of our movement to God. But equally there is no pretence that this is of any avail without his movement to us. The New Testament makes it perfectly clear that the meetings now and the marriage then are much more the result of his movement to us than of our movement to him. The church is the bride to whom the bridegroom comes. 'Thy kingdom come' and 'Maran atha' show the secret of the final triumph of grace, which is always prevenient, however much it may also be co-operant. The long pilgrimage of Dante through purgatory to heaven does less than justice to the long pilgrimage of God to earth, which is its prior condition and alone makes it an endurable, let alone a thrilling and a Christian prospect. It also does less than justice to the secret of that first meeting with Beatrice, out of which its inspiration came.

The traditional adherence of both simple evangelical pietism and catholic mysticism to the 'gentle Jesus' and the 'sacred heart' of Jesus may change its vocabulary and emphasis from one generation to another but remains proof against all the rigour of the anti-sentimentalists. For behind the outward sentimentality lies the inward mystical experience, which remains a permanent embarrassment to the anti-mystic, and a perpetual reminder of the validity of the analogy of human love as a pointer to something which lies at the very heart of the Christian gospel.[1]

It is easy to criticize, but no amount of abuse can justify the disuse of the terminology of love in describing the relationship of the soul with God and with its fellow men. In the end the final

[1] Cf. J. Burnaby, *Amor Dei* (Hodder and Stoughton, 1938), pp. 3 ff.; C. Chavasse, *The Bride of Christ* (Faber and Faber, 1940), *passim*.

meeting with our Lord at the parousia, which will be embodied and not disembodied, and corporate as well as individual, will involve such a revelation and liberation of love as will result in a transformation limitless in its scope and dimensions. Earth will be transformed, for God's kingdom will come on earth. We shall see Jesus Christ as he is and we shall be like him. We shall meet him, and with him of course all who are his, for they cannot be separated from him.

In that day the world of objects, things and ideas will all step up to us and find its fulfilment in that one world of I and Thou, in which all life finds its consummation. It will be a thrilling surprise, however much we may expect it. It will be a terrible prospect, however much we may look forward to it: for then there will be no cover from the eyes of him with whom we have to deal.[1] Therefore with no cocksureness, but with the true assurance which is not based on anything in ourselves, we look forward with trembling hope to that final vindication on earth of the purpose of God so far as it conerns the earth.

On the yonder side of this lie the indescribable blessings of the 'new heaven' and 'new earth' awaiting all creation in so far as it is not stampeded by a guilty conscience into sharing the terror of the whole expanding universe, rushing away from him whom it does not want to meet, but whom in the end it cannot help meeting.[2] But these blessings are no mere future compensation for what is not present here and now. They are the fulfilment of what is here and now, whether we realize it or not.

Only if we believe in victory here can we meet the Marxist challenge on its own battlefield, and having defeated it there move on to the triumphs beyond of which it has no inkling. To this hope of God's triumph on earth we are committed, if our hope is genuinely Christian. But to the hope of God's triumph solely on earth we are not committed. The Christian hope is the *telos* of human history, and even the crude apocalyptic millennium is a better symbol of it than the communist commonwealth. But it is also the *finis* of human history and as such beyond the horizon of any outlook limited by time and space.

Out of the final meeting, on which parousia, judgment and resurrection all focus, a new world will dawn upon our astonished eyes. It is the world of love, the world of the childlike, the world of those who by the magic of tribulation have regained innocence with experience, the world whose sign is the cross and whose power is the Spirit. It is the world in which Jesus lived and which he brought to earth

---

[1] Isa. 2, 19 ff.; Rev. 6, 15 ff.   [2] Rev. 20, 11.

and embodied two thousand years ago. The veil which now hides it from our eyes will then be taken away when 'he shall be manifested' and 'we shall be like him; for we shall see him even as he is'.[1]

Then mysticism and eschatology will find together the fulfilment which is only partial and one-sided in the one apart from the other. Now mysticism alone needs the balance of the future hope to keep its inner secret from degenerating into selfish individual indulgence. And now eschatology alone needs the balance of the present mystical union with Christ to keep its future hope from barren intellectual dogmatism. Then, but not till then, the mystics' faith and the prophets' hope can find their fulfilment in that lovers' meeting, which precisely because it involves the love of God himself will issue in a limitless transformation both of nature and of man.

Then will be 'the revealing of the sons of God',[2] to catch a glimpse of which the whole creation is even now craning its neck. In proportion to our present love of God and of our fellow men and of nature too we shall understand that glorious climax of the purpose of love to be near, and may even help to bring it nearer. But when it comes in the end, we shall know that it is not our doing, but God's. Our hope should be in him now and it can be nowhere else then.

For those who have in this eschatological sense fallen 'in love' and who know therefore something of the reality of the Pauline mystical secret of being 'in Christ', there is a fusion of eschatology and mysticism, which is inexplicable in logic but inescapable in love. The secret of those who have made this discovery is first of all their awareness that nothing they can do can produce the new consciousness of which they are aware.[3]

The monastic way from which Luther rebelled was a way which had come to be interpreted as a ladder reaching from earth to heaven, up which the monks began to ascend in this life and up which they hoped they would continue to ascend after it. Theoretically the prior movement of God from heaven to earth was recognized as essential, but practically there was no vital permanent interrelationship between the two. Their relation was external, and there was no integrated wholeness at any rate in the popular understanding of the way of salvation.

Luther's monastic way may be paralleled by the rabbinic way, from which St Paul recoiled after his vision on the Damascus road, and also by the neo-Platonic mystical way, from which St Augustine

---

[1] 1 John 3, 2.   [2] Rom. 8, 19.

[3] It is here that the distinction between acting and re-acting mysticism is quite invaluable, for there is all the difference in the world between them. Cf. C. A. Anderson Scott, *Living Issues in the New Testament* (C.U.P., 1933), pp. 62 ff.

was converted under the fig-tree at Milan. It may have been true
that it was the only way the neo-Platonists knew: it certainly was
not the only way the rabbis knew or the Christian mystics of the
mediæval or any other age. But it is the agelong temptation of
ecclesiastical and spiritual pride to try to make its own way to heaven
and to refuse the humbler way which is offered to it from heaven.

It is quite fundamental, however, to both the Jewish and the
Christian faith to assert that the way is first from God to man in
order that it may then be from man to God. The doctrine of the
imitatio Dei justifies the notion that God was 'in the beginning' in
order that man might make a beginning.[1] Man must create if he is
made 'in the image of God', but he can only do the creative work
which is his birthright if he acknowledges his dependence upon the
Creator even for his own pro-creative initiative.

The Creator's own initiative is not an initial push which starts
creation off and then leaves it to its fate: it is also its continual
support and inspiration, which alone enables it to go on to any worthwhile goal. Being the support of love, this initial and continuing
activity of God is not advertised or ostentatious, and therefore it is
very easy for man to ignore his continual dependence upon God's
self-effacing help. But to contract out of his creatureliness is man's
besetting sin, which blinds him to the reality of the world to which
the little child's eyes alone are open. It is indeed to fall into the
root of all evil which etymologically as well as scripturally is to be
found in man's excessive claims for himself and ideas of himself.[2]

To fall into sin of this sort and to persist in it is to contract out of
the world of mutual love which is the kingdom of God and, however
high the aims and spiritual the ambitions of those who do contract
out of that world, there is no way forward along such a route towards
the reality revealed in its essence by Jesus Christ crucified. This was
St Augustine's discovery just as it had been St Paul's and as it was
to be Luther's. However unbalanced may be in some cases the
reaction from a previous mode of life caused by such a discovery,
nothing can obscure what lies at the heart of such experiences. And
it is the reality which eschatologically is safeguarded adequately
only by the doctrine of the parousia.

Without the parousia, immortality or eternal life is arrived at
via purgatory and judgment, and these latter are stages on the way
from man to God and, although lip-service is paid to the priority of
the movement of God to man, both in prevenient and co-operant

---

[1] Cf. M. Buber, *Mamre* (Melbourne University Press and O.U.P., 1946), pp. 42 ff.
[2] Cf. *The Concise Oxford Dictionary*, 3rd ed. (O.U.P., 1934): s.v. 'evil . . . perh. f.
root of *up*, w. sense "excessive"' (p. 391).

grace, both in holy baptism and in holy communion, and in all the means of grace, the fact that this movement has no decisive significance in any of the Christian eschatological symbols or dogmas of the end at all proves that it has no effective or vital significance on the way to that end. For either eschatology informs the whole of life or it is not the genuine article at all. As a mere appendage to doctrines, the significance of which it reverses, it is at best a harmless sleeping draught and at worst a fatal drug.

It is 'the mystical factor in salvation'[1] which takes St Paul's rabbinic exegesis of justification by faith and lifts it into the living reality of our Lord's parable of the Pharisee and the publican.[2] It is the same with St Augustine and, in so far as Luther caught the spirit of St Paul, it was the Augustinian tradition which carried the mystical element in religion, as the fertilizing factor in the otherwise arid intellectualism of the later scholastics, right down to the cloister at Erfurt at the close of the fifteenth century.

As an interpretation of the reality of the way in which the soul meets God, the mystic path may easily become a three-runged ladder of purgation, illumination and union, set up on earth to reach to heaven. But at the heart of reacting Christian mysticism there lies its inner secret, which no words can better express than the bare outlines of the traditional biblical dogma of the movement of God to man, expressed in the Abrahamic covenant, confirmed in the Mosaic, revived in the Davidic and sealed in the blood of the new covenant at Calvary.

The fact that this priority of the divine initiative has been exhibited day by day in the eucharist all down the history of the Christian church should have safeguarded the dogma from the barrenness of a theological speculation and converted it into the secret of a real and personal presence. But all too easily the eucharist has itself become an objective demonstration in rite designed to be as effective to the sight as was the logic of the spoken dogma to the ear. And the result is that the secret of any meeting of the soul with God is obscured, for this is essentially dependent upon the coming of God to the soul with a reality of love which is quite incapable of logical comprehension. It is beyond all apologetic proof, though it is the heart of all truly apostolic witness.

This is the real presence of Christ which is the secret of living Christianity and which by its very nature of love always points forward to his real parousia. It is the lack of the former in the present which relegates the latter to an obscure corner of the future eschatological scheme, of which it is often regarded to-day as a piece

[1] C. A. Anderson Scott, loc. cit.   [2] Luke 18, 9 ff.

of out-of-date mythological *naïveté*, to be quietly dropped by the church if its presentation of the last things is to have any effective relevance to the modern world.

So far, however, from this being the case, the parousia is in fact the one eschatological symbol which safeguards the truth which lies at the heart of all genuine Christian experience; for the secret of the meeting of the soul with God is that it depends much more upon God's coming to man than upon man's going to God. This is the divine reality of grace, to which every human experience of falling in love is a faint analogy. And it is to no disembodied individual spirituality that the parousia bears witness, for by its necessary connection with the doctrine of the resurrection of the body it has a social and a material as well as a spiritual significance.

It is not the secret of the end of a road of emancipation from the material limitations of a life in space and time, but it is the secret all along the road of that transformation of the material limitations of space and time which is the purpose and the possibility of each stage of life from the cradle to the grave and of every age of history from its beginning to its end. It is no refuge of escapism into another world, known conceivably to the soul before it entered this world,[1] but having no reality in this world except in so far as the soul can get out of it partially here and now and longs to get out of it altogether one day hereafter.

Any such doctrine of a present mysticism and a future immortality lacks just those elements both of mysticism and of eschatology which are distinctively Christian. It is only when mysticism is genuinely reacting and when eschatology is an integral part of the whole revelation of God, past and present as well as future, that either is distinctively Christian and that both together by their interaction can produce that confidence in the presence of the love of God in Christ which leads inevitably to the hope of his parousia.

Whenever either mysticism or eschatology loses the clue to real love which is found neither in the one-way traffic street of giving nor in the one-way traffic street of taking, but in the two-way traffic street of mutual give and take, the result is fatal. It is the mutual reciprocity of meeting and of communion which is at the heart of the doctrines not only of the trinity and the atonement but also of the eucharist as well, and it is as vital to mysticism as to eschatology.

Without it mysticism becomes so easily either an effort to secure just exactly the very thing which Jesus refused to secure, when he 'counted it not a thing to be grasped to be on an equality with God',[2]

---

[1] Would traducianism imply this? Creationism of course would rule it out.
[2] Phil. 2, 6, R.V. margin.

or else an attitude of such sheer passivity as to be more akin to the Moslem *kismet* than to de Caussade's vital and creative *Abandonment to Divine Providence*.[1]   Similarly, an eschatology bereft of the secret of reciprocal love is bound to leave us with a future prospect focused either upon a dim and distant goal which we hope to reach after immense toil, or else upon an immediate and magical gift to us after death, entirely unrelated to anything which has gone before in this present life.

If this life and the next are to be integrally related, and if the secret of their interrelation is the secret of mutual and reciprocal love, and if that secret as between God and man can only be revealed through the divine initiative, then the eschatological symbol which expresses it in the future coincides in meaning with the eucharistic rite which enshrines it in the present.   It is the eschatological parousia which confirms the real presence and it is the real presence which affirms the eschatological parousia.   The one without the other is inconceivable if the reality of either is love.   The presence without the parousia is an idol, whether enshrined in outward rite or inner experience: and the parousia without the presence is phantasy, whether characterized by the optical and acoustical pomp and circumstance of an apocalyptic imagery or by the clear-cut definitions of a prophetic programme.

We cannot say how Christ will come, and therefore we cannot rule out either the literal fulfilment of apocalyptic symbolism or the dramatic demonstration of prophetic or mystical vision. St Paul's experience on the Damascus road should make us pause before we even think of doing so.   But to make that exceptional experience the norm of the manner either of the presence or the parousia of love is to make the exception into the rule, whereas in fact it is the exception which proves the rule that the presence and the parousia of love are self-effacing and not ostentatious, and therefore each is bound to be and to remain a surprise.

If the presence gives the clue to the parousia, then the surprise will be after the manner of the revelation to Elijah on Mount Sinai, which was disclosed not in the whirlwind nor in the earthquake nor in the fire, but in the 'sound of gentle stillness'.[2]   And this after all was the essence of the surprise which overwhelmed St Paul on the Damascus road.   His fellow travellers saw the light and heard 'the sound',[3] but only he understood its meaning.   If the revelation

---

[1] J. P. de Caussade, *Abandonment to Divine Providence* (The Catholic Records Press, Exeter, 1921); cf. R. Hudleston, *The Spiritual Letters of Dom John Chapman* (Sheed and Ward), pp. 82 f.
[2] 1 Kings 19, 12, R.V. margin.
[3] Acts 9, 7, R.V. margin.

is of love and if love is mutual and reciprocal, then it cannot be otherwise either with the eucharistic presence or with the eschatological parousia. There will always be a proportion between a revelation received and the mental and spiritual state of the receiver. If we seek to eliminate either the eucharistic or the eschatological surprise, we eliminate something which is of the very essence of love itself.

Mysticism is at the heart of all real religion: awareness of God, whatever the medium he uses, is no prerogative either of the Quakers or of the great contemplative saints of catholicism. It is the life-blood of all the vital traditions of Christianity. It is given not as the logical terminus of a long search conducted along 'the proper channels', but as the initial surprise awaiting those who do not dodge the daily cross of God's appointment, through which crucifixion with Christ becomes not an apostolic idiosyncrasy, but a universal possibility for all members of the body of Christ and for all the redeemed community of the new Israel. It is the inescapable corollary of holy baptism, in so far as the latter retains any of its original significance of identification with the death of Christ.

It is the approach of God to the soul, which is fundamental to the Christian good news, and not the approach of the soul to God, which is derivative and secondary. It is practical forgetfulness of this fact in catholic mysticism which always provokes protestant and evangelical reaction, and inevitably means that a whole section of Christendom nurtured on the inner secret of justification by faith, in which a mystical factor is a vital reality, ignores the spiritual treasures of the great catholic mystics, who are at heart so very evangelical. Nothing is more needed in the church to-day than the liberation of these treasures of the three stages of the mystic way of catholicism so that they become accessible to the great pioneers of the protestant tradition. And on the other hand nothing is more needed than the liberation of those who are toiling in the steps of St John of the Cross up the *Ascent of Mount Carmel* [1] by the rediscovery of that prevenient movement of God to the soul, which is at the heart of the wonder of justification by faith when that doctrine is no mere talisman of Christian initiation but the centre of Christian living and of Christian eschatology as well.

How can the fusion of eschatology and mysticism be effected in such a way as to arrest neither the onward progress of the former nor the upward progress of the latter? How can both be revitalized

---

[1] E. Allison Peers, *The Complete Works of St John of the Cross* (Burns, Oates and Washbourne, 1934), vol. i, pp. 9 ff.

by their mutual cross-fertilization? Can some contribution be made in this way towards that eschatology of the community in history and of the individual beyond it, of which the church is in such sore need?

Such questions drive us back to rediscover the essential focus of New Testament eschatology. By its focus upon the coming of a person it corrected any tendency of ecclesiasticism to imagine that God's presence could be so secured by rite or formula as to be possessed after the manner of lust and of idolatry. At the same time it corrected any tendency of mysticism to imagine that his presence could be so secured in experience as to be possessed after the manner of the blasphemy which denies the very nature of love itself. For love cannot ever be so possessed as an object or, if it is imagined so to be, it is lost for ever. At the same time also it safeguarded that essential personal relationship which is at the heart of all biblical religion, for it made inconceivable any notion of God which depersonalized him or reduced him to a mere object of contemplative or meditative speculation or of philosophical investigation.

It was because the kingdom of God was revealed in Jesus Christ and so intimately bound up with him that for St Paul 'to be "in Christ" was to be in the kingdom. The historic idea became the mystic reality, and the future became the present. The apostolic preaching of Christ therefore took the place of Christ's own preaching of the kingdom. He was now identified with the kingdom',[1] and to be 'in Christ' was to be 'in the kingdom', and when we try to make sense of what either being 'in the kingdom' or 'in Christ' meant for the New Testament church, we cannot do much better than use the analogy of the deepest experience of human love.

To be 'in Christ' meant for St Paul to be in such an intimate relationship with him as can only fitly be described as being 'in love'. St Paul found he was 'in love' and love for him meant Christ, and so he was 'in Christ'. If in fact he thought it out the other way round as a result of his vision on the Damascus road being interpreted in terms not of love, but of Christ, he came to the same conclusion. The process of his thought by which he arrived at his conclusion does not materially matter, though the conclusion matters immensely.

This mystical relationship of being 'in Christ' was not something he could maintain by his discipleship any more than he could achieve it by his devotion. No technique of mysticism had given it him, and no rule of worship or system of thought or code of behaviour could keep it from him. As far as his conscious experience was

---

[1] P. T. Forsyth, *The Person and Place of Jesus Christ* (Hodder and Stoughton, 1909), p. 122.

concerned, it was originally given [1] as a surprise and it was constantly renewed as such.

St Paul's relationship with Jesus Christ was one of vivid and dynamic reciprocal intimacy: it was never an absorption in static contemplation. So he lived in the present, and in the present he knew the presence in such a way as to hope for the future and long for the parousia. The love he knew in the present gave him the certainty of the love he looked for in the future. Present presence and future parousia do not disappear or coalesce in a timeless eternity. They are two inseparable but irreducible elements in that single reality of love, of which the more you have in the present the more you know awaits you in the future. Such love comes because it is here, and in our conscious experience it comes and goes (exactly after the manner of the biblical God of the Old Testament as well as of the New) even if in its own unchanging reality it is always here as a presence, though never as a possession.

It is the peril of the church either to believe in an eschatology which in fact if not in theory offers a presence one day in the future to make up for an absence to day in the present, or else to believe in a mysticism which in fact if not in theory offers a presence to-day in the present which leaves no room for any further significant reality on any future day. But when in love eschatology and mysticism come together, then there is room for a real present presence and a real future parousia. But in each case the reality is the reality of love, and of love the apostolic word is supremely true: it is only those who are in the happy position of 'having nothing' who do in fact possess 'all things'.[2] That is why the first beatitude is pronounced on the spiritually [3] (and perhaps materially [4]) poor and bankrupt, and why the supreme demonstration of the reality of love upon this earth was marked by a sense of total dereliction.[5]

The mystic who possesses the presence and leaves no room for the parousia is as much astray as the apocalyptist who hopes for the parousia but has no experience of the presence. The connection between the essence of Christian mysticism and the essence of Christian eschatology does not involve a clear-cut logical division, leaving mysticism to enjoy the present and eschatology the future. To append a theoretical future eschatology to an unbalanced present mystical experience is no more the corrective that is needed than

---

[1] Nothing is more important than to stress that love, like the Spirit, is given and not got. If only Confirmation addresses stressed the cross which is not to be dodged rather than the Spirit who is (as can so easily be said) to be got! Jesus was not baptized to get the Spirit. The Spirit was given as the sequel to his baptism: and the gift was a surprise, as the gifts of love must always be.

[2] 2 Cor. 6, 10.   [3] Matt. 5, 3.   [4] Luke 6, 20.   [5] Mark 15, 34.

to prefix a definition of present mysticism to an unbalanced future eschatology. The connection between mysticism and eschatology must be vital and interpenetrating, or else the secret of the relationship of love on which each depends and which neither itself adequately interprets is quickly lost.

At the same time the real continuity between present and future and the vital link between mysticism and eschatology is not something which can be secured after the manner of the religion of the Baals, in which people and god were indissolubly bound up in an unbreakable organic unity. Even the most categorical promises of Yahweh are always morally and spiritually conditioned. It was not in an indissoluble organic unity with him that the old Israel lived, but rather under a constantly renewed covenant.

And it is the same with the new Israel as with the old. Christians have no more right to fall back upon the categorical word and promise of God in Jesus Christ than have Jews to rely upon the categorical word and promise of God given by Abraham or Moses, if such a word or promise is regarded as guaranteeing either to the community or the individual a security which is absolute and not morally and spiritually conditioned. The security of love can never be had on such terms, and the security of love is the only eschatological security there is.

The old covenant (despite the priestly code, which turned it in fact, if not in theory, into a contract) reveals the pattern of God's working, and the new covenant confirms it. The good news is not primarily of an unbroken continuity of organic life, but of a broken and restored covenant relationship. But the bond of the covenant is too fragile to hold except within an area of at least potential organism. That is why the resurrection of the body, which is a corporate and not merely an individual doctrine,[1] is needed to balance the parousia of the Lord in the full eschatological perspective.

Without the doctrine of the resurrection mysticism is bound to tend to degenerate into a flight of 'the alone to the Alone', the soul's one aim and object being to get rid of the encumbrance of the body. On the other hand, without mysticism, an eschatology focused on the doctrine of the resurrection is bound to tend to degenerate into a kind of materialistic magic, conditioned as to its working beyond space and time as we now know them by our knowledge of space and time. The corrective both of such mystical apostasy and of such eschatological idolatry is to be found in the recovery of the central significance of the parousia,

[1] Cf. J. A. T. Robinson, *The Body* (S.C.M., 1952), pp. 49 ff.

which the resurrection may support but for which it is no substitute.[1]

It is the resurrection of the body which safeguards the relative reality of the material order, but it is the parousia which opens up the possibilities not of its temporal continuity but of its eschatological transformation into the absolute reality of the spiritual order. The concept of the millennium may safeguard the historical process from complete ultimate unreality and meaninglessness: only the doctrine of the meeting with the Lord Jesus Christ (not of our initiative and going to him, but of his initiative and coming to us) can open up the transcendent prospect which will fulfil surprisingly both the purpose of history and the vocation of every human soul.

That at least is all that we can say with certainty out of present experience. It is only in meeting, in conversation, in communion and in intercourse that the deepest reality of love is made known to us. That is the secret of the presence here and now, and that will be the secret of the parousia there and then. What lies beyond such meeting we can never know in advance, even in human relationships in this life, let alone in the divine relationship in the life beyond.

All we can say as Christians is that the end cannot contradict the revelation of God in Jesus Christ. That revelation is an eschatological revelation. If anything in the future seems to contradict it, as it well may, that is only because our understanding of that revelation is so very far from being complete. The clue to eschatology is not found by curious speculation about the future: it is found in mystical awareness of the present. But mystical awareness of the present has nothing to do with the presence of love unless it is indissolubly bound up with eschatological expectation of the future parousia of love. Both present and future depend on God, and presence and parousia are always given and never got. Each is a mode of the manifestation of God in Jesus Christ, his only Son. He is the key to Christian eschatology just as he is the key to Christian mysticism. To get away from him may leave us an eschatology and a mysticism as well, but neither will be distinctively Christian at all. That is the meaning of the poet's vision of the truth, which has been already quoted:

> For the end of the world was long ago—
> And all we dwell to-day
> As children of some second birth,
> Like a strange people left on earth
> After a judgment day.[2]

---

[1] This is precisely the apostolic attitude in the New Testament towards the resurrection of our Lord. Cf. A. M. Ramsey, *The Resurrection of Christ* (Geoffrey Bles, 1945), pp. 72 f.   [2] G. K. Chesterton, *Ballad of the White Horse*, Bk. I.

A picture of present living in the words of such poetry brings vividly before us a glimpse of the meaning of Christian eschatological mysticism, and it is a challenge to the need of nothing less than rebirth if we are ever to see, let alone enter, the kingdom of God's love. It vividly suggests the child's world of poetic imagination into which we are now invited out of the materialistic common-sense sophisticated prose world of a twentieth-century adult. It is the sort of jolt in words that a Trappist monastery or a Jewish *kvusa* or *kibbuz* [1] provides in deeds.

To walk through the gate of the Trappist monastery of Latrūn at the foot of the Judæan hills and to be confronted with the mosaic inscription, *Pax*, and then to go through the rooms and the library and the unfinished chapel and the vineyards and the vaults of this silent adventure in dying to live, was an experience which many chaplains during the 1939–45 War felt was a complete challenge to their entire worldly-wise and semi-Christian way of looking at life. Here was something wholly and utterly different. There was a peace about it and it was not an idle peace.

But not far away were the communal experiments of the Jewish agricultural colonies. To enter one of these colonies was also to enter a new world and to realize what in fact it means to have few, if any, possessions of one's own. Here was an experiment which had not yet failed.[2] Here was a community gripped with the enthusiastic hope of creating a new home for their race and of pioneering a new and voluntary way of communal living for, perhaps, the whole world. In its own way this was quite as much a challenge to our contemporary democratic western ideas of living as was the Trappist monastery.

It would be unfair to condemn the latter as an otherworldly escape from material life: its vineyards alone would be a sufficient refutation of the charge. And it would be equally unfair to condemn the former as a materialistic escape into hard manual work from that concentration upon the world of the mind, which was all the eastern European ghetto could offer the best spirits of Jewry for so long. To see the colonists at a concert of the Palestine orchestra would be a sufficient refutation of any glib allegation of mere materialism. Not yet have material conditions in the colonies allowed time for much reflection. But this will come, and when it does, who can prophesy whether it will produce the cynicism of disillusioned despair or the reformulation in our day of the ancient material and spiritual hope of the prophets of the Old Testament?

[1] Cf. M. Buber, *Paths in Utopia* (Routledge and Kegan Paul, 1949), pp. 139 ff.
[2] *Ibid.*

It may always be easier to produce an Ecclesiastes than an Isaiah, but that is no excuse for cheap Christian criticism of this Jewish experiment: it is rather a challenge to pioneer some 'more excellent way'. If the Christian church is to have any message whatever for the volcanic futurism which grips not only the Jewish colonists but also so much of the non-western and non-white world to-day, and if it is ever going to be the reinvigorating source of life within the western world and the white peoples, then in either case it is hope which it must offer: a truer hope for those who are deluded by a false hope and some hope for those who have none.

Without the mysticism of which the Trappist monastery of Latrūn speaks so eloquently by its silence there is no chance of the discovery of such a hope. But mysticism, like patriotism (in Edith Cavell's famous phrase), 'is not enough'. Eschatology is needed as well, if the church is to save itself from self-indulgence in the present and the world from self-delusion about the future. A Christianity orientated towards the past, as Latrūn must necessarily appear to be to the Jewish colonies around, has a salutary corrective to offer but hardly a constructive alternative. And it is precisely the constructive alternative of hope which the Christian gospel offers the world, if only the church can rediscover its secret.

There is no short-cut to the secret, which can only be found by way of the three great purgings of intellect, memory and desire which lie at the heart of the classical expression of Christian mysticism by St John of the Cross. Only on the yonder side of understanding shall we move out into the darkness of faith and discover its reality when, with Kierkegaard, we tread water with 70,000 fathoms beneath.[1] Only on the yonder side of memory shall we move out into the darkness of hope and discover its reality in a truly eschatological understanding of the eucharist. Only on the yonder side of desire, even for good things and spiritual, shall we move out into the darkness and total dereliction of love and discover its secret in the poverty of spirit of the first beatitude and the agony of the cross.

The necessity for such purgings is not likely to pass unchallenged either by the theological dogmatist in the case of faith or by the rigid sacramentalist in the case of hope or by the popular evangelist in the case of love. But if they are necessary, then it is not sufficient to map out a pattern of New Testament eschatology which eliminates the absurd *naïveté* of the second coming and still imagines it safeguards the essentials of the gospel. For if it has in fact, if not in theory, eliminated the glorious hope of the early church, then it has been guilty not only of critical sharp-practice in its handling of the

---

[1] Cf. J. E. Fison, *The Blessing of the Holy Spirit*, p. 28.

15

scriptual evidence, but also of spiritual treachery in cutting the nerve of the very element in the Christian gospel, which is most relevant to the needs of to-day.

Appearances look as if this is in fact the case and, if so, the question at once arises as to how that hope can be recovered. The purging of the mystic way strongly suggests that we shall not find it by seeking it. The surprises of love are never got: they are always given. And it is *via* the purging of memory that hope is given and in no other way. This means that the clue to the future is to be found in the past, for it is only with the past that memory has to do. What fills our future for us will depend upon what fills our past.

There are those whose memories are stored with things they wish they could forget. But the truth in the eschatological symbol of judgment is that nothing in fact can be so forgotten, however much it may disappear below the level of consciousness. It will all 'catch up with us' in the end and then, face to face with the memory of it, our only security will manifestly lie in the mercy and the forgiveness of God. That is where it lies now in fact, though we so often do not realize it. Face to face with the Lord Jesus Christ the truth will be inescapable, and that is the great eschatological significance of the doctrine of justification by faith.

But there are other memories of the past besides those we would like to forget, but which only God can forgive. These other memories are those we do not want to forget: we treasure them and do everything in our power to cling on to them. But if the purging of bad memories of the past is essential to a living hope in the future, then the purging of good memories is no less essential. It is this which religious people so often fail to realize, and the remorseless rigour of St John of the Cross is not at all too extreme to demonstrate its absolute necessity.

It is the clinging by a child to the memory of its parent which so often blights its life after the parent's death. It is the clinging likewise of husband or wife to the past memory of the other, instead of looking forward to the reunion, which so often blights the widow's or the widower's life. It took the Jubilee to remove the long blight that thus settled on Queen Victoria after the Prince Consort's death. And it is just the same with the holy communion itself. Without its eschatological significance the *anamnesis* can be deadly in its effect upon the soul.

But how different is the effect of the good memories of the past when they are purged into hope! Parents and children, husband and wife, the church and her Lord, the Christian and his Saviour— each and all need no longer cling to the past. They can live for the future and the reunion which will 'exceed all that' they 'can desire'. That is the secret of the New Testament hope. The early Christians lived for the reunion not of Christendom but with Christ—and the difference between the church of the first century and the church of the twentieth century in this respect is significant. Their memories were filled with one they loved. They did not cling to them, but hoped for him and turned his prayer, 'Thy kingdom come',[1] into their own 'Maran atha'.[2]

It was he who filled their memories. They could not forget him, but they did not cling to him, for he would not let them. St Mary Magdalen received the rebuke [3] against any attempt to cling to him which might have been meant for them all. He could only return if he withdrew. He could only stimulate future hope if he gave no encouragement whatever to those who wanted to cling to their past memories, however holy they might be, and it was love that made him ruthless here.

But how were the first disciples to look for their Lord and Saviour in the reunion? How were their purged memories likely to express their hopes? Quite apart from the deep theological reason that the fundamental truths of the divine initiative and of prevenient grace justify the eschatological expression of the future hope in terms of a coming of Christ to earth rather than a going of Christians to heaven, there is another and much more intimate psychological reason for the way in which the early Christians expressed their vivid expectation. This is drawn from the way in which memory works or, at any rate, seems to ordinary men and women, like the first disciples, to work.

If we want to remember something we have forgotten, how often the worst thing to do is to make a great effort to try to remember it! The more we try the less we succeed. But if we stop trying, how often 'it all comes back to us', as we say colloquially, but expressively, in the light of early Christian eschatological convictions! The first Christians formulated their hope in just this way, though for them it was not couched in impersonal but in personal terms, for of course their memories were not filled with any 'it' or thing at all, not even with the kingdom of God. They were filled with the one 'he', who personally gave content and reality to all that they most valued and whose person filled the memories they treasured most.

Therefore, on psychological as well as on theological grounds, the secret of the purging of the memory of the early Christians could not have been better expressed than in terms of Jesus' personal coming back to them, provided that such a return is interpreted not after

---

[1] Matt. 6, 10.   [2] 1 Cor. 16, 22.   [3] John 20, 17.

the manner of any ostentatious display but in the light of the self-effacing intimacy with which all love's self-disclosures are made. It is the little self-effacements of the past that are treasured in the memory of any dear one, then it can almost be said that it is the great self-effacement in the future, which is looked forward to as the secret of the manifestation of love in the day of reunion.

It is quite in agreement with this self-effacing nature of love's revelation that it is only Christians, with some knowledge of Jesus Christ either from personal memory or from recollections passed on to them and believed by them, who can look for his return. Only those who (whether they are aware of it or not) have some present understanding of him can hope for any future revelation of him. But they are bound to do so, and are well aware that their present experience does not rule out their future surprise. On the contrary they know that it ensures it, for it is in the nature of love to delight to fulfil our hopes surprisingly beyond all our expectations.

It is useless for us to try in advance to secure such fulfilment or to make ourselves into self-appointed manipulators or artificial hasteners of the coming of our Lord. But if we live as we should and love as we should, there is no telling how much we may in fact hasten that coming without being aware that we are doing anything of the sort. Our behaviour in the present in some way prepares us and so prepares the whole universe for that final coming manifestation of love, which cannot even in the end be forced upon anything but depends for its revelation upon the degree of preparedness for it. That is why Christian future hope so inspires Christian present faith and love, and why Christian present faith and love so kindle Christian future hope.

It is this relation between present and future which suggests a most striking psychological parallel with the Marxist hope. Bertrand Russell has set out its details, and says that

> to understand Marx psychologically, one should use the following dictionary:
>
> | | |
> |---|---|
> | Yahweh | = Dialectical Materialism |
> | The Messiah | = Marx |
> | The Elect | = The Proletariat |
> | The Church | = The Communist Party |
> | The Second Coming | = The Revolution |
> | Hell | = Punishment of the Capitalists |
> | The Millennium | = The Communist Commonwealth |
>
> The terms on the left hand give the emotional content of the terms on the right hand, and it is this emotional content, familiar to those who

have had a Christian or a Jewish upbringing, that makes Marx's eschatology credible.[1]

The parallel may be overdrawn, but nevertheless there is something very thrilling and very terrifying about it, and the important thing to notice is that the real lever motivating the dynamic hope of the Marxist is that he is in the revolution.   He is actually able to take a part in it and he can contribute something towards its final inevitable and imminent triumph.

It is striking that in Bertrand Russell's dictionary the parallel between the emotional content aroused by the revolution among the Marxists is that aroused by the second coming among Christians. When it is realized that the apostolic expectation of the parousia of Jesus Christ is their translation of Jesus' own expectation of the kingdom of God, then it becomes clear that it is not something merely future, but something in some sense already here.   The eschatological panorama is already unfolding, and just as the communist derives his hope from the imminent prospect of the victory of the revolution in which he is already actively taking a part and perhaps even a decisive part, so the Christian should derive his hope from the imminent prospect of the parousia of Jesus Christ, the immediacy of whose triumph, if not its inevitability, in some measure depends on his co-operation.

It is the feeling that nothing can be done about the situation of the world and humanity to-day which is killing responsible creative activity and initiative in the democratic western world.   If the church can give people a grounded conviction that they can do something that matters and something which may in fact make all the difference, if not to the victory or defeat of the cause of God, at least to the speed or the slowness with which that victory may be won, then she has already half won the battle against inertia and lethargy.   But where is such grounded confidence to be found except in the New Testament doctrine of the parousia of our Lord? The missionary enthusiasm generated among the early Student Volunteers by St Matthew 24, 14 was based not upon the conviction that they would bring in the kingdom of God upon earth, but upon the confidence that they could do something towards hastening its coming.   Here is the inspiring Christian parallel to the secret of the Marxist hope.

Such a hope is needed by the whole church, and it is in the New Testament.   But it is a hope grounded not upon the logic of reason, but upon the intuition of faith and love.   Its credibility does not

[1] B. Russell, *A History of Western Philosophy* (George Allen and Unwin, 1946), p. 383.

lie in its rationality, but that does not invalidate it any more than it invalidates its Marxist parallel, which is impervious to the sensible criticism of reasonable democrats that there are no grounds whatever for imagining that the outcome of the revolution and the establishment of the communist commonwealth will have any other result than the inevitably corrupting influence of power upon whatever persons in society wield that power.

The attempts to undermine either the Christian or the Marxist hope on grounds of irrationality are beside the point, for in both cases that hope is in origin biblical and therefore it is strictly eschatological, and eschatology is a frontier subject and uses a frontier language. No logic or reason of space or time (which is all the logic and reason we possess) is adequate to interpret a reality which is neither limited to the temporal nor lost in the eternal.[1] Only the language of love can speak with relevance and intelligibility on both sides of the frontier of space and time. And the language of love is never merely objective, as the theologians might wish, or merely subjective, as the psychologists might desire. It offers neither the objective security of dogma nor the subjective security of experience. Any attempt to rest in one is bound to provoke a reaction from the other, as the pattern of the New Testament development of eschatology so clearly shows.

The eschatology of the earliest strata of the Synoptic gospels tingles with the hope of imminent fulfilment. Here love knows it has all it needs and yet is simultaneously aware of the incredible possibilities that await it. But as soon as love grows cold, or even when first-hand experience attempts to translate its secrets so that others may share them, then inevitably the objective futurist comes on the scene, solidly basing his hopes for what will be upon something or someone now absent from his subjective experience. This in turn produces the subjective transformation of the future into the present and the dissolving of eschatology into a timeless mysticism, which claims for the present all that there is to be in the future.

This dialectic does not discredit the New Testament, for it is the best that theologians can do. They have to deal with ideas and objects and symbols which are not themselves the reality of which they speak, but only the transcription and translation of that reality. Record and revelation are indistinguishable in personal love, even if they are distinct in its propositional interpretation. Therefore we do grave disservice to the cause of personal truth if we

---

[1] The fact that Marxism denies the eternal does not alter the fact that the strength of its conviction is derived straight from the Hebrew messianic hope, which is thoroughly eschatological.

deny either the New Testament futurism or the New Testament mysticism. But we do even graver disservice to the cause of truth if we imagine that either the objective futurist eschatology or the subjective mystical experience could give away by itself the secret of the coming one (ὁ ἐρχόμενος).[1] He can only be met and he can never be defined.

If the heart of living is meeting, and if in the meeting of mutual love we enter into the fullness of life (and in no other way), then at the end the unlimited world of meeting will open to us, streaming in upon us along all the avenues of its divine and human and natural approaches to us. However much we may protect ourselves from the perils of such encounter here and now, in the end we cannot escape this unlimited responsibility. Now we can all too easily retire within the safeguards of a world which we can certainly delimit objectively and perhaps experience subjectively. Thus we avoid all personal contact with the world of persons which we can neither delimit nor experience but only meet. It is at our peril that we so replace the terrible and fascinating possibilities of a loving *tête-à-tête* with a person by a logical plan or blue print of the *rendezvous*.

In evangelism, in the eucharist and in eschatology, neither in subjective terms alone nor in objective terms alone can we rightly speak the truth of the gospel. For in all such spheres of real living we can never prove: we can only bear witness. The apologist for love is a very different person from the apostle of love. If the proof of the apologist is often obvious and ostentatious, the witness of the apostle must often be obscure and always self-effacing.

To the final lovers' meeting, where eschatology and mysticism combine, the whole New Testament bears an apostolic witness, though it rarely offers any apologetic proof. It is no selfish meeting of man with God alone, but a meeting in which God and man and nature too all come together. That is what the parousia means, for it is not the climax of a merely individual but of a truly cosmic salvation.

Where the witness to it is misinterpreted as proof of it, eschatology disappears either in a temporal event or in an eternal experience and the Christian hope is lost. But where the witness to it is understood for what it is, there it ministers to our souls the living hope, which is as true for every individual soul as for the universe as a whole. 'Journeys end in lovers meeting',[2] but no one has ever arrived there without finding that the end was in fact a new beginning. This is what the Christian is meant to find here and now and believes that

[1] Matt. 11, 3.
[2] W. Shakespeare, *Twelfth Night*, II, iii.

he will find hereafter. The trysting-place of God's appointment with us is marked by a cross and it is not far from any one of us. 'Behold, I stand at the door and knock'—that is the inescapable fact of the presence: 'if any man hear my voice and open the door, I will come in to him and sup with him, and he with me' [1]—that is the indescribable possibility of the parousia. It is impossible to have the one without the other, for mysticism and eschatology are joined together in the indissoluble union of love.

[1] Rev. 3, 20.

CHAPTER VIII

THE SHAPE OF ESCHATOLOGY

So often Christian eschatology is taken in isolation as the final term of Christian doctrine and is quite unrelated to the rest of its structure and itself consists of apparently quite disconnected elements, some in this world and some in the next, some corporate and some individual. As such an appendage it really consists of a series of optional extras to the essential Christian dogmas.

Nothing could be more disastrous, not only for the true significance of eschatology itself but also for the saving efficacy of Christian truth as a whole. For the whole must be eschatological if it is to be really Christian: and therefore eschatology itself must be an integrated whole if it is to permeate the whole. It cannot be such a whole unless each part of the traditional subdivisions of the subject falls into its right place in the whole. What is central must be kept central: what is circumferential must remain circumferential.

Quite clearly in the course of the argument of this book the central place in the Christian future hope is occupied by the doctrine of the parousia or the coming of the Lord. Next to this comes the doctrine of the resurrection of the body, the longest statement of which in the New Testament is, as we have seen, introduced because of problems arising in connection with the delayed parousia.[1] Then come the twin doctrines of particular judgment at death or of general judgment at the last day, both of which in our view should be closely related to the parousia as the obverse or the reverse of the same truth, but each of which in traditional dogmatics has been either substituted for it or separated from it.

Finally, on the edge of Christian conviction come on the one hand the doctrine of some kind of millennium and on the other that conviction of the immortality of the soul, which is based more on psychological than on spiritual grounds and which has its roots rather in Greece than in Palestine. Such are the main aspects of Christian eschatology which deal with the frontier beyond which (either with or without purgatory) open up the inescapable and final alternatives of heaven and hell, which no serious biblical study can possibly ignore.

[1] 1 Cor. 15, 18; 1 Thess. 4, 16.

If such an eschatological prospect is to be regarded as a living whole, every part of which has something to offer towards the full Christian hope, then it must be vitally related to the present life both of individual souls and of society as a whole. Can such a vital relation be found and, if so, can it be expressed? Eschatology in the right perspective may help towards the attempt to see psychology and ecclesiology in the right perspective too. And likewise a truer understanding of the soul and of society may help towards a truer understanding of the end of both the soul and also of society as a whole.

There is a psychological pattern which I owe to a lecture given by the Rev. Dr. F. W. Dillistone in Oxford in 1947.[1] Dr. Dillistone did not pretend that the six ways of human behaviour which he outlined were exclusive. They are a logical analysis, which does not attempt to provide more than some help towards an understanding of attitudes, which never in fact run strictly true to any one type.

To begin with, there is the behaviour which is unconscious. Not only when we are asleep but also when we are awake much of our behaviour is unconscious. No one who has watched the crowd of spectators at the centre court at Wimbledon can fail to have noticed the movement of heads from side to side, following the flight of the ball as it crosses and recrosses the net. Everyone is moving his head, although no one knows he is, and the movement is quite unconscious.

Slightly higher up the scale of consciousness is the subconscious behaviour, which fills so much of everyone's life. A typical illustration is a marching column of troops, whose movements are far from being subconscious before they have learned to march in step and indeed, to begin with, are very self-conscious. However, after a time they become almost automatic, and there is no conscious thinking about their behaviour. It has become so much a part of them, second nature as we say, that they would almost be able to carry on with their instinctive motions when half asleep on a route march.

Further up the scale of consciousness is the traditional pattern of behaviour, which comprises the greater part of every normal human being's life. Each of us gets up and washes and dresses and eats and works and plays and sleeps and in countless ways our life conforms to a traditional pattern. This pattern is partly of our own devising and partly a conforming to the family or social and local pattern. In our work, whether it be manual or academic, in our worship, whether it be private prayer or public liturgy, and indeed

[1] J. E. Fison, *The Blessing of the Holy Spirit* (Longmans, 1950), pp. 208 f.

in the whole of our life our normal behaviour is largely traditional.

So much is this so that in some cases, as for example in the bondage of a rigid caste system or of a rigid school custom, a man may never dare to break the traditional mould and so do the creative work to which he is called if he is made in the image of the Creator.[1] Yet it is only if he dares to break the traditional mould, despite all the odds on the result being the prodigal's descent to 'the husks that the swine did eat',[2] that there is any chance of his ever doing the creative work which is his true vocation. To be content with the safety-first mechanical fulfilment even of a traditional pattern of life and conduct and behaviour is not worthy of a man and it does not satisfy him.

He disregards the traditional at his peril, as we shall see, but it is on the yonder side of the traditional pattern or of convention, as Jung would say, that creative living begins.[3] This is as much true of great artists and great scientists as of great saints. It is true of Shakespeare's plays and of Jesus' sermon on the mount. The price of such creativity is high. It is the meaning of the cross: the severing of the deepest tie of loyalty, family love or personal friendship in obedience to the call of the unknown beyond, to which we must respond.

Unfortunately, rather than face this, the true and often humdrum cross of God's appointment, which is the gateway to the working of the creative Holy Spirit, the Lord and giver of life, many will volunteer for the cross of their own choosing and so seek that selfsame Spirit by a pattern of behaviour which is at best eccentric or superconscious and at worst little less than idiotic.

The superconscious eccentric deliberately flouts tradition and flaunts his break-away from it, whether it be by the clothes he wears or by the manners he adopts, or even by the religion he professes. He must be different from other men and he is not content to remember that he is; he must make sure that he is. And so by conscious effort and deliberate planning he seeks to maintain a way of life which is a break-away from the traditional pattern to which he is meant to conform until the creative break is not chosen or worked for but forced upon him, if he does not dodge it.

The trouble with the eccentric is that, even at his best, he prefers

[1] That God is creator is all we know about him at the time of the Genesis reference to the *imago Dei*. This strongly suggests that it is not in virtue of any distinctive psychological or other quality that man has the high distinction of this unique resemblance to God, but simply and solely because of his powers of procreation (taking that term in its widest possible sense).

[2] Luke 15, 16.

[3] This is why so many communists come from safety-first jobs with guaranteed incomes and good pensions. Without the risk of creative experiment no life is satisfying.

to volunteer for the heroic cross of his own choice rather than respond to the humdrum cross of God's appointment. Even Christian saints may lead us astray in this direction unless they fulfil their true rôle of pointing not to themselves but to their Lord and ours. To copy someone else's creative pattern of living is more likely to mean a life of eccentricity than of creativity. For creation is always original and yet never a stunt. That is why it is the work of God the Holy Spirit to correct the notion that true sanctity consists in a slavish *imitatio* of even Jesus himself.

This does not mean that there is no room for eccentricity in life. The world would be a poorer place for the elimination of its lovable eccentrics. The pressure of tradition is so strong upon the unconscious and the subconscious that few are able to break away to fulfil their creative vocation without a trace of self-conscious effort about their action. But the fact that, human nature being what it is, such eccentricity is usually to some extent inevitable should not blind us to the perils of its deviation from the true creative pattern, if it is obstinately persisted in.

Finally, on the extreme edge of consciousness comes the idiotic pattern of behaviour, which is not so much a culpable sin as a private and solitary [1] experiment which frustrates the true purpose of man's life. All of us sometimes behave idiotically, just as we act unconsciously; and probably we are more often idiots than we know. But though God despises none (and idiots are sometimes very near to him), there is something astray with the man who, so far from being an integrated whole, is in fact on the way to becoming a split personality, a schizophrenic or a superman. Here is the supreme nemesis of conscious or unconscious *hybris*, which awaits all who contract out of their limitations and seek to trespass on the Creator's own forbidden ground.

None of these patterns of behaviour, unconscious, subconscious, traditional, creative, superconscious and idiotic, exists by itself in complete isolation from the others. Only by artificial abstraction from life can they be thus sharply distinguished. In fact all overlap, and the success or failure of life for each of us depends on the right proportion and balance being maintained not in the static rigidity of a fixed plan but in growing conformity to a dynamic purpose. Life is an adventure in responsibility, and responsibility is no mere conforming to a less than conscious tradition imposed on us or a more than conscious originality chosen by us: it is literally a response to the will of God, mediated in devious ways to us, and progressively understood in its deepening significance by those of us who are

---

[1] Cf. H. G. Liddell and R. Scott, *A Greek-English Lexicon*, s.v. ἰδιώτης.

prepared to walk by the faith it demands rather than by the sight we for ourselves or others on our behalf would prefer.

These six patterns of human behaviour obviously must find expression in society. And here, quite independently and without in his book [1] any suggestion of any relation between them, Dr. F. W. Dillistone has added a second most suggestive series of patterns, this time not of individual behaviour but of society as it has in fact been organized by human beings in general and by Christians in particular. Dr. Dillistone does not connect his two series, but the connection seems to exist, though of course rigid analysis is even less likely to provide watertight compartments to separate different types of society than to distinguish different types of individual behaviour.

The six types of society in which Christians have organized themselves may be described (in Dr. Dillistone's analysis) as the monastic, the imperial, the organic, the covenantal, the contractual and the sectarian. They begin at the unconscious and they end at the superconscious or idiotic level of individual behaviour. It is important that the parallels suggested should not be taken as implying moral censure upon any type of society any more than upon any kind of individual behaviour. There is, or there should be, room for all within the Christian whole, but room for none in isolation from that whole. This is as true of the patterns of human society as of individual behaviour. A society which aims at the forcible suppression of cranks will destroy genius, and one that aims at the elimination of monks runs the risk of eradicating saints.

Integration is a grand ideal, but it can be used to destroy originality. On the other hand, originality in isolation is completely sterile. A society of cranks, though conceivably impressive as a stunt or even as a 'sport', can never be a demonstration of fellowship or of love. In the whole in right proportion each has a place: in isolation all are fatal. The aim must be to see each type fulfilling its part in a greater whole, which itself has a purpose, which holds all diversities together in true proportion and growing harmony.

The existence of the monastic type is self-evident. Its essential characteristics are not necessarily Christian at all. Its most Christian expressions provide a pattern of living for lack of which the whole church and indeed the whole world would be the poorer. Here is the peace which goes down to the depths of the unconscious and can produce in the few who have the genuine monastic vocation a creativity perhaps unsurpassed in any other type.

But the essence of the monastic life is that conformity with the

[1] F. W. Dillistone, *The Structure of the Divine Society* (Lutterworth Press, 1951).

rhythm of nature which eliminates the strains and frictions of so much human effort. It is for man to work with nature and not against it: it is for grace to crown nature and not destroy it for, as von Hügel used to teach, those who are enamoured of grace should not despise nature.

In many ways the monastic sacrifices seem to go clean contrary to such a principle. In fact they are made to enable the monks to conform to it. Even the sharpest exception, the night office, is in St Benedict's original intention no exception at all. For his rule puts the monks to bed at sunset and to sleep at lighting-up time and only gets them up seven or eight hours later.[1] The rest of the day is governed by hours, modified according to the seasons so that the length of the day's hour is not sixty minutes, but a twelfth of the time between sunrise and sunset. In a life lived in this way the deepest needs of the unconscious have been met again and again in the history of Christendom on its catholic side.

Then there is the imperial pattern of society, with its secular model in the pyramid and its sacred expression in the papacy. The whole structure is rigid and institutional, and the framework is designed so that a push from the top sets the whole in motion. The lower strata of the structure fulfil their rôles not indeed on the almost purely mechanical model of the monastery, but in at least a way which demands of necessity little more than subconscious activity on the part of most of the individuals who go to make it up.

Here is the direction of the confessor, the discipline of the institution and, if not the corpse-like response of the Society of Jesus,[2] certainly the semi-automatic functioning of a well-run machine. Like any machine, which sooner or later becomes obsolete, by itself the imperial or hierarchical structure is doomed to the impressiveness of an imposing monument, well ordered, but dead. Seen in the perspective of a wider whole, there is a permanent or vital place for the discipline and efficiency of a pattern of society which could produce not only the civilizations of ancient Egypt and Rome but also the classic expressions of catholic and orthodox Christianity.

But its vitality will be in proportion to the closeness of its relation to that third conception of society, the organic, which is as old as ancient India and is the typical catholic interpretation of the structure of the divine community. Here is tradition at its best and an unbroken continuity of structure vitalized by an inner energy. In it the individual members of the body serve the well-being of the whole body, and for this type of society, whether in ancient India or ancient

---

[1] C. Butler, *Benedictine Monachism* (Longmans, 1924), pp. 275 ff.
[2] Cf. H. Bettenson, *Documents of the Christian Church* (O.U.P., 1943), p. 364.

Greece or modern catholicism, it is the whole that matters most: the parts are secondary and serve the whole.

Such an organism will live so long as it is rightly and reciprocally related to its environment. If it fails in this relationship and itself harms its environment it will commit suicide. If it does not fail in this, it commands an allegiance from its members which may degenerate into the frozen rigidity of a caste system but which can develop into a beautiful harmony giving exquisite æsthetic satisfaction by its integrated wholeness. No wonder the Epistle to the Ephesians crowns the great apostle's conversion from his individualistic superconscious eccentricity by his ever deepening and widening vision of the body of Christ, the fullness of him who all in all is being fulfilled![1]

But this is not the only way of looking at the church of Jesus Christ. To see it merely as his body and the extension of the incarnation is to miss the grandeur of its greater glory, for it is also the people of the new covenant. If it is the social organism of the divine Logos manifested in time, it 'is also the covenantal community of the divine Redeemer constituted through his cross'.[2]

Where this is forgotten either inside catholicism or outside it creativity is killed, for this is the secret of the relationship which does not exist by nature or by mere identification with some traditional and organic continuity of life. It involves something more, the creative step out of tradition on its yonder side, which may seem to break the continuity of the organism but in fact alone perpetuates its creative life.

It means breaking the ties of milk to establish the deeper tie of blood. It means forsaking father and mother to marry a wife,[3] and it means forsaking father and mother and wife to follow God.[4] It is the secret of 'here stand I: I can no other, so help me God', which perhaps only once on Calvary was ever with complete truth expressed in silence if not in speech. It is the spirit of the true and positive protestant side of Christendom, wherever inside or outside the catholic church that spirit has been found.

Without this forward-looking balance of a dialectical society, the inevitable tendency of any organic society is to cling to the past and avoid the future, whereas the essence of a dialectical or covenantal society is that it looks to the future and its very basis presupposes the hope of a future that is better than the present. It is the pattern of society which gives scope for the creativity which

---

[1] J. Armitage Robinson, St Paul's Epistle to the Ephesians, 2nd ed. (Macmillan, 1904), p. 37; on Eph. 1, 23.
[2] F. W. Dillistone, op. cit., p. 232.   [3] Mark 10, 7.   [4] Luke 18, 29.

springs not so much naturally out of the being of an organism as creatively out of the meeting of one person with another or of one society with another in a dialectical relationship or conversation.

This is the heart of the biblical understanding of the divine society, which is a gospel enshrined not in two bodies, but in two testaments or covenants. It is what completely separates the religion of Yahweh from the religion of the Baals. The Baal and his people were one by nature and their unity was organic and indissoluble. It always had been and it always would be. The end of one meant the end of the other. Yahweh, on the other hand, was one with Israel not by nature but by grace, not by any natural ties but by free choice. In fact it was the covenant which brought him and them together in that peculiar unity which depended for its maintenance not upon any racial or biological continuity of heredity but upon a continued loyalty to the progressively revealed will of God.

It is not without significance that the central words of the central act of worship of the Christian society should be in two forms (like the two great commandments), which at our peril we combine into one. 'This is my body' is matched by 'This is my blood of the new covenant'.[1] It is a striking fact and perhaps more than a coincidence that wherever in Christendom the organic conception of society is allowed so to dominate the scene as to exclude the covenantal, there the incarnation dominates the atonement and the way is opened up for that denial of the sacramental cup to the laity, which involves the denial of the covenantal word which is spoken over it.

But covenants are forward looking and of grace (not less at Sinai than elsewhere). They live in hope of better things to come. They depend on promise rather than on law. They offer the *fascinans* of the *mysterium* on the yonder side of the challenge of its *tremendum*. It is but a step to move out of this truly and livingly sustained dialectical relationship into another and a different type, in which a superconscious attempt is made to safeguard society by the clearest possible expression of its contractual basis.

Whether this basis is enshrined in the Thirty-nine Articles or in the Westminster Confession or in some quite different creed or formula, there is always the grave danger of losing the covenant in the contract. Instead, then, of a personal relationship based on a promise there develops a contractual relationship based on strict conditions. 'To promise oneself without explicit conditions—that is covenant: to promise a gift upon explicit conditions—that is contract.' [2]

---

[1] I use the form of words of Institution hallowed by the Book of Common Prayer. But my point does not depend upon the exact original form of those words.

[2] F. W. Dillistone, *op. cit.*, p. 134.

It is a *quid pro quo* bargain. It is fixed and irreformable: it must never be changed. Such was the fate of the Sinai covenant at the hands of the post-exilic priests. Such has been continually the fate of portions of the Christian church and especially of protestantism. There is a place for such contractual terms, but only as the temporary clarifications in propositional form of the personal reality behind. Once the proposition becomes the end and ceases to be the means, it is the most effective insulator from the grace which it is meant to convey and interpret. 'The lady doth protest too much, methinks',[1] could be written over so much superconscious Christianity.

Finally, there is the sectarian pattern of society, which ceases any longer to claim the whole for Christ, but is in fact, if not in theory, content with a part, and seeks to make the part the whole or even without knowing it to pretend that it is the whole. Having ceased to be the way of looking at all life, which it was at least in the monastery even if the whole it looked at was a partial whole, religion becomes a department of life.

Sectarian leaders always tend to narrow the wholeness of life down to the particular part of it in which they are interested. It may be some psychological peculiarity, like speaking with tongues, which dominates their interest. Or it may be some social or economic peculiarity which determines for example the erection of so many chapels in the hey-day of British nonconformity. Or it may be some spiritual concern which governs all their energies, as for example where the whole of religion seems to consist in evangelism either at home or overseas.

Such sectarian religion cuts adrift from its past natural roots altogether and strikes out for the rootless unknown future with all the solitary loneliness which in extreme cases can lead to idiocy. It is at the other extreme from monasticism: each is a minority ideal by its very nature. Within the greater whole each may have a rightful place, but by itself in isolation neither is an ideal to be imitated.

Surely the parallel between Dr. Dillistone's two patterns of social and individual behaviour is not imaginary. And if it is real, then at least the central emphasis of each finds its obvious expression in the human family, in which tradition is presupposed by any creative activity whatever and which only lives and grows by combining within itself both the organic and the covenantal or dialectical principles.

And if it comes finally to an ultimate issue and choice, then the

[1] W. Shakespeare, *Hamlet*, III, ii.

16

centre of the picture which the six types present must be given not
to the organic and the traditional but to the covenantal and the
creative. Without this priority no marriage, which involves the
breaking of the organic to establish the dialectical relationship,
would ever take place, and without marriage the family is doomed.
It loses its life to save it, and there is no other way, for it is not the
continuity but the resurrection of the body which is a dogma of the
Christian creed.

This brings us to the application of those patterns of present
individual behaviour and of present community living to our conception of the future. What bearing, if any, have they on eschatology? Can they help to give shape and coherence to its
otherwise apparently haphazard and disordered and disconnected
truths?

It is vital to get an answer to this question, for an eschatology
totally divorced from either the present experience of the individual
or the present character of society cannot claim to represent
adequately the Christian future hope, which springs straight out of
present faith and love and cannot for one moment be separated from
them. If the modern idea of revelation is at all right and true to
the biblical record, then it is given, as we have seen, in event and
in interpretation of event. That being so, a revelation that is valid
for the future can only spring out of the present and the past.

Biblical eschatology is just like that, for in it the conclusions drawn
about the future are derived from the convictions given about the
present. In so far as present convictions are not only true, but
also seen in proportion, 'according to the proportion of the faith',[1]
they will lead to future conclusions which are also true and not
only true, but seen in proportion, according to the proportion of the
hope. In so far however as present convictions are false or seen
out of proportion, they will tend to lead to an even more false and
an even more distorted future hope. Eschatology must be seen in
proportion: its shape is all-important.

If it is to be so seen, the present patterns of individual and community living, which we have been discussing, seem to provide a
clue as to that proportion. To begin with there is the unconscious
behaviour of the individual finding its perfect expression in
the monastic type of society. This surely leads straight to the
eschatological doctrine of the immortality of the soul, conceived
either psychologically on a low level of bare survival or continuance
in Sheol or Hades or some other vague hereafter, or else at a far
higher level as a virtual absorption in the divine in a union of the

---

[1] Rom. 12, 6, R.V. margin.

soul with the One, in the flight of the alone to the Alone, in a beatific vision.

This is the climax of those solitary experiences of illumination, whether in sought or given trance or ecstasy, which are so often considered to be the goal of the mystic and of the contemplative way. Here is St Anthony's final rest: φύγη κόσμου οἰκείωσις θέου.[1] This is not necessarily a Christian conviction or a Christian hope. The Orphic and the Dionysiac mysteries gave it to Greece, and found in the ecstasy of earth the clue to eternal life. It was an ecstasy won by Greek initiates and entered by Greek philosophers, and it came via neo-Platonism and 'Dionysius the Areopagite' and St Augustine to exercise a powerful and permanent influence upon Christian eschatology.

As long as the Platonic and Augustinian tradition remained alive in the Catholic church, unsubmerged beneath the hair-splitting Aristotelianism of the later scholastics, so long this mystical vision fertilized all Christian theology and not least Aquinas' own. For St Thomas Aquinas was himself a great mystic, and the value of his propositional interpretation of truth lies very largely in its being the outward expression of an inner core of vital personal experience.

The tragedy of later scholasticism is that it tended inevitably to take the propositional interpretation without the personal experience. The inevitable hardening this produced drove the great catholic mystics of the counter-Reformation to found schools and systems of mysticism in order to survive. The result was the danger of a forced and hothouse spirituality, standing over against the cold hard logic of the general post-Tridentine outlook of catholic theology.

This split between mystical and dogmatic theology may have served to clarify the systematization of both, but it has certainly hardened the intellectual life of the one and narrowed the spiritual life of the other. The essential cross-fertilization has so largely ceased, and without such cross-fertilization the mystic concentration on the vision of God as the almost solely operative eschatological concept of hope inevitably becomes lopsided, and for many Christians besides monks and nuns this is exactly the tragedy which has occurred. For them it is axiomatic that the vision of God is the focus of Christian eschatological hope.

But a moment's reflection on the scriptural evidence will provoke the query: is such an outlook true to the New Testament perspective? As a matter of strict verbal phraseology it certainly is not, for the proof-text, 'Blessed are the pure in heart: for they shall see God',[2]

---

[1] My authority for this is a text in the chapel of the monastery of Mar Saba in the wilderness of Judæa. [2] Matt. 5, 8.

is certainly the exception that proves the rule, though Dr. Kirk naturally takes it for the opening text of his monumental study of *The Vision of God*.[1] As a summary of 'the Christian doctrine of the *summum bonum*', as Dr. Kirk's sub-title expresses it, the vision of God is in grave danger of distorting the New Testament perspective.

A survey of any manual of mysticism [2] will confirm the impression, which von Hügel's judgment on Evelyn Underhill's attempt to turn the Gospels into mystical treatises still further underlines.[3] There is tangential Christian eschatological truth in the doctrine of the immortality of the soul, based on psychological grounds. There is much more Christian eschatological truth in the doctrine of the vision of God, but when this is considered as meaning essentially a union of the soul with God reached *via* the mystic way of purgation and illumination and interpreted, as the best Christian mystics do not interpret it, in terms of virtual absorption instead of communion and relationship, then it cannot rightly claim a central place in the Christian eschatological perspective.

It is interesting in this connection to compare Dr. Kirk's handling of his theme [4] with Dr. Newton Flew's survey of 'the Christian ideal for the present life'.[5] A comparative quantitative survey of these two books will raise questions on bare statistical evidence as to whether Dr. Kirk's emphasis will bear the weight he places upon it. For the centre of the New Testament hope is certainly not based in so many words upon the vision of God. Indeed, the striking absence of such mystical terminology from its vocabulary suggests a deliberate reorientation of spiritual perspective, conscious or unconscious, from that of the already traditional mystical outlook. Certainly neither the heart of Jesus' teaching, the kingdom of God, nor the heart of his living can be easily so interpreted.

That mysticism is a vital element in a fully orbed Christian outlook it is a major purpose of this book to affirm. But the mysticism affirmed as central is not the distant goal of an individual soul's relation with God, but the here and now response of that soul to

[1] K. E. Kirk, *The Vision of God* (Longmans, 1931).
[2] E.g. A. Tanquerey, *The Spiritual Life* (Desclée and Co., Tournai), E.T. 1930. Contrast the appendices (pp. 751 ff.) with what has gone before.
[3] F. von Hügel, *Essays and Addresses on the Philosophy of Religion* (Dent, 1924). 'It is profoundly impressive to note how intractable the Synoptic Jesus remains to all purely mystical interpretation: Evelyn Underhill's recent attempt is as able as it is unconvincing' (p. 132). (The reference is to Evelyn Underhill's book, *The Mystical Way*, published in 1913.)
Von Hügel goes on immediately to say that 'the fact of course is that nothing could be more anti-mystical than is the Proximate Futurism of the authentic Jesus'. The aim of this book is to deny this.
[4] K. E. Kirk, *op. cit.*
[5] R. Newton Flew, *The Idea of Perfection in Christian Theology* (O.U.P., 1934).

God's approaches to it in the contemporary facts and circumstances of everyday life, whether sacred or secular. It is a mysticism of reaction rather than of action, an embodied mysticism rather than a disembodied one, a mediated mysticism rather than an unmediated one.

Such at least appears to come nearest to the pattern of our Lord's own interior life, so far as the gospels give us any hints as to its nature.[1] Of spiritual experiences of the kind St Paul refers to in 2 Corinthians[2] there is hardly a hint. Of any technique or system of approach to God there is only the merest semblance in the Lord's prayer and hardly anything anywhere else. Of any seeking for a distant goal of vision, certainty and blessedness there is hardly a trace.

On the contrary, Jesus' whole life was filled with the response he felt himself called to make to the everyday activities, needs, obligations and opportunities which came his way and were more often of a secular than of a sacred character. Even when he came to die, it was not the cross volunteered for, but the cross not dodged, which the agony of Gethsemane showed was the secret of his abiding union with his Father. Here is no absorption, but an unbroken intimacy of mutual relationship beyond the highest range of mystical experience. There is no improvement upon his holiness if we truly follow the great mystical saints of Christendom.

The most intimate Christian relationship with God can never be any absorption into him, if we remain loyal to the pattern of Jesus' own spirituality and to the clear implications of the doctrine of the Trinity. Love does not so absorb its beloved, and it is to the true nature of any relationship of love that we shall be led if we seek to redeem debased and semi-Christian mysticism to its authentic and fully Christian significance.

If we go this way, then we shall not allow the mystic ladder to God ever to blur in fact or theory the way of God to man, which always precedes man's way to God and can alone provide the inspiration and the help which will see the mystic through to his journey's end. This is bound to raise the eschatological problem of purgatory. When the purgative way is extended beyond this life so as to emphasize the movement of the soul on its long pilgrimage to God to such an extent as virtually to ignore both God's movement to us, which is basic and far more important than our movement to

---

[1] Our Lord's personal reticence as to his own inner spiritual experiences and his complete refusal to use such experiences as levers for evangelism is in marked contrast to much shallow contemporary thinking to-day.

[2] 2 Cor. 12, 1 ff.

him, and also our interrelationship with other souls and with nature too,[1] then the essential Christian perspective has been lost.

This is no gateway to a living hope: it is much more like the refuge of despair. This is not the way in which memory is purged into hope. For if that memory is at all Christian, it will be filled with the wonder of the essential Christian doctrine of the divine initiative and of the priority of grace to every human effort. And what it knows to have been essential in the past, it will not readily discard in the future.

This is where the biblical and the Christian idea of the future is so radically different from the ordinary outlook of the twentieth century, even when the latter is itself nominally Christian. The latter may pay lip-service to the hope of the coming of the kingdom of God upon earth, but the authentic gospel 'aim and the manner of its realization are fundamentally different from our rational idea of future aims and therefore totally different from the modern interpretation of the kingdom of God and its coming'.[2]

Dr. Brunner follows this quotation with words which I have already partly quoted. The biblical picture, he says,

is just the reverse of ours. This is not a movement going on from where we are, step by step, until the goal is reached, not a movement going upwards, as it were on a ladder until the highest point is reached, the movement of Dante from hell through purgatory to heaven; but on the contrary, it is a movement starting from heaven, starting from where God is, and going downwards to us until we are reached.[3]

Dr. Brunner sees the point at issue with crystal clarity, but because of his refusal to come to terms with the mystical element in religion, his theology offers an intellectual rather than a living hope. His future focus is on the resurrection [4] rather than the parousia. But the biblical 'living hope',[5] which is begotten of 'the resurrection of Jesus Christ from the dead', does not so much look forward to the resurrection as to the parousia. Its origin and source may be Jesus' resurrection: [6] its end and fulfilment is his parousia.

Dr. Hunter's quotation from Dr. Vincent Taylor is nearer the mark: the parousia, he says, 'includes all that is meant by the resurrection, but is a more ultimate concept'.[7] But he succeeds no

[1] Cf. J. Dalby, *Christian Mysticism and the Natural World* (James Clarke, n.d.), pp. 53 ff.
[2] E. Brunner, *The Scandal of Christianity* (S.C.M., 1951), p. 104.
[3] *Ibid.*   [4] *Op. cit.*, pp. 94 ff.   [5] 1 Pet. 1, 3.
[6] But to say this is seriously misleading unless we remember that it was not the empty tomb but Jesus' post-resurrection comings (parousiai) to his disciples, which gave them back their hope.
[7] A. M. Hunter, *The Work and Words of Jesus* (S.C.M., 1950), p. 109.

more than Dr. Brunner in giving reality to the theological concept because again he ignores the mystical approach to the doctrine, which alone can give it living content.

Purgatory has taken us far afield, but it is such an essential element in the traditional catholic eschatological scheme that it cannot be lightly dismissed or ignored. There is deep down in the depths of the unconscious in every man a desperate hunger for that purging from sin, to which it ministers. Whatever we may superficially think or say, in the depths of our souls we all carry a sense of guilt, which no cheap or glib assurance of forgiveness can remove.

The vital question is not whether purgation is necessary either here or hereafter, but whether it leads to the vision of God or springs from the vision of God. It is a question of the relation between renunciation and reconciliation, and John Oman has said the relevant word on that relation. 'Renunciation', he says, 'in other religions, is first and for reconciliation: in Christianity, reconciliation is first and renunciation of value only as it is from reconciliation.' [1] That is where the good news of Christianity so utterly transcends the good advice of morality. And if eschatology is not to contradict the rest of Christian theology, it must bear its own distinctive witness to this fact.

When we move to the next type of individual behaviour and community living we find the subconscious individual in the imperial or hierarchical society. It can hardly be fortuitous that the crowning glory of the imperial structure on its ecclesiastical side, the mediæval papacy, conceived the end primarily in terms of a last judgment (after a general resurrection) invested with all the tremendous imperial trappings of a Byzantine *pantokrator* or of Michelangelo's paintings in the Sixtine Chapel or of Thomas of Celano's version of Zephaniah's doomsday.

Here is the future eschatological sanction of the present ecclesiastical set-up. Only by a long process of purification from sin achieved through a whole series of instrumental rites appointed by the church could the soul reach the safety of the haven where mediæval man so greatly longed to be. There was no future in history and time, but only out of both. There was no future for society as a whole, but only for its individual members. There was no future for matter, but only for spirit. If the strict Orphic *soma sema* was not *de fide* and *de jure*, it was certainly *de facto* the ruling principle of Christian doctrine. This life had value only for the next.

The resurrection of the body was believed in, but it was largely

[1] J. Oman, *Grace and Personality*, 4th ed. (C.U.P., 1931), p. 118.

an irrelevant article of faith. Every mediævalist in the vast hierarchical structure was, as has so often been said, a monk at heart.
The structures of ecclesiastical society might claim relevance even
in the next world, or at least they might more presumptuously and
less humbly than the Russian *Contakion for the Departed* dare to
hold the next world to some extent in their embrace.

Whatever the upper orders of the great imperial or hierarchical
structure of society hoped for for themselves, they made quite sure
that the final prospect in general for the common people was a
terrifying one, well calculated to keep the lower orders of society
in their proper place. Not only in this life did the hierarchy claim
the power of the keys, but also in the life to come. It is true that
the poignant Russian *Contakion for the Departed* as well as the
lovely late mediæval chantries in our English cathedrals witness to
the at least æsthetic satisfaction that this facet of eschatological truth
gave to the subconscious cravings of the human heart. But as a
whole it bred a spirit of timid fear and sometimes obsequious respect
far different from the 'balanced rapture' and tonic hope of the
genuine New Testament outlook.

No wonder its corrective came with a crashing blow in the rediscovery of the truly eschatological doctrine of justification by faith!
For much mediæval catholicism, as for much Tractarian anglicanism
in the nineteenth century, it was true that (as Dale wrote of Pusey)
'the absence of joy in his religious life was only the inevitable effect
of his conception of God's method of saving men : in parting with
the Lutheran truth concerning justification, he parted with the springs
of gladness'.[1] St Francis is a glorious exception to prove a rule
that held for Newman and so many lesser men.

Over the whole approach to the doctrine of the last judgment
there is a suspiciously selfish tendency to call 'the New World into
existence to redress the balance of the Old'.[2] It is true that the
need for law and order on the one hand and the peril of anarchy on
the other are often so great that almost any government is better
than none and almost any sanctions used by the government can be
justified by the grimness of the facts.[3] There is ample New Testament evidence that the early church was well aware of this.[4]

But that this justifies the grim panorama of the last judgment and
its prominence in ecclesiastical tradition is a much more debatable
point. Certainly the last judgment does not so decisively dominate

[1] H. R. Mackintosh, *The Christian Experience of Forgiveness* (Nisbet, 1927),
p. 243.
[2] George Canning, Speech, December 12, 1826.
[3] The communist revolution in China is a case in point.
[4] Rom. 13, 1 ff.; 1 Pet. 2, 17.

the whole of the New Testament eschatological outlook, unless we are prepared to accept such a twist of exegesis as would force all attention in the allegorical parable of the sheep and the goats not upon the 'Inasmuch' [1] to which it all leads up, but upon the 'Depart from me',[2] which is relatively incidental to the grand finale.

Furthermore, as so often ecclesiastically proclaimed, the one thing that the last judgment is never allowed to do is the one thing that in the New Testament it is most designed to do. Its purpose there is to spring a complete surprise not upon the lost pagan souls outside the pale of the church, but upon the complacent ecclesiastical souls whose entire confidence is based upon the fact that they are well within it.

Where such souls are sensitive, they are well aware of their peril, for they see only too clearly the abiding significance of the fact that judgment 'must begin at the house of God'.[3] All the last judgment does to them, when it is devoid of any living connection with Jesus himself and is only nominally administered by him, is to cut the nerve of certainty and hope and joy and to kill the inspiration for creative and adventurous living by inspiring a perpetual morbid and scrupulous introspection.

We move nearer the centre of the New Testament eschatological panorama when we come to the next pattern of behaviour. For the traditional type finds its expression in the organic society, which in turn finds its fulfilment in the eschatological hope of the resurrection of the body, a hope which is not, it must be repeated, in continuity but in resurrection.

The continuity may depend on ministerial succession or even upon the existence of bibles or written statements of apostolic belief. But can it seriously be maintained that the gates of hell would finally prevail against the church, if all its apostolic ministers died and all its apostolic books were destroyed? The marks of continuity of form and structure are very important for the body, but if they were essential for its life, would Christ have died and would his body have been broken? What had to happen to his natural and physical body may have to happen to his spiritual and mystical body.

In fact he sacrificed his existence, as it appeared, to save its meaning. Who can say that the church might not have to do the same or exempt her from the universal principle that 'whosoever would save his life shall lose it: and whosoever shall lose his life for my sake and the gospel's shall save it'?[4] There is no guarantee whatever in the Christian faith that the worst, as we understand it, may not happen.

[1] Matt. 25, 40.   [2] Matt. 25, 41.   [3] 1 Pet. 4, 17.   [4] Mark 8, 35.

On the contrary, it is the Christian faith that the worst that could happen did happen and was turned into something better than if it had never happened. From the human standpoint that is the meaning of the crucifixion and the resurrection of Jesus Christ. No doubt from the divine standpoint, which we never completely share, except at least in retrospect, the crucifixion itself was the triumph, as St John clearly realized long afterwards[1] and as we may well believe Jesus himself understood at the time.[2]

But this does not alter the fact that at our peril we put in advance a limit to the extent of the spiritual as well as the physical disasters that may befall not only ourselves and those we love, but also the whole church and the whole creation itself. At our peril from the human standpoint, even with scriptural and ecclesiastical sanctions behind us, do we rule out the possibility of some very unpleasant and very terrible surprises being in store for us not only individually but also corporately too. In advance such things always appear to be going to contradict the declared and promised purpose of God. Only in retrospect are they seen never in fact to do so. If God is love, this is one of those things which cannot be otherwise, and it would be our blessedness not to wish it so.

The fulfilment of the organic hope of society which satisfies the traditional type of human behaviour is in the resurrection, not the continuity of the body. But it is in the resurrection *of the body*, and therefore it includes far more than those imagine who think of a future only in terms of the immortality of the soul. Being 'in Christ' is now a present possibility for everyone: being 'in Christ' will one day be a universal possibility for everything.[3]

That is the grandeur of the future eschatological climax to the organic and traditional types of present behaviour. It opens up a gradual and almost inevitable progress to a glorious finale, but by being based upon a doctrine of resurrection rather than of continuity, it prevents the twisting of the Christian eschatological hope into the likeness of any merely human evolution. It is the genuine expression of the fulfilment of one element in the memory of every Christian, but though it secures for the future the best that has been in the past, it hardly indicates the limitless surprise that all those who believe in the controlling purpose of creative love must look for in the future.

It is to this last point that the next pattern of behaviour bears its witness. For the creative finds expression in the covenantal or dialectical, and the covenantal finds its eschatological fulfilment in the coming of our Lord Jesus Christ. The good news of the New

---

[1] John 12, 23; 19, 30.   [2] Luke 23, 46.   [3] Eph. 1, 15 ff.

Testament is centred on the fact that God has come down to man and found him and rescued him where he is and ungodly sinner though he is. This is 'the Gospel of the Outcast',[1] and the measure of the advance of the New Testament upon the Old can be seen in the fact that Dr. Montefiore can actually say (with probable exaggeration, admittedly), 'that God loves the sinner *before* he repents and while he is a sinner is never suggested by any Old Testament writer'.[2]

Whether this is true of the Old Testament or not, its complete reverse is certainly true of the New Testament. And in the light of the New Testament at least it is this gospel which can be seen to be the basis of the covenantal society as much of the old Israel as of the new. 'When Israel was a child, then I loved him, and called my son out of Egypt.'[3] Here is the mystery of election and of prevenient grace interpreted in terms of the romance of falling in love. It is not the goodness of the elect which evokes the grace of God: on the contrary, it is part of the inscrutable mystery of the God of love and his great delight to show mercy to those who do not deserve it and even to send his Son to die 'for the ungodly'.[4]

It was the wonder of all this, as Jesus had revealed it to them by his life and teaching and still more by his suffering and his death, which filled the memories of the first Christians. And therefore it was to the fulfilment of this that they looked forward with their memories of the past purged to give them their hopes for the future. To them, the amazing thing about the gospel was that Jesus had come to them and not that they had gone to him. If he had done that in the past and was doing it in the present, then they were sure he would do it in the future. So they lived in the wonder of his presence and looked for the wonder of his parousia.

The secret of the people of the covenant had always been that God had 'visited'[5] them. He had met them through their representatives, and through those meetings undreamt-of possibilities for the future had opened up. The secret of all this was not to be denied in the very end: it was to be fulfilled. The covenantal society of the new Israel looked for the parousia more than for anything else in the world. This was the only item in their eschatology of which no one outside their society could have any inkling at all. It was the new thing, the creative thing and the distinctive thing in the future, of which they alone had the secret.

[1] T. W. Manson in *The Mission and Message of Jesus* (Ivor Nicholson and Watson, 1937), p. 574: 'the L material in chapters 15–19 (of St Luke) might be called in a special sense the Gospel of the Outcast'.
[2] C. G. Montefiore, quoted by C. A. Anderson Scott, *Footnotes to St Paul* (C.U.P., 1935), p. 227.
[3] Hos. 11, 1.   [4] Rom. 5, 6.   [5] Luke 1, 68.

They did not deny the other items in the shape of current Jewish eschatology, but this was the key to the coherence of all the rest and in the light of this all the rest looked different. It takes a long time to alter the shape of eschatological doctrine, just as it takes a long time to alter the pattern of funeral practice. Therefore in eschatology more than in any other branch of doctrine it is the new thing that matters. And the new thing in Christian eschatology was the parousia of Jesus Christ. Others had immortality and looked for a millennium, and the Pharisees believed in the resurrection of the body and the 'abiding consequences' of heaven and hell after the judgment.

Certainly Christians alone knew that Jesus would be their judge, and therefore to some extent the judgment, as Christians understood it, was a new element in the shape of current eschatology. But it was bound up with the much more new and the much more wonderful expectation of the parousia. It was the latter that involved and carried with it the former as its necessary and inevitable corollary. The parousia was at the heart of the primitive eschatological hope of the Christian church. The early Christians were in love with their Lord, and they knew they were not worthy of his love outstretched and freely offered to them. They had never been and they never would be. They knew that they could never make themselves worthy, however long the effort and however heroic the struggle. Yet such was the wonder of the love extended to them that their sense of unworthiness did not crush them. On the contrary, sinners though they were and knew they were, they were lifted up to a glad and not self-centred joy and to a radiant thrilling hope.

They did not cling to their dearest memories of the presence but lived in hope of the parousia, never imagining that they had glimpsed more than a fraction of its meaning and therefore being fully prepared for the inevitable surprise that it would be. It is the final meeting 'in the air',[1] which, for all its crudity if taken literally, symbolizes better than any other eschatological doctrine the fulfilment of all creative individual and of all dialectical corporate living.

It is out of the meeting between God and man, between heaven and earth, between Christ and his church, that the creative leap up and on occurs. It is out of intercourse that new life is born, just as it is out of conversation that new truth is seen. That is why, as we have seen, the Bible still seems to retain a kind of temporal time-table even for its most ultimate eschatological dogmas. And in this time-table the parousia is at the beginning rather than the end.[2]

It is true that the organic conception of society offers through the body of Christ the glorious possibility of the consummation of

---

[1] 1 Thess. 4, 17.　　　　[2] 1 Cor. 15, 23 f.

all things in him. That is part of the biblical perspective, but it is not true if it is taken out of its context, and its context is on the yonder rather than the hither side of the parousia. It is *via* the parousia and only *via* the parousia that the prospect of the cosmic consummation 'in Christ' is offered as a Christian hope. Leave out the parousia and the prospect is inconceivable, except to the wishful thinking of evolutionary utopians or to the catastrophic imagination of those who believe in the resurrection of the body. But in the evolutionary view there is nothing necessarily Christian at all, and in the catastrophic view the cart is put before the horse.

It is true that in 1 Thessalonians and in 1 Corinthians St Paul speaks of the resurrection of the body in a context in which it is the necessary prelude to the parousia rather than its sequel. But he is thinking in both cases only of the particular resurrection of those Christians who have died before the parousia: he is not thinking of that general resurrection which may legitimately be interpreted in a cosmic sense, and which is what the cosmic consummation in Christ necessarily involves.

This latter is the surprising possibility that opens up out of the parousia rather than leads up to it. Its indescribable wonder dawns on the other side of the parousia, if the expression may be allowed. If the existence of the new Israel is based not on a contract which binds it to the past but on a covenant which points it to the future (and it is no covenant society at all unless this is true), then the fulfilment of its hope in the parousia itself looks on into the future beyond. The forward-looking principle of the covenantal society is affirmed and not denied at the end.

The final meeting will be the climax of all the meetings that have gone before, not only in and through the sacrament but also in and through the word and in countless other ways as well, for no one can limit the ways in which God visits his people. He is always *ho erchomenos* (ὁ ἐρχόμενος), and he is first spoken about with an exclamation mark as 'He!' and only then interpreted as 'I am that I am'.[1] Substitute propositional logic for personal love and the whole of eschatology becomes a barren and a baseless dogma, for the mystical element has gone out of it, and this alone by relating it integrally with the present is able to make it live.

But how is this mystical element in the present finally realized in the future? It is not so much in the beatific vision, conceived of as the ultimate possibility of the soul's purgation here and hereafter, as in the beatific meeting, conceived of as an immediate possibility at any time and as a final possibility at some time, which is much

---

[1] Exod. 3, 14.

nearer the beginning than the end of the soul's pilgrimage to God and may perhaps surprise the soul before it knows it has begun to go to God at all.

In this way the end confirms and does not contradict the beginning. It fulfils its movement and it does not reverse it. From the very beginning the biblical God has been on the move in grace to man and in the very end he will be on the move in grace to man. The coming of our Lord Jesus Christ is at the heart of the eschatological Christian gospel. His presence now guarantees his parousia then.

From the creative and the covenantal and the eschatological parousia, which is the centre of the whole pattern of individual and corporate life here and now and its climax hereafter, we move on to the circumferential types of behaviour and of society. The superconscious person must express himself in a superconscious society, and each, because it deliberately takes its stand somewhat apart from the traditional pattern of individual or corporate behaviour, is obliged to define its basis and *locus standi* over against its parent body in terms of superconscious detail and exactitude.

This is where the contract comes in, for whereas the covenant always points to the future, it is the function of the contract to bind to the present, which itself immediately becomes the past. If we look for the eschatological sanction and fulfilment of such a superconscious attitude, we find it in the proximate judgment conceived as the immediate sequel to death and portrayed rather after the manner of a Puritan merchant, examining his account books, strictly made up to the day. It is this proximate judgment which fills the future prospect of the superconscious soul and of the members of the contractual society. Any attempt to get round the strict letter of the contract here and now is checked by the forcible reminder that there will be no getting round it there and then.

This is the Puritan protest against all easy-going cocksureness, whether of evangelical antinomianism or of catholic ecclesiastical sharp practice. Here is the goal of a true pilgrim's progress, but all too often without the secret of how he lost his burden on the way.[1] It makes a grim prospect out of the Puritan motto, 'Forefancy your deathbed', for it so often lacks the assurance of the Puritan 'dying grace'. But if the superconscious expectation of the judgment kills something of the radiant hope of the New Testament, there is nothing cheap about it. It may breed a grimness which is foreign to the gospel, but at its best it can breed a grandeur too.

And in this it stands in sharp contrast with the superconscious attitude of the evangelical pietists. If the Puritan in face of the

[1] J. Bunyan, *The Pilgrim's Progress* (R.T.S., 1914), p. 46.

immediate particular judgment shares something of the Tractarian fear and trembling in face of the lengthened purgatorial process hereafter, and if each of them lacks something of those springs of joy and hope which mark the authentic New Testament outlook, the evangelical and sectarian pietists fall away from the gospel in the opposite direction. Their joy and hope tends to be shallow and cheap, and their cocksureness is as far removed as the timidity of the Tractarians from the true assurance of the New Testament. They believe in justification by faith alone. But their justification so easily lacks that mystical element which alone lifts it into the world of loving relationship and makes it moral.

To live under the law is not to live in love, no matter whether the law be that of faith rather than of works. It is to imagine that by reckoning that we are justified here and now we are thereby justified. In the superconscious cocksureness which such a doctrine engenders, those who imagine they are justified await the judgment with as much presumption about their own salvation as about the damnation of everyone else.

If the last judgment can so easily destroy hope and certainty and breed a timid apprehension at best and a terrifying cocksureness at worst, it is because Jesus is no longer in fact the judge, and because the whole eschatological prospect has been taken clean out of any vital connection whatever with any present relationship of love. That is the inevitable danger of the superconscious attitude. The bud of love may not come to flower if the unconscious and the subconscious do not come to the surface in the traditional and the creative, but at least it may be there as a closed bud. But the super-conscious can so easily kill the lovely bloom by forcing it prematurely into the open.

This is what happens when faith is pinned on to a quite fictitious and imaginary magical transformation of life and character by a sudden speeding up of the processes of God. Leaving the world of lovers' meeting, the superconscious soul lives in the world of legal fiction. It believes it is now miraculously changed into something quite different from what it was. There is something akin to the Jesuit *excæcatio* [1] in the false confidence of fideism. The law can be our schoolmaster or 'tutor' [2] to bring us to Christ: but it is only when it is that its ethics are as gracious and generous as those of the Puritans are grim and those of the pietists are sentimental.

The superconscious individual, living under the law, with his rule of life more like an end than a means, and the contractual

---

[1] Cf. K. Heim, *Spirit and Truth*, E.T. (Lutterworth Press, 1935), pp. 112 f.
[2] Gal. 3, 24 f.

society with its basis of membership, more like a threat than a privilege, have a place in the entire wholeness of the present purpose of God. So also in the future has the particular and proximate judgment to which superconscious souls look forward either to confound their fears or to confirm their hopes. But when the superconscious attitude dominates society as a whole and tries to clamp the hatches down on all creative ventures by reference back to the terms of a fixed and immutable contract, the result is legal bondage and it is deadly. It is as much a fatal twist in the present, if society is so fettered and individuals so bound, as it will be in the future, if the last judgment is along such lines allowed to dominate the Christian hope and distort its true perspective.

Finally there is the idiotic type of human behaviour and the extreme sectarian type of society, and these express their hope in an eschatological prospect, which is not in any sense the fulfilment of the present but in every way its complete reversal. Here the future means something for which no memory of the past or experience of the present provides any clue at all. Here the idea of the second coming of our Lord has no relation whatever to the fact of his first coming: in every conceivable way it is its exact opposite.

The millennium likewise has no point of contact with anything in the present at all. It offers this world's outcasts the prospect of ruling in this world in the future, not as Jesus himself offered it to the apostles,[1] in terms of a kingship won by suffering and sacrifice and exercised in service, but as idiots imagine themselves to be Napoleons or Christs. Here is the supreme example of the eschatological sanction of the religion of compensation as opposed to the eschatological fulfilment of the religion of reality.

It may perhaps be able to meet the Marxists in this respect on their own ground, and perhaps that is why the Marxists pay so much attention to Jehovah's Witnesses. As a corrective to those who would abandon this world to the devil, the hope of its redemption by a *deus ex machina* intervention has a value, just as the ruthless single-mindedness of the sectarian protest against the entire worldly pattern of behaviour and the whole natural order has its value as a corrective to the attitude of a church which can so easily become absorbed in the world and indistinguishable from it.

It is therefore true that such an idiotic [2] outlook and such a sectarian society may at moments of crisis act as salt within the whole and save it from corruption. But to do this they each must stay

---

[1] Matt. 19, 28.
[2] In the technical sense of the word, without moral stigma attached to it.

within the whole, and to stay within the worldly or even the ecclesiastical whole is what the idiot and the sects, in which he bands together his clique of regimented followers, will so seldom do. By a false compulsion [1] rather than by a true vocation, the idiot feels he must go out into the wilderness alone. It is heroic and it is hard. It may have produced as many saints as the monasteries and as many missionaries too. But if the peril of the monastery is to produce cogs in a machine rather than men in a community, the peril of the sect is to produce prigs or cranks on their own. While the former is comparatively harmless even if it can be completely sterile, the latter is extremely dangerous and may be terribly destructive.

The idiot and the sect can reveal a facet of the whole truth, but it is a facet which is in fact fatal to the truth if it claims to be the whole truth. As such it is wholly irrational and unrelated in any coherent pattern with the rest of life. Seen out of all proportion, it makes any interpretation of life as a whole impossible. Therefore it shuts itself off from life as a whole, and in the isolation of idiocy the tiny fraction of life or truth which the idiot perceives is taken to be the whole.

There can be no coherence on such a view of life, for nature is wholly despised in order that a narrow sector of grace may be cultivated, and every other truth except the fraction held fanatically to the last is either denied or disregarded. Such an outlook may lead to the cross, but all too often to the public and compulsive cross of self-chosen immolation rather than to the secret and unavoidable cross of divine appointment. The idiot may be crucified, but all alone of his own choice in public like Stylites on his pillar rather than with Christ unavoidably in secret in Gethsemane. His splendid isolation can be an impressive testimony to the cross for which we may volunteer, but it lacks the inner dereliction of the often quite humdrum cross, which we may not dodge.

It is not for us to exclude the idiot or the sects from the final eschatological purpose of God or to eliminate from the shape of that eschatology their contribution to it. Dostoievsky's Idiot [2] has his place secure in the end and very near the centre it will be. There is room for all, but for none in isolation. It is the tragedy of man's sin of pride and of ecclesiastical man's pride more than all the rest that, if he has an eschatology at all, he so often believes himself entitled to exclusive rights to that part of it upon which he has set

---

[1] This compulsion is psychologically indicative of the resistance of the lower levels of consciousness to the claims of the superconscious and the idiotic.

[2] Cf. Z. Maurina, *A Prophet of the Soul* (James Clarke, n.d.), pp. 142 ff.

17

his heart and fixed his hopes. It is the discipline of love to cease to claim such rights without ceasing to have such hopes.

It is precisely the sectarian notions of judgment on the cheap and of the millennium in a trice which need the corrective of the long-drawn-out process of the purgatorial way, while those, who think the mills of God's judgment grind so very slowly in his imperial way, need to come to grips with the possibility that he may render his account at any moment.

If the superconsciousness of so much protestantism was balanced by the subconsciousness of so much catholicism, and if each could move together towards the traditional creativity of Jesus Christ himself, then the eschatological prospect of the Christian hope would not be envisaged as either a long-drawn-out or a magically speeded-up process in calendar time. It would be seen in its mystical context as the imminent hope of lovers' meeting in lovers' time, which is the best description that we have of how all journeys end.

SCRIPTURAL INDEX

17*

259

GENERAL INDEX